Urbanization and Environment

Urbanization and Environment

The Physical Geography of the City

Thomas R. Detwyler and Melvin G. Marcus,
University of Michigan

And Contributors

Line Drawings by Peter Van Dusen

Duxbury Press *A Division of Wadsworth Publishing Company, Inc.*
Belmont, California

Duxbury Press *A Division of Wadsworth Publishing Company, Inc.*

L.C. Cat. Card No.: 72-075110
ISBN 0-87872-034-0
Printed in the United States of America
2 3 4 5 6 7 8 9 10 – 76 75 74 73

CONTENTS

PREFACE

In man's history this is an era of exploding environmental and urban problems. To a large extent our environmental ills are caused by the demands, functions, and expansion of cities. Conversely, healthy urban life requires understanding of, and wise accommodation to, the complex physical environment in and near cities. This book is about the dynamic physical geography of the city, the interaction between urbanization and environment.

Specifically, *Urbanization and Environment* aims (1) to demonstrate how man has changed the natural environment by urbanization, (2) to suggest how physical features and processes influence the growth and function of cities, and (3) to reveal some of the feedback between man's actions and environmental processes. Numerous examples (mainly North American) are used to give insight into the complexity of the urban ecosystem.

A definitive treatment of these subjects is impossible at present. They have scarcely been studied until recently. Further, existing facts have not been drawn together in a comprehensive, meaningful, and readily understandable way. Our awareness of this situation led us to organize an experimental course (consisting primarily of seminars and lectures by invited experts) at the University of Michigan. This book has evolved from the initial enthusiasm shown by participating students and faculty alike, because it appeared that much of the presented material would otherwise remain unpublished or in fugitive papers.

We have extensively edited the contributed chapters to integrate the content and approach and to strike a similar level of treatment. We hope that the book's level, together with its subject, will make it useful to both concerned citizens and students in a variety of college courses. With this audience in mind we have incorporated numerous photographs, maps, and other drawings, provided lists of references for further reading (at the end of each chapter), and included a detailed index.

The introductory chapter provides the conceptual fabric for the following chapters, which are organized according to environmental subsystems. This arrangement should facilitate the use of the work as either a core or supplementary text in diverse courses, including physical geography, urban studies, environmental science, ecology, urban geography, urban planning, landscape architecture, cultural geography, and so on. With several of these fields we share an ultimate concern: improving the quality of urban man's life through judicious management. It is not our objective here to specify how the urban ecosystem should (or even may) be controlled. But achievement of this goal is dependent on first understanding how the system operates.

We and other contributing authors gratefully acknowledge the following help: Ann Larimore for critically reviewing Chapter 1; Charles R. Foster, Harry Close, Bob Paullin, and Squire Williams of the Office of Noise Abatement, U.S. Department of Transportation, for various information in Chapter 8; William Benninghoff, Jack Matthews, and Forest Stearns for critically reviewing Chapter 9; the National Science Foundation for a grant on Collaborative Research on Natural Hazards supporting some work reported in Chapter 7; and numerous individuals, public agencies and companies, specified in the captions, for providing photographs and other illustrations. We appreciate the many suggestions made by Nancy Clemente, who copyedited the entire manuscript. Peter Van Dusen made numerous suggestions for improving the substance of both text and illustrations, in addition to drawing the charts, graphs, and other line illustrations. Special thanks are due to Pat Bosma, Merikay Bryan, and Judy Spencer for their typing and editorial assistance.

Thomas R. Detwyler
Melvin G. Marcus

Urbanization and Environment

CHAPTER 1

Urbanization and Environment in Perspective

Melvin G. Marcus and Thomas R. Detwyler

Cities are nodes of man's greatest impact on nature, the places where he has most altered the essential resources of land, air, organisms, and water. The city is the quintessence of man's capacity to inaugurate and control changes in his habitat. Through urbanization man has created new ecosystems within which the interactions of man, his works, and nature are complex. This complexity — and the importance of our understanding it — grows as cities burgeon in the modern world.

For much of the world, the twentieth century is an urban age. Today the majority of people in industrialized countries live in cities; and in emerging nations, industrial expansion and urban growth are seen as keys to prosperity. In the context of man's biological development over a million years or so and a history of urbanization spanning perhaps 10,000 years, urbanism has burst forth overnight. By the year 1800 the world's population had grown to almost one billion, but only some 20 million people (less than 3 percent) lived in cities of more than 100,000. The Industrial Revolution, accompanied by a dramatic population explosion, has since produced an even more dramatic rise in urbanization (see Figure 1.1). Today more than 20 percent of the world's population lives in urban places of more than 100,000, and the figure for those living in cities of 20,000 people or more is rapidly approaching 30 percent (United Nations 1970). Urban growth has been most impres-

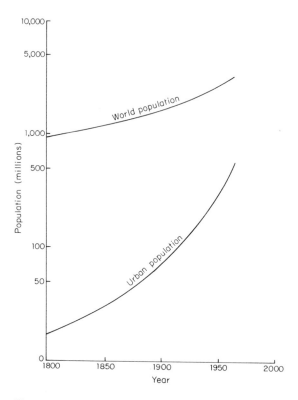

Figure 1.1. Urbanization compared with world population growth since 1800. The steeply rising urban population curve reflects the growing proportion of people living in cities of 100,000 or more. (After Davis 1965.)

sive in industrialized countries — England and Wales together and the United States, for example, have some 80 and 70 percent, respectively, of their populations living in urban places.

In recent years the converging forces of population, urbanization, technology, and environment have come into serious conflict. At a time when man's control over nature is apparently increasing, each new day brings fresh evidence of his potential to create havoc and make the world less livable. Seldom in the past have crises been as visible as they are now, and seldom in the past have the problems of city and environment concerned us as they do now. There is an increasing awareness that man's works — his buildings, his highways, his dams and canals —

are not divorced from environment, but are artificial or altered environments subject to many of the same physical processes that operate in undisturbed nature. Conversely, it is recognized that nature must be understood not only in its pristine state, but also in terms of man's impact on it. Nowhere is this interaction between man and his environment more apparent than in the city.

This book's major purpose is to delineate the dynamics of these relations and portray the physical geography of the city, placing particular emphasis on the North American city. In pursuing this goal, we continually encounter pressing and recurrent problems in urbanizing societies, and hence we are compelled to extend our discussion to questions of wise management and recommendations for future planning.

Before discussing in each chapter the major physical elements in the city and their linking processes, it is useful to view urbanization and environment in perspective. This chapter defines some important terms, touches on reasons for our present ignorance about the physical geography of the city, and suggests a conceptual view of the city as an ecosystem.

SOME DEFINITIONS

In order to discuss man's interaction with his urban environment, it is necessary to define some basic terms and their relationships. Words such as "city", "environment", and "urbanization" may have different meanings for different people. In common usage, for example, "city" may mean a political unit, a settlement exceeding a certain population, or an aggregation of dwellings or other structures; or sometimes the city is seen only as its inhabitants: Shakespeare asked, "What is the city but the people?" Because of the multiplicity of definitions of terms such as *city*, it is necessary to establish the meaning of terms as they are used in this book. We do not pretend ours are the only definitions, but they do help clarify our discussion.

A city is a special combination of a place and its people. *City* is broadly defined here to include the totality of natural, social, and artificial components aggregated in populous places; the population has a highly organized culture including varied skills but lacking self-sufficiency in the production of energy (including food). The city may also be thought of functionally — as an open ecosystem for perpetuating urban culture by exchanging and converting great quantities of material and energy. These functions require a concentration of workers, an elaborate transportation system, and a hinterland that can supply the resources required by the city and absorb some of the city's products. These definitions purposely avoid arbitrarily defining a city on the basis of a minimum number of inhabitants. We use the term *urban place* generally, as a synonym for "city" or the space occupied by a city. We use the term *urban area* to mean a group of coalescent cities or the space occupied by them.

Urbanization is the process of city establishment and growth; the term commonly connotes population increase in the city, resulting from both internal growth and immigration, as well as spatial expansion of the city. We employ this broad definition because typically population growth and spatial growth of an urban place go hand in hand and because both kinds of growth importantly affect, and are affected by, environment. Our major concern in this book is the physical implications of urbanization rather than the growth and movement of populations or the relative numbers of urban and rural residents.

Environment is the aggregate of external conditions that influence the life of an individual or population, specifically the life of man; environment ultimately determines the quality and survival of life. This is an ecological definition that includes both physical and cultural components. Although environmentalists often emphasize one or the other, there is significant overlap between these two environmental classes. A house, for example, is a feature of both the physical and cultural environments — on the one hand, it is made of materials subject to the work of physical processes; on the other, it is largely a cultural fabrication. In this book we are interested in aspects of the physical environment, including those that are material products of culture. Nonphysical facets of the environment — for example, behavioral and social attributes such as language, religion, and social order — are beyond our concern here.

The city consists of two components: urban man and urban environment. An understanding of the dynamic interactions between these two elements is facilitated by recognizing that the city is an ecosystem. The ecosystem concept allows us to view the city in systematic, operational terms — to evaluate the flows of energy and matter

into and out of the city and to trace their circulation within it. In a
broad sense, an *ecosystem* is defined as the organisms of a locality
together with their related environment, considered as a unit. Within
the urban ecosystem three self-evident interactions are apparent: (1)
urbanization involves a modification of environment; (2) physical
(or "natural") environment may influence the form, functions, and
growth of the city;* and (3) continuous feedback occurs in the city between man, culture, and physical environment. A major purpose of this
book is to exemplify and explain these three generalizations.

Feedback is an important process discussed later in the chapter,
but a brief example here will illustrate its nature. For instance, men
may build expressways into the city and use physical environmental
criteria such as topography and bearing strength of the surface material
in the road-planning decision. By clearing, excavating, filling, and
paving, men create a new environmental surface, but natural processes
continue to operate across this new interface and unexpected repercussions may occur. Local flooding and erosion by surface waters are
typical consequences that may require new engineering adjustments,
such as the placement of new culverts and storm drains. These, in turn,
may trigger additional environmental effects of importance to man,
such as sedimentation or change in the water table. And so on, feedback ad infinitum: extended consequences of man's actions force new
human adjustments and, with them, further environmental repercussions.

NEGLECT OF THE SUBJECT

Given the importance of environmental problems related to
urbanization, it is remarkable how little is known about the subject.
This ignorance is only one specific manifestation of the generally widen-
ing gap between environmental change and environmental understanding
(Detwyler 1971). Insight into the reasons for this gap — specifically,

---

*There is great variability in the degree and type of urban response to the physical
environment. Our concern in this book is to show examples in which this causal relationship is clearly at work. To understand these influences in detail is beyond the
scope of this book and would require intensive study of human perception and its
translation into action in different cultural realms of the world.

why we have neglected learning about interactions between man and environment in the city — can help us overcome past neglect and focus attention on the environmental problems of the city. Hence it is useful to look briefly, and broadly, into the history of urbanization and environment as a subject of study.

The existing gap between environmental change and environmental understanding is primarily an outgrowth of the traditional Western concept that man and nature are separate, rather than inseparable (White 1967). This distinction has largely been sustained during the last hundred years, as the modern natural and social sciences have emerged. Unfortunately, a primary lesson from Charles Darwin was overlooked: that man cannot be separated, intellectually or physically, from the rest of nature. Man — like all organisms — is an integral part of nature and a product of natural selection through evolutionary time. Largely ignoring man's role in nature, most natural scientists focused undivided attention on the operations of "natural systems," that is, those relatively unaffected by man.

These practices became entrenched in the natural sciences before the massive environmental effects of the Industrial Revolution were experienced. But why have they persisted so long after intensive urbanization spurred these effects? Part of the answer lies in the fact that man is a complicating factor when it comes to studying environment. Man's actions are not easily reduced to sets of physical and chemical laws. Even the more complicated biological models that have been developed in the past few decades have proven of little use in explaining man's environmental actions. Furthermore, until very recently both natural scientists and the general public have ignored the work of social scientists, while revering physics, chemistry, and the other sciences on which technological progress has been founded. A final part of the answer probably lies in the excessive research specialization that has developed to the near exclusion of broad, interdisciplinary investigations of linkages between man and environment.

Typically, physical geography, although bridging many of the natural sciences, has been slow to recognize the influence of man in nature, especially in the city. Further, until recent decades the subject was primarily descriptive rather than analytical and process-oriented. Descriptions of physical geography have long served as bases for studies by cultural (including urban) geographers, but not much geographical research has specifically investigated the ties between man and environment (with the noteworthy but unfortunate exception of environmental determinism, which flourished as an interpretive model in geography for several decades before World War II). Within the past decade things have begun to change, however, and recently geographers have advanced our understanding of phenomena such as human perception of, and adjustment to, environmental hazards.

The social sciences, like the natural sciences, have shown narrowness in their development. Specifically, social scientists have neglected the interaction of urban man and physical environment because they considered the city to be almost wholly a construct of man, a cultural phenomenon. As cities have grown, so has man's local domination over nature and with it the idea that man is independent of nature, rather than an integral part of it. But, without reverting to social Darwinism, Konrad Lorenz, Desmond Morris, René Dubos, and others have rekindled interest in the question of biological determinism relative to culture, and have demonstrated that free will is not the sole determinant of culture. And yet, just as natural scientists have tended to "assume away" man, so too have social scientists tended to "assume away" environment.

A major objective of this book is to cut away these assumptions on both sides, to cut away the inertia of historical circumstance — in short to show both how environmental considerations are necessary to an understanding of urban man and how urban man is a potent force of environmental change.

THE CITY: AN INTEGRATED SYSTEM OF MAN AND ENVIRONMENT

A basic theme — that the relation between man and environment in the city is extremely complex — has already been stated. It is reiterated throughout this book because it is impossible to isolate completely the elements and processes within the urban environmental system or to separate them from each other. Explanatory discussion of one inevitably leads to others. For example, air pollution, a by-product of human activity, is intimately associated with climate; furthermore, the condition of the atmosphere (and, therefore, pollution) is locally influenced by topography, distribution of surface water, vegetation, and human factors. Thus, although individual chapters perforce focus on specific environmental elements within the city, other significant factors must be remembered and considered in each case.

In order to develop an appreciation of the range and complexity of the interactions between urban man and his environment, we present here a conceptual overview. We hope that placing the individual elements and processes in the perspective of an integrated whole will enhance understanding of the specific chapter subjects.

The City as an Ecosystem

In one sense the urban system is no different from other ecosystems: it is subject to the principle of *environmental unity*. This concept states that all the elements and processes of environment are interrelated and interdependent, and that a change in one will lead to changes in the others. This principle is frequently used as a framework by physical geographers and other earth scientists to understand the complex relations that occur in nature. It is apparent, for example, that because of environmental unity, a variety of environmental elements are altered in response to a lightning-triggered forest fire. Increased runoff and erosion usually follow the burning and removal of vegetation. These conditions, in turn, change physical and chemical properties of the underlying soil, possibly reducing soil fertility. Without a forest cover, the surface is also exposed to climatic extremes of radiation, temperature, and wind, from which the forest previously provided protection. These and other modifications significantly affect future plant and animal populations, which in turn exert effects upon the physical environment.

The same kinds of relationships exist in the city; however, in the city man is commonly the primary operator who initiates the train of environmental modifications. Also, because changes induced by modern man tend to occur more rapidly than those in undisturbed nature, the effects are sometimes more dramatic. Repercussions such as increases in flood runoff or traffic volume are easily observed over a single generation; more recently, some detrimental effects have been discernible in a few years or even months or days.

In short, the city — population together with environment — is a relatively new kind of ecosystem on the face of the earth. As in other ecological systems, the organism (man) is self-driven — drawing environmental resources to itself on the one hand, expelling its

products and wastes on the other. Energy and matter are the basic
stuff of any viable ecosystem, and like other ecosystems, the city
must concentrate, store, transform, and diffuse energy and matter.
There is not widespread recognition that the city is indeed an ecosystem, and therefore these flows and transformations have been little
studied and are poorly understood. Thus, our outline of the city as
an ecosystem is tentative. We present it to suggest what the major
pieces of the system are and how they are functionally related.
Further research using this viewpoint should modify and deepen our
initial interpretations presented here.

In the parlance of systems analysis, the city is an *open system*.
This means that the city is not self-contained; that is, that it cannot
function independently and in isolation from other parts of the world.
Some men would like to believe that the city can subsist on its own
juices and perpetuate itself — a not unexpected belief when the city
is viewed as the acme of human achievement. Reality tells us that
urban places cannot exist without exchanging matter and energy with
a much larger environment. Self-contained, or *closed*, ecosystems
cannot persist as durable units of our environment. The egg and the
space capsule are examples of temporarily closed systems — but even
they require heat and other energy from outside their shells and
must inevitably open in order to gather nourishment and guarantee
survival.

Urbanization, as an open system process, can be illustrated
using the familiar "black box" analogy, wherein the city is thought of
as a box that receives *inputs* of energy and material. Most of the inputs are transformed or stored within the city, although some flow
through the system with little alteration or resistance. Eventually
a portion of the transformed products and wastes (along with some
unused energy and matter) is sent out from the city as *outputs*. The
balance between various inputs and various outputs provides a simple
measure of the urban metabolism; it indicates whether the city is
in a state of growth, equilibrium, or decay.

There is some risk, however, in oversimplifying descriptions of
input-output systems; most ecosystems are extremely complex. There
are within the city, for example, numerous *feedback loops*. Maruyama
(1963 p. 176) has shown that "in a loop, the influence of an element
comes back to itself through other elements." Some feedback loops

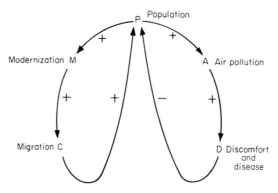

Figure 1.2. Positive and negative feedback loops.
(After Maruyama 1963.)

are recognized as *positive* and others as *negative*. Maruyama illustrates positive feedback with an example that (even though it operates on a priori notions) is instructive here (see Figure 1.2):

> Some of the arrows form loops. For example, there is a loop of arrows from P to M, M to C, and C back to M. A loop indicates mutual causal relationships . . . In the loop of P-M-C-P, an increase in the number of people causes an increase in modernization, which in turn increases migration into the city, which in turn increases the number of people in the city. In short, an increase in population causes a further increase in population through modernization and migration. On the other hand, a decrease in population causes a decrease in modernization, which in turn causes a decrease in migration, which in turn decreases population . . . Whatever the change, either an increase or a decrease amplifies itself. This is so when we take population as our criterion. But the same is true if we take modernization as a criterion: an increase in modernization causes a further increase in modernization through migration and population increase; and a decrease in modernization causes a further decrease in modernization through decreased migration and decreased population. The same holds true if we take migration as the criterion.

In other words, positive feedback is the phenomenon sometimes referred to as a "vicious circle" or as "deviation amplification"; changes occur in the same direction at a compounding rate. Many urban processes tend to produce positive feedback and so disturb the existing "balance of nature."

Negative feedback loops also are at work in the city. These loops are *equilibrating*; that is, they tend to dampen fluctuations in the system and maintain a steady state. The thermostat is a commonly used example of a mechanical device that produces negative feedback, or equilibration. As the temperature in a room drops, the thermostat activates a furnace, which in turn heats the room to some desired level, deactivating the thermostat until the temperature again falls; a tendency to a steady state is thus maintained. Similarly, in Figure 1.2, it can be seen that increased population (P) leads to increased air pollution (A), which leads to increased discomfort and disease (D). This may, in the long run, lead to decreased population, which in turn decreases air pollution, and so forth. This is, of course, only one of very many equilibrating, or negative feedback, systems within the urban ecosystem.

It should be noted that positive and negative feedback *do not* represent measures of "goodness" or "badness." No value judgments are involved; these terms simply indicate whether a loop is deviation-amplifying or equilibrating.

The open system approach to environmental analysis is widely accepted by physical, biological, and social scientists today. This is not surprising (although closed systems were once in vogue), because this common sense perspective provides a convenient "bank balance" by which conditions and change may be evaluated for any part of a system or for a system as a whole. Geographers and sociologists, for instance, utilize open system models to describe the spatial aspects of urban economy or demography in terms of inputs and outputs. Similarly, open systems are used by biologists to describe the life cycle of an organism and by hydrologists to delineate the seasonal behavior of a river. Such cases, which can be complicated, treat subsystems within larger ecosystems. Large ecosystems are incredibly complex and almost defy understanding because such a large number of operative variables and feedback loops must be identified and assessed.

Like other large ecosystems, the urban ecosystem as a whole is poorly understood. Nevertheless, we believe that a tentative and simplified description of the city ecosystem, although lacking complete substantiation and much detail, is helpful in several ways. It holds promise as a better model than most other existing ones for understanding how man and environment dynamically interact in the city; and it suggests avenues for research that, in turn, can improve the model. Even at this stage the major components and their relations can be seen clearly. A tentative and general model of the city ecosystem is illustrated in Figure 1.3 and discussed below.

The Requirements of Urban Man

City functions place many demands on man and nature. Two broad categories of requirements may be noted: (1) biological needs essential to survival of the urban population, and (2) cultural requirements necessary for city functioning and growth. Some critical biological and cultural requirements are listed in Table 1.1 and schematically illustrated in Figure 1.3.

Biological Requirements

The biological needs of man in the city are essentially the same as those he requires in any situation; but mainly because of high population densities, the requirements cannot always be met by the immediate environment in the city. It is a rare urban place that does not draw food, energy sources, and materials for shelter from an extensive hinterland. Except in arid and semiarid regions, water usually is available to cities from local rivers, lakes, or the ground; but in highly urbanized areas increasing levels of consumption and pollution of these resources are forcing urban man to seek water at ever greater distances and expense.

Space is a biological requirement of urban inhabitants that has received slight attention until recently. It has always been obvious that cities consume space as they grow physically. It has been less apparent, even when the efforts of city planners, architects, and social scientists are taken into account, that living and working space for the individual inhabitant is also a significant biological need. Laboratory rats are not the only creatures that can be driven to irrational and murderous or suicidal behavior by overcrowded living conditions. In the past few

Table 1.1. Some requirements of the urban ecosystem.

Biological Requirements	Cultural Requirements
Air	Political organization
Water	Economic system (including labor,
Space	capital, materials, and power)
Energy (food and heat)	Technology
Shelter	Transportation and communication
Waste disposal	Education and information
	Social and intellectual activities
	(including recreation, "cultural"
	facilities, religion, sense of
	community, etc.)
	Safety

years, research by John Calhoun (1962) and others and the popular works of Konrad Lorenz and Robert Ardrey (not to mention recurring incidents of individual and group trauma in the city) have focused attention on the need for living territory and the possible danger of very high population densities. Perhaps it is in the provision of space and adequate kinds of shelter that the urban ecosystem has most seriously failed to meet its residents' biological requirements.

Systems for supplying the requirements of air, water, and waste disposal are also under stress — especially because of increased pollution. Contamination of air, water, and food poses problems to human health, causes repercussions on other environmental elements, and threatens the general quality of life. More and more our cities are diffusing noxious outputs and absorbing adulterated inputs. It sometimes seems that the net effect on the balance of the urban ecosystem and surrounding countryside is inevitably deleterious, that urban places destructively impinge on the biological environment that permitted them to exist in the first place.

However, this is not necessarily the case. Although urbanization places the local physical environment under considerable stress, it also provides man with biological requirements that might not be available to large populations in pastoral or rural societies. In short, the cultural and technological attributes of urbanization allow a greater number of people to maintain themselves.

Cultural Requirements

The word *culture* has many meanings and uses; its use here encompasses the totality of man's ways of living built up by a human group and transmitted from one generation or group to another. The cultural requirements of the urban ecosystem are listed in Table 1.1. It is apparent that neither urban populations nor urban functions can be maintained without some degree of social, economic, and political organization. The urban ecosystem has survived under a variety of political and economic systems; each leaves its unique imprint on the city's characteristics.

Technology (including invention) and transportation have advanced with, and in fact allowed, urbanization. Without them the modern city could not exist. It is transportation and technology that allow the city to absorb basic resources, remake them, and distribute them to a marketing hinterland. Once energy and material resources are in the city, technology provides the means by which construction, industrial production, and communication are achieved. And most important, technology and transportation have made it possible for the city to concentrate the resources needed to fulfill the biological requirements of its dense population.

The modern city is very dependent on technological apparatus, which means that mechanical breakdowns can have serious repercussions in the ecosystem. The ever present danger of atomic holocaust has led many persons to assess their abilities to survive without the usual life-support of urban civilization. The chances for urban man would be slim because without a fully working technological system he probably could not obtain adequate food, power, or heat. In some cases even water would be unavailable.

But isolation by nuclear war is, we hope, an unlikely and avoidable event. Dramatic examples of the impact of temporary technological collapse have already become rather commonplace. Generally, technological breakdowns affect the city's ability to provide the biological requirements of the urban population. Power failures are a case in point. They are occurring with greater frequency owing to expanding use, overloading, and machinery failure. Huge populations periodically are cut off from various services, such as heating, air conditioning, and light. Thirty years ago the loss of air conditioning would have been merely a nuisance, entailing few serious repercussions, but now it is a serious occurrence. Today many office buildings and apartments are constructed so that it is almost impossible to obtain natural ventilation when the air-conditioning equipment shuts off; and today's cities are more effective heat traps than they used to be. Thus power failure during a heat wave can threaten the lives of many inhabitants.

Beyond technology, cultural attitudes and economic values may strongly influence a city's ability to supply its biological requirements, such as water. Cities that draw river water for domestic use are a good example. For many years it has been a bad joke that people living along the Mississippi River have been drinking the sewage of their upstream neighbors. This is not far from the truth, because a river cannot naturally purify itself of huge loads of organic sewage or even small amounts of some inorganic wastes. To ensure potable water each city downstream must invest in expensive water treatment facilities. The same cities, in turn, may dump their wastes into the river. Before disposal most cities' wastes are only partially treated, and many cities eject untreated wastes into the river. The consequent pollution not only presents problems for downstream users, but it may destroy other river values, such as aquatic life, recreation, and aesthetics.

These water problems could be significantly reduced if waste effluents were properly treated: downstream communities would receive clean water and the river environment would be protected. Unfortunately, the cultural subsystem strongly inhibits enactment of such a rational program. The reasons are complex but may include the following:

1. *Effective* sewage treatment is very expensive.
2. Taxpayers generally are unwilling to pay for improving a resource someone else will use.
3. An effective regional program is almost impossible because of the complex legal and jurisdictional conflicts existing between cities, townships, counties, states, the federal government, and the private sector.
4. Most of the citizenry give short-term economic considerations a higher priority than regional water management, long-term ecological values, and aesthetics.

Thus, the quality and quantity of a major biological requirement, water, strongly reflect the social, political, and economic characteristics of the urban ecosystem and usually the interaction between cities. Similarly, cultural conditions (both within and without the city) affect the amount and suitability of the other substances that are available to fulfill the biological requirements of urban man.

Factors Affecting Biological and Cultural Requirements

Examples have been given of some ways in which an urban ecosystem's biological requirements and cultural conditions interact. It is important to note that the exact cultural and biological needs of a given city are, in large part, controlled by at least three other conditions — stage of cultural development, population size and density, and energy flow. All are intimately linked and function jointly throughout the evolution of cities. They exert great influence on the urbanization process.

The conditions and functions of the ecosystem are partly reflections of the city's stage of cultural development. Generally, the more complex the material culture, the greater are the amounts of raw materials needed for transformation into artifacts and energy. Obviously urban man's biological requirements are simplist in the initial stages of urban development and increase in complexity as urbanization proceeds. As a city grows, its dependence on technology (and raw materials to support it) grows, and the complexity of consequent environmental repercussions also increases.

Cultural and biological requirements also are influenced by population factors. Larger absolute populations and higher densities have a direct relationship to the ecosystem's needs; a city with 100,000 people is a simple system compared to a megalopolis. Also, as indicated earlier, high population densities are difficult to maintain — because of complex interdependencies — without frequent breakdowns in the biological and cultural subsystems.

Finally, input, storage, and output are functions of the rates at which energy flows through the ecosystem (a phenomenon discussed further later). Here the expression "energy" refers to the power to do work within all the sectors of the ecosystem: cultural sphere, biosphere, atmosphere, lithosphere, and hydrosphere. The human element is most important in the manipulation of this energy. The growth, productivity, competitive success, and even physiognomy of cities are strongly influenced by the rates at which energy is imported and utilized.

The Role of Environment in the Urban Ecosystem

Some major functions and requirements of man in the city ecosystem have been described (albeit briefly), but environment has been treated only peripherally. With urban man's basic needs in perspective, it now is appropriate to view the total urban ecosystem and the role of environment in it. Figure 1.3 presents a schematic representation of the urban ecosystem, divided into input and output components. Some feedback loops resulting from interaction of the environmental and cultural subsystems also are suggested in the diagram. In reality, all components are subsumed by the larger earth ecosystem that is the totality of man and his environment.

Environments of the Urban Ecosystem

In order to analyze the urban ecosystem, it is useful to identify its component parts. There are many ways in which the urban environment — the aggregate of external conditions that influence the life of urban man — can be classified into subsystems. Such classifications necessarily are arbitrary, and the one presented here is no exception. The urban environment is herein divided into two broad classes, cultural

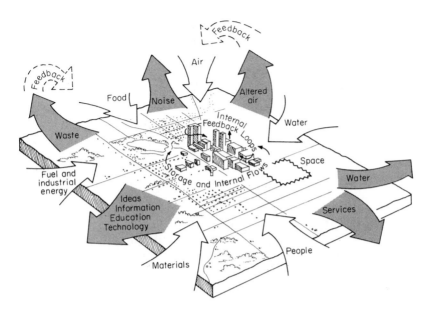

Figure 1.3. Schematic representation of some inputs and outputs of the urban ecosystem.

and physical subsystems, which reflect respectively the basic interests of social and physical scientists, discussed previously. Actually, of course, the cultural and physical subsystems are interlocking and in some cases only arbitrarily distinguished.

The *cultural environment* is that essentially formed by man; it comprises the external cultural attributes of a given community. The cultural environment in the city may be categorized in a number of ways — functionally, structurally, locationally — but such schemes are beyond our purpose here. Many of the material aspects of culture — for example, roads and buildings — have important physical environmental implications, especially the alteration of physical processes such as heat flux, runoff of rain, and so on. Such attributes of the cultural environment will receive appropriate attention throughout the text.

The *physical environment* consists of nature's omnipresent elements; these exist whether or not man is on the scene. In the city these elements commonly are modified by man, though their essential characteristics are not destroyed. This is the environment on which man ultimately depends, both biologically and materially. All artifacts are, of course, molded from the physical environment. Several major components (or spheres) of the physical environment traditionally are recognized:

1. The *lithologic* environment, consisting of the solid, nonliving portions of the earth, which include landforms, bedrock, and soil;
2. The *atmospheric* environment, the gaseous envelope of air (and suspended small solid and liquid particles) that surrounds the earth;
3. The *hydrologic* environment, consisting of the water portions of the earth;
4. The *biological* environment, which is that part of the world consisting of living things.

These four environmental components are not mutually exclusive, of course, but are spatially interfused and tied together by various earth processes. Some water, for instance, is a constituent of organisms, some is chemically bound in rocks, and some exists as vapor in the air.

This environmental classification provides a useful framework for chapter subjects in this text. Thus, we consider urban man's interactions with the lithosphere in chapters on the geologic and topographic setting of the city (Chapter 2) and soil in the city (Chapter 6); with the atmosphere in terms of the city's climate (Chapter 3) and problems of climate and urban planning (Chapter 4); with the hydrosphere in a chapter on water in the city (Chapter 5); and with the biosphere in essays concerning vegetation and wildlife in the city (Chapters 9 and 10, respectively). Other appropriate chapters discuss urban noise (Chapter 8) and the perception by man of natural hazards in the city (Chapter 7).

Now, having recognized component physical environments within the urban ecosystem, we can examine some important aspects of the system's dynamics. The relations between urbanization and physical environment may be clarified by identifying the flows — inputs, outputs, and storage — of energy and materials that occur in the city.

Inputs, Outputs, and Storage

The urban ecosystem draws and utilizes large quantities of human and environmental resources from the area around it. The most important of these inputs are illustrated by the input arrows in Figure 1.3. The imported materials help provide both basic biological necessities and the materials and energy required for production. Within the urban ecosystem energy and material are redistributed locally and transformed.

Tremendous quantities of resources must be imported into the modern city. The average urban dweller in the United States, for example, uses (directly or indirectly) about 150 gallons (1,250 pounds) of water, 4 pounds of food, and 19 pounds of fossil fuels *each day* (Wolman 1965, p. 180). Largely to satisfy the metabolism of cities, the United States transports about 9,000 ton-miles of freight per person yearly. Also, on the average each American consumes 1,400 pounds of steel, travels some 5,300 miles between cities, receives nearly 400 pieces of mail, and makes more than 700 telephone calls per year (Brown 1970, pp. 121–122). In an average day the city's inputs are converted into 120 gallons of sewage per person, 4 pounds of refuse per capita, and 1.9 pounds of air pollutants per inhabitant (Wolman 1965, p. 180).

Once resources flow into the urban system, they are subject to a number of possible uses. Some are consumed directly, either by the population or by the construction necessary for urban expansion. Much of the resources is either stored for future use or transformed into exportable products and waste. Finally, a large-volume input of air and water is transient in the city. It passes quickly through the system, and only a small amount is actually consumed or used for more than merely diluting wastes.

Unfortunately, the urban ecosystem seldom treats air and water resources by riparian standards; that is, they are not returned to the ecosphere in the same condition in which they were received. As a result of this economic expediency, some waste outputs of the city mingle with atmosphere and water to contaminate both city and surrounding countryside. Some liquid waste is pumped back into the ground beneath cities. Some solid waste is transported beyond the city for dumping, and some is used as landfill to restructure the city's topographic base.

We do not mean to imply that all outputs are undesirable. A primary function of cities is to produce and export goods. These include the items manufactured or processed by the city as well as the commercial and professional services that are concentrated in urban places. Most important, cities are the focal points of civilization, where

man's intellectual activities are concentrated. Urban ecosystems are
the seats from which political and economic power, information, ideas,
and education are diffused.

Repercussions within the Ecosystem

In pursuing an analysis of the city as an ecosystem, feedback
loops become apparent, and it becomes difficult to separate cause and
effect. Quite clearly, the concept of environmental unity is illustrated;
the elements and processes of the ecosystem are interacting and
interdependent. In a large city many outputs become inputs. The citizen
is made aware of many feedback loops that have "bad" repercussions
(although, as previously stressed, feedback itself is not a bad thing). Man
requires better understanding of repercussions resulting from urbanization (that is, the feedback loops) if he is to predict them and correctly
adjust for them.

Many repercussions within the urban ecosystem are described
and explained in following chapters; by way of example here, we present a brief description of repercussions involving just one element
in the ecosystem — water. Figure 1.4 schematically illustrates relations
between water and the city. The figure reveals that the flow of water

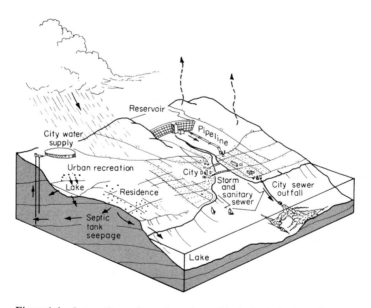

Figure 1.4.   Interactions of an urban place with the hydrologic cycle.

is subject to both physical processes and human alteration; some is simply deflected, some is recycled. Typically, the water that leaves the urban system is quite different in quality and quantity from the water that arrived.

Water is carried to the city by natural means (rivers, springs, precipitation, lakes) or by engineering works (canals, wells, pipes, pumps, and so forth). Once in the urban area, water still is subject to physical processes, and some will be lost to immediate use by runoff, evaporation, and infiltration into the ground. Within the city most water flows in pipes, drains, gutters, and modified watercourses; only vestiges of natural watersheds remain in most urbanized landscapes.

There are two types of water use in the city: consumptive and noncomsumptive. Consumptive use removes water from the system and depletes the outflow; the beverage industry and evaporative air coolers are typical consumptive users. More water is required for nonconsumptive uses, and theoretically such water is returned to the system undamaged. In reality, most nonconsumptive uses alter water quality; even so-called clean uses (for example, recreation, navigation, and cooling) generally result in chemical or thermal modification.

A high proportion of water leaving the urban ecosystem is transported in sewers and drains, but eventually most is dumped in rivers, lakes, or the sea. Thus, human and industrial wastes (which usually are partially treated at best) and sediment-heavy runoff contribute to further pollution and eutrophication of our primary water resources. The case of Mississippi River cities cited earlier is only one example of such repercussions.

Feedback can occur internally within the same city. In the city depicted in Figure 1.4, for example, some water is pumped into the city from the ground water immediately below. In this particular case (and it is not an uncommon one), the city also pumps liquid waste back into the ground in another area. In yet another part of town suburban residents utilize septic fields for waste disposal. A combination of shallow wells and local topography may lead to unintentional contamination of the city water supply. Corrective measures, such as alternative sewage disposal or tapping of new water supplies, will then be required, but these, in turn, may create new problems elsewhere in the system. For example, it is apparent that the lakeside recreation area is seriously polluted; the addition of more waste — as by the seepage of sewage along the bluffs where subsurface waste escapes — may terminate its use.

In this brief discussion of water in the urban ecosystem, we have not specified negative and positive feedback loops, but rather focused on various important interactions between the city and water and between man and water in the city. So, too, throughout the book discussions of other environments generally are not couched expressly in terms of inputs, outputs, storage, and positive and negative feedback loops. Rather, these valuable concepts are implicit. As man's attention toward the problems of urbanization and environment increases in the future, explicit analysis of the constituent processes will improve. We hope that the conceptual and methodological framework presented here will prove useful in that development as well as immediately beneficial in putting the chapters that follow in perspective.

REFERENCES

Ardrey, Robert. 1966. *The territorial imperative.* New York: Atheneum.

Brown, Harrison. 1970. Human materials production as a process in the biosphere. In *The biosphere*, ed. Editors of Scientific American, pp. 115–124. San Francisco: W. H. Freeman.

Calhoun, John. 1962. Population density and social pathology. *Sci. Amer.* Feb.: 139–148.

Chorley, Richard, and Barbara Kennedy. 1971. *Physical geography: A systems approach.* London: Prentice-Hall.

Dansereau, Pierre, ed. 1970. *Challenge for survival; Land, air, and water for man in megalopolis.* New York and London: Columbia Univ. Press.

Davis, Kingsley. 1965. The urbanization of the human population. *Sci. Amer.* Sept.:40–53.

Detwyler, Thomas R. 1971. Modern man and environment. In *Man's impact on environment,* ed. T. R. Detwyler, pp. 2–9. New York: McGraw-Hill.

Gottman, Jean. 1961. *Megalopolis: The urbanized northeastern seaboard of the United States.* New York: Twentieth Century Fund.

Lorenz, Konrad. 1963. *On aggression.* New York: Harcourt, Brace & World.

Maruyama, Magoroh. 1963. The second cybernetics: Deviation-amplifying mutual causal processes. *Amer. Scientist* 51:164–179.

McHarg, Ian L. 1969. *Design with nature.* Garden City, N.Y.: Natural History Press.

Mumford, Lewis. 1961. *The city in history: Its origins, its transformations, and its prospects.* New York: Harcourt, Brace & World.

Smock, R. B. 1971. Man and the urban environment. In *Environment: Resources, pollution and society,* ed. W. W. Murdock, pp. 339–359. Stamford, Conn.: Sinauer Associates.

Thomas, William L., Jr., ed. 1956. *Man's role in changing the face of the earth.* Chicago: Univ. of Chicago Press.

United Nations. 1970. *United Nations demographic yearbook, 1969.* New York: U. N. Statistical Office, Dept. of Economic and Social Affairs.

White, Lynn, Jr. 1967. The historical roots of our ecological crisis. *Science* 155 (3767):1203–1207. (Reprinted in Detwyler 1971.)

Wolman, Abel. 1965. The metabolism of cities. *Sci. Amer.* March:179–190.

Yeates, M. H., and B. J. Garner. 1971. *The North American city.* New York: Harper and Row.

CHAPTER 2

The Geologic and Topographic Setting of Cities

Donald F. Eschman and Melvin G. Marcus

The geologic and topographic setting of cities plays a major role in their location and growth. First, the physical landscape is a major factor in the initial selection of sites for settlement. Second, topography and landforms strongly influence the early growth and development of settlements, particularly the evolution of their spatial pattern. Last, even though in these days man's technology allows him to move mountains, the economic costs of overcoming geologic and geomorphologic factors continue to impose directional and aerial constraints on urbanization. Thus, although the greatest impact of physical environment on human activities such as urbanization may be found in the historical past or in less developed cultures today, the basic landscape on which cities are situated continues to play an important role in modern urbanization.

This chapter considers the geologic landscape on which cities are built. Because the criteria by which sites for settlement are selected are extremely complex, attention is first directed to the multitude of locational factors in order to place the physical factors in their proper perspective. Basic topographic and geologic questions are then considered. They involve a variety of interactions between cities and their topography, geomorphic processes, and geologic composition. The feedback between human activities and the parent landscape is critical, and therefore examples are given throughout the chapter.

THE LOCATION OF CITIES: RESPONSE TO SITE AND SITUATION, CULTURE AND ENVIRONMENT

Cities are not simply where you find them. They are located in response to a complex set of interacting processes and forces that encompass a range of factors extending well beyond those presented by the physical landscape. The larger the city, the more complicated are the economic, political, and social factors that influence its location and growth. It is important to recognize, however, that man has only recently acquired the ability to bring a sophisticated technology to bear on the selection and development of his settlements. Although in the long run the survival and growth of urban places must depend upon economic and social factors, success is seldom achieved if rational decisions regarding physical locations are ignored.

Urban geographers often group the factors of urban location as being those of site or those of situation. *Site* refers to the features of the local environment on which settlements are established and over which they grow. The initial conditions of site are modified by human activities; the alteration of site is particularly evident in large urban areas. *Situation* refers both to the physical conditions relative to the site that extend over a wider area than the actual settlement occupies and to man's cultural characteristics within and around the city. Except as the initial site of a city may be altered by man, site tends to remain static, whereas situation changes through time in response to urban expansion and the development of new activities within the city.

The parent material and topography on which cities are built are major site factors, although other elements such as water resources, land-water boundaries, and climate commonly are important. In the case of New York City, for example, the original European settlement was on Manhattan Island, then an area of wooded, bedrock hills, interspersed with low-lying marshes and tidal flats. The island's drainage pattern and shoreline were qualities of site. As the population grew and more space was required for human activities, the site was altered by draining and filling the marshes. The dramatic expansion that New York City experienced, however, was not a simple response to its initial site characteristics. Rather, its broader physical situation — expressed in such features as the Hudson River, good harbors, and access to the interior of North America (via the Hudson River and the Mohawk Lowlands) — provided a physical setting favorable to the growth of industry and commerce. The human situation was even more significant in that it provided the social, economic, and political needs and potentials that allowed a great city to evolve upon and spread from the initial site. In short, the city required a physical base, but it was the broader relationships of that site to human activities and distant landscapes that proved most significant in the city's evolution.

The growth of every city can, in large part, be explained in terms of human determinants. It has been suggested by some urban geographers and sociologists that there is little point in attempts to classify the geological and topographical attributes of urban places, because each city responds to a unique set of environmental and human conditions. According to them, generalized explanations of urbanization that are based on a physical typology must inevitably be fruitless exercises that do not address the major social and economic processes at work. Though these arguments are in some part true, the fact remains that cities are built on earth materials that have topographic expression — and the rational use of this physical base is profitable to man. Conversely, topography and geology may place constraints on human activities that require an expenditure of time, money, and effort to overcome.

ENVIRONMENTAL CONSIDERATIONS IN EARLY SETTLEMENT

Historically, man has sought city locations that provide: (1) access to good water transportation or overland routes; (2) protection from natural hazards such as floods, storms, and landslides; (3) security from enemies; (4) water supply; (5) building materials, fuel, and other usable resources; and (6) a stable base for construction. Other factors, some of which may provide commercial and industrial advantages, such as water power, natural breaks in transportation routes, local food sources, and of course historical accident, are also important. Nearly all of these settlement criteria are dependent on geologic and topographic conditions.

The settlement history of North America clearly reflects the need to satisfy some or all of these environmental conditions. New

York, Providence, and Boston are good examples of settlements built at the site of a well-protected harbor, while Baltimore and Charleston, South Carolina, are examples of settlements bordering a large estuary (resulting from the drowning of a river valley). In each of these locations, protection from storm waves is provided by deep coastal indentations and offshore islands — landforms created by the recent post-glacial rise of sea level relative to the land. It is interesting that 22 of the world's 32 largest cities are located on estuaries.

Another locational requirement — that settlements be easily defensible — is as old as the first cities. Hilltops are excellent defensive positions, especially if they are nearly surrounded by steep slopes that rise from water or wetlands. Such sites are defensively strengthened if routes of land access are narrowly constricted and can be closed off by strong walls and a gate. Island locations, such as Manhattan or the Ile de Paris in their early urban periods, also enhance a city's defensive capability. Moats are, after all, nothing more than human efforts to create islands where nature has not provided them.

Town sites that not only provided fortified heights but also controlled waterways or harbors were particularly important to pioneer settlers. Quebec was such a city, and its major role in controlling the St. Lawrence region is described in Jesuit journals:

> Quebec, therefore, is the key to North America, and as I have said, a very firm bulwark of New France, because it is first a rock, secondly a height, thirdly a promontory; and, lastly, because it is fortified by two rivers in a manner of a trench and a moat. The rock serves as a very solid base for the citadel and town founded upon it, and prevents them from being washed away by the waves or undermined by sappers. The height offers a steep and arduous ascent, almost unscalable by enemies. The promontory, jutting out into the river Saint Lawrence, forms a secure haven for Our own ships, but a dangerous port for those of an enemy; for cannons, on the level space at the base of the cliff, and in the Citadel above, can protect or defend our ships and hinder the others from approaching or passing.
>
> For from the mouth of the river, that is, for a distance of three hundred and sixty miles, the shores are not within cannon range of each other; here, for the first time, one bank defends the other. Finally, the river Saint Lawrence on the east and south, and the Saint Charles, the other river, flowing into the St. Lawrence on the north, form as it were a moat and a wall. From these points it is evident how great is the Natural strength of the Citadel, and the stability of the town. (Thwaites 1899, p. 185)

Numerous large inland cities are located on rivers and lakeheads; confluences of major rivers are particularly desirable. Great cities abound, for example, along the Mississippi, the Danube, and the Yangtze rivers. The general situation that makes rivers good locations for settlement does not, however, determine the exact physical site on which a city is located. Local geologic and topographic circumstances must also be considered. The situational factors at the confluence of the Missouri and Mississippi rivers, for example, were encouraging to the development of a major settlement in the nineteenth century — the situation offered water transportation, access to the northern and western interior of the United States, and centrality. The actual place selected for the settlement (St. Louis) was a response not only to this situation but also to site characteristics. The original city was built upon the first dry, nonflooding bluff downstream from the confluence rather than at the confluence proper.

Finally, some cities are established upon or near desirable mineral resources. Such cities are often ephemeral, rising dramatically only to waste away to relic ghost towns as their mineral wealth is depleted. North American history is replete with examples of once teeming boom towns — Virginia City, Deadwood, Dawson, and Eldora — that today are skeleton cities surviving on the tourist dollar.

GEOLOGIC DIVERSITY INFLUENCES URBAN GROWTH

Once a settlement has been established, its continued growth commonly is influenced by the geologic and topographic attributes of its site. In an urbanizing area environmental factors such as steep slopes, poorly drained ground, flowing or standing bodies of water, and aesthetic characteristics constrain or bar development of certain areas. Patterns of urban expansion may develop a bias in a particular direction or favor certain landforms; transportation can be similarly affected. Barriers are most apparent during a city's expansion phases, and considerable technological and economic effort is required to overcome them. As long as the least cost and effort can be achieved by building the city on favorable physical locations, problem terrain is avoided. Eventually, if population pressure and economic and political circumstances demand it, urbanization will spread to less desirable landscapes.

Where the City Grows

It has been economically sensible for cities to expand, especially in their early stages of growth, along the lines of least topographic and geologic resistance. In areas of relatively flat or rolling, well-drained

land, cities tend to spread rather evenly in all directions. Examples
abound in the Great Plains and Central Lowlands of North America,
where only rivers and lakes commonly present major barriers to growth.
Houston, Texas, and Saskatoon, Saskatchewan, are good examples of
cities where topographic resistance is low and the cities have expanded
without interruption and about equally in all directions from the CBD's
(central business districts; see Figure 2.1, top). Chicago and Detroit
have sites where only water has been a major obstacle to urban growth;
flat, open land has otherwise allowed quite uniform expansion into
the rural countryside (Figure 2.1, center). In fact, once the lakefront
effect has been accounted for in Chicago, the flat terrain so nearly
approaches an isotropic surface that that city has become a major focus
of studies which attempt to explain patterns of urbanization by various
theoretical models. For example, the classical urban studies of Ernest
Burgess (1925) and Homer Hoyt (1939) focused on Chicago.

In some regions geologic structure presents formidable obstacles
to urban growth. The dramatic relief between ridges and valleys in
the Appalachian Mountains has clearly influenced patterns of human
settlement. Cities located along the valley floors, on water courses
and overland routes, tend to spread longitudinally. Rosary-like strings of
towns accompany many rivers, leaving sparsely populated spaces on
intervening slopes and ridges (see Figure 2.2). The urban area of Bluefield–South Bluefield, West Virginia, in the Appalachians illustrates
the elongation that accompanies urban growth in this region (Figure 2.1,
bottom).

The urban pattern of Los Angeles, California, is another example of the constraint that topography can place on urban growth.
This city, which has experienced phenomenal population growth in the
last half century, exemplifies urban man's determination to subjugate
the environment. The population boom seemingly forced the city to expand from the lowlands of the Los Angeles basin onto nearby slopes
and hills. The city has become an impressive testimonial to man's technological ability to overwhelm his environment – but only if one
blindly ignores the risks from landslides, earthquakes, and storms. Even
in Los Angeles, though, some steep mountainous areas (those that
continue to present physical and economic barriers to urbanization) remain unsettled (Figure 2.1, bottom).

Hills and slopes are not the only kinds of geologic resistance to
urban growth. Low, poorly drained areas, such as flood plains, marshes,
and tidal flats, also present problems. In the New York metropolitan

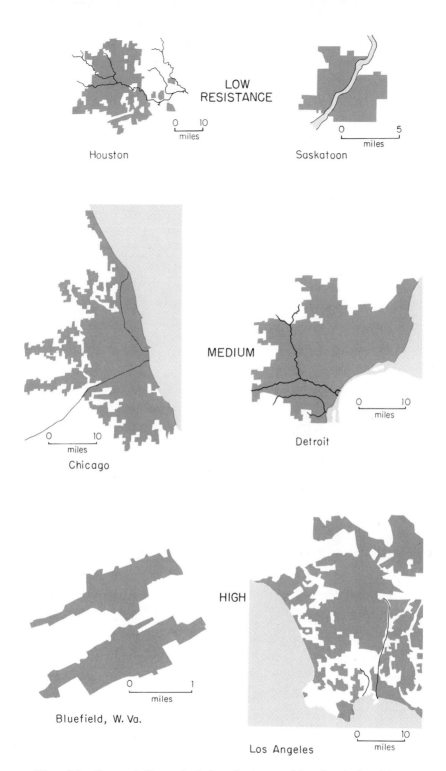

Figure 2.1. Shapes of cities on land of varying topographic and geologic resistance.

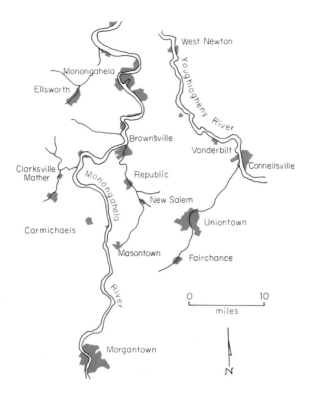

Figure 2.2. Many cities in the Appalachian Mountains are arranged in rosary-like strings in valleys.

region, for example, some 15,000 acres (of an original 30,000 acres) of the water-saturated open lands called Hackensack Meadows remain relatively unsettled and unused in the midst of densely populated and industrialized land. Despite dramatic economic pressures, this land is only slowly being drained, filled, and turned to human use. Areas made suitable for some construction by land-filling are not suitable for all types of constructions. Some low-lying fill zones of Manhattan Island, for example, cannot support the skyscrapers that rise on firm bedrock in midtown and lower Manhattan. For many years Chicago was forced to expand horizontally because a means could not be found to soundly support high-rise buildings on the unconsolidated sediments along the lake shore. In recent years this problem has been solved, and vertical growth has become a major feature of Chicago's urbanization.

Suburban expansion is particularly sensitive to geologic conditions, because few home owners have the capital to invest in a major technological battle with the environment. Yet the suburbanite who pioneers residential housing on the outskirts of a city must cope with such problems as water supply, septic disposal, and drainage (these problems are discussed in Chapters 5 and 6). This is one of the reasons that most prospective owners of suburban homes wait until they can move into new subdivisions where instant connections to urban utility systems are available and the environmental costs are spread over a larger population. Individuals who do build on environmentally difficult terrain commonly represent income extremes within the population. Families with high incomes can afford to clear and build on virgin terrain and to invest in expensive systems for water supply and sewerage. The advantages — privacy, a more natural landscape, perhaps scenic outlook, as well as avoidance of the environmental and social liabilities of the city — are considered worth the additional investment. Low-income families also move into these fringe areas as long as property values remain low; in fact, in many areas of the world the urban fringe is occupied by "land squatters" (see Figure 2.3). It has been suggested that low-income groups cope with such an environment because they are willing to do with less elaborate utilities and provide their own labor and construction. Thus, the edge of the city can present the incongruity of neighboring tarpaper shacks and elaborate homes.

This residential arrangement has been described for the "dormitory" area of central New Jersey, where commuters who work in cities reside. Plainfield, Bound Brook, and Somerset are burgeoning communities adjoining the southern edge of the Watchung Mountains (see Figure 2.4). Two landform types characterize this area: (1) low, rolling hills composed of erodible shales and sandstones and (2) resistant ridges of basalt (the Watchung Mountains). Until a decade or so ago, the majority of suburban growth had remained in the low-lying areas where the ground is easily worked by bulldozers and groundwater and septic fields were readily available. The ridges remained sparsely populated until population pressures and economic conditions pushed subdivision and development there.

Whenever man moves onto the hillsides and ridges, a particular set of physiographic factors become important. Construction on hill sites must take into account the stability of slopes (which is dependent on the nature of the bedrock or surficial deposits constituting the surface layers), the extent and character of weathering of the material,

Figure 2.3. Urban slums (or *favela*) on a steep slope in Brazil. (Courtesy of Planned Parenthood Federation of America.)

its suitability for water supply and sewage disposal, the likelihood of slope failure due to future undercutting (by streams, waves, or man), earthquake activity, and other processes discussed in Chapters 5, 6, and 7.

Finally, it is important to recognize the impact that topography and local watersheds have on suburban expansion. In the city of Ann Arbor, Michigan, for example, good construction sites have remained unannexed and largely undeveloped for many years because they are located in watersheds draining away from the city's principal sewer systems. Subdivision development is prohibitive until a major intercept sewer line breaches or circumvents the hydrologic divide to provide gravity flow. The connection to city sewer and drainage systems also is essential to urban expansion in areas where the substrate is relatively impermeable. In such areas the cost of construction of suitable disposal fields is often prohibitive, and only a limited number of housing units can be served without serious health threats from contamination.

Transportation

Many of the geologic factors that affect the selection of city sites and influence urban growth also are significant in the development of urban transportation. This is true particularly in the early stages of urbanization, when space is not at a premium and the lines of least geologic and topographic resistance are the most economic ones. Later, as social and political interests override environmental considerations, transportation is routed wherever the people (or the politicians) decide.

Inside the city, as in the countryside, cost per mile of road or railbed is a critical criterion in route determination. Some of the environmental factors that significantly affect cost are right-of-way drainage, slope, need for and difficulty of excavation, and requirements for fill. It is often cheaper to follow a longer, circuitous route from one point to another than to shorten the path by excavation, filling, and tunneling; bridges, of course, add greatly to the cost. Hillsides are usually avoided, both because of increased construction cost and because of danger from slope instability. Depending upon the type of rock, the geologic structure, and the covering surface materials, either ridges or valley bottoms may be preferred.

Ridges are especially desirable when valley bottoms are poorly drained or subject to periodic flooding. The selection of ridge routes is apparent in the early patterns of transportation and settlement in

Figure 2.4. Relations between land use (aerial photo on left) and geology and topography (map on right) in the Watchung Mountains area, New Jersey. Urban and agricultural land uses predominate in the low areas, which are underlain by shale and sandstone. Recently residential development has commenced on the hills. (After Marcus and Robbins 1970. Courtesy of Association of American Geographers and the Macmillan Co.)

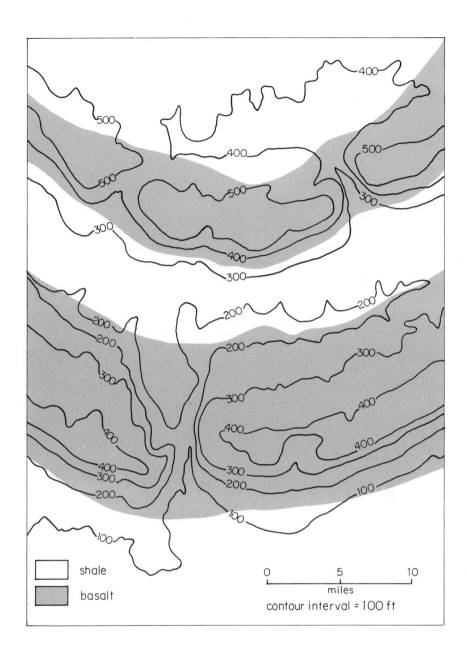

shale
basalt

0   5   10
miles
contour interval = 100 ft

southeastern Michigan and northern Ohio. The topography of this
region, adjacent to Lake Erie, is characterized by several broad, poorly
drained plains, consisting of lacustrine sediments deposited by late
glacial and post-glacial lakes. Relic beach and dune ridges ring the
former lake bottoms, providing higher, well-drained paths for travel.
These were the routes of prehistoric trails; the Indian, like today's highway engineer, preferred to travel the ridges rather than the intervening
wet and clayey flats. Many of the major transportation routes in metropolitan Cleveland and Detroit still follow these old trails.

In hilly or mountainous areas man's roads commonly follow the
valleys. These are natural routes, which avoid the difficulties of higher
relief and also pass through the areas of greatest human activity.

In the long run, the transportation demands of urbanization
overcome most geologic and topographic obstacles. Then, in the large
city, the ways in which environment influences transportation become
secondary to the question of how transportation influences environment. It is a rare road that does not require removal of earth from one
place and the build-up of land in another. Thus, the basic topography
and material of the city's surface is altered constantly by civil engineers.
The cost and availability of the basic materials from which the roads
and railbeds are made also contribute to the alteration of the environment: The low unit value of rock, gravel, and sand dictates that they be
transported the shortest possible distance; thus many urban roadways
are built at the expense of gouging the nearby landscape into which
cities eventually expand.

THE MODERN CITY OVERCOMES ITS SUBSTRATE — BUT AT A PRICE

Modern man is a major agent of landscape alteration. Although
on the one hand his cities respond to their physical setting, on the other
man often sees fit to tear down and remold the urban land. He ac-
complishes this by scraping and filling, by changing the structure, composition, and properties of soil and unconsolidated earth mantle, and by
conquering unstable hillsides. Thus, the modern city overcomes its
substrate — but at a price. The cost is sometimes simply economic and
can be expressed in terms of capital, labor, and investment in technology. At other times, it is the price of negative environmental feed-

back, repercussions from a landscape whose equilibrium has been disturbed. As man has the ability to profoundly alter nature, so nature has the capacity to disturb and even destroy man's works. This section discusses both how man has significantly altered the physical base of his urban environment and how that environment has, in turn, affected man.

Remolding the Land by Scraping and Filling

The present city of Boston, Massachusetts, occupies a peninsula between the Charles River and Dorchester Bay (Figure 2.5, right). Topographic relief within the area of Old Boston is low, and even such famed landmarks as Beacon Hill are but gentle rises. The land broadens to the south, where the city extends into its major metropolitan area.

A citizen of colonial Boston would have difficulty associating the above description with the town he knew. In 1775, Boston was restricted to a peninsula that was connected to the mainland on the southwest by only a narrow neck of land (Figure 2.5, left). Within the city were several fortified hills. Most of these rises were drumlins, hills molded from glacial deposits; only Beacon Hill was in part comprised of bedrock. The peninsular site had favored early settlement and growth of the city not only because of its excellent, protective harbor, but because at that site (in contrast to the surrounding lands) good spring and well water could be obtained from porous gravel beneath the glacial deposits.

As has been true with many of the world's great port cities, Boston's growth demanded additional land space in the vicinity of the harbor and commercial districts. The logical direction for expansion was into surrounding marshes, where the land could be built up with fill. Thus the hills were either leveled or reduced in height to procure fill. Mill Pond was first filled, followed later by the salt marshes on both sides of the peninsula. The former shallow-water zone on the west is known today as Back Bay. Not all the filled areas were constructed at the expense of the former hills and glacial drift, however. Some of the fill consisted of solid wastes from early urbanization and commerce — the brick, stone, and mortar derived from buildings as they were replaced and the ballast from ships that arrived to carry off goods produced and sold in the city.

The topographic changes wrought by man in Boston are not unusual. Rather they typify the manner in which man remolds the land-

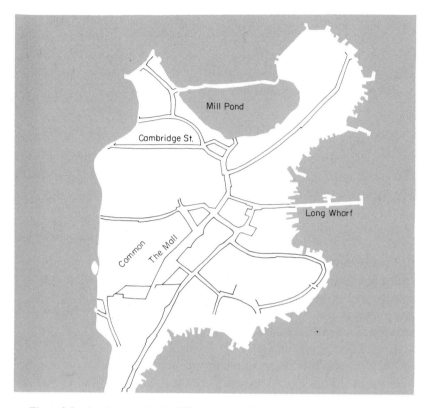

Figure 2.5. Land expansion by filling, Boston. The two maps, depicting the same area and drawn at the same scale, show the change in shoreline and land area (in white) between 1775 (left) and the present (right).

scape to suit his cities. And much of this new landscape is not nature's material but instead the waste products and discarded junk produced by man (discussed further in Chapter 6). Without such deposits we would have a much poorer idea of how our ancestors lived; archaeology learns much from ancient trash heaps and dumps, for which it uses the less disagreeable term "midden."

The geologic factors already discussed as important to location of settlements and their subsequent growth continue to place some restrictions on urban expansion in contemporary times. The influence on the pattern of cities is much less impressive, however, because of man's present ability to move great quantities of material from one place to another. For example, dune sands are now being barged across Lake Michigan to provide new urban space along the western shore

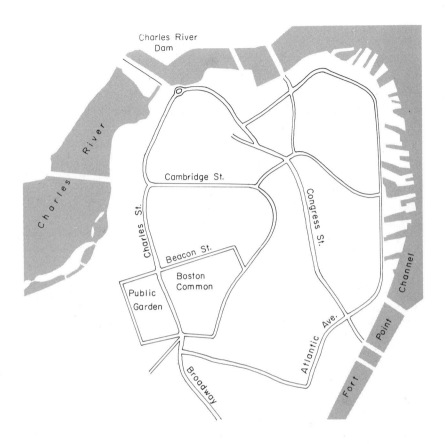

at Evanston, Illinois. Almost 40 years ago Chicago constructed a world's fair on land largely built from the city's waste. In New Jersey bogs are filled, and in Los Angeles hills are beveled and terraced to accommodate suburban developments. What formerly would have required years, decades, or even centuries to accomplish is a short-term project with today's technology.

The modern city does, however, have one requirement that is dependent upon the geologic resources of its region; that is, sand and gravel to construct buildings, utilities, streets, and highways. Those cities located in sites of limited or exhausted supply of such aggregates either have to import them from ever-increasing distances or else develop industries to make aggregate from crushed stone, clinkered shale and clay, or industrial waste and slag. Long-distance transport of sand and gravel or the manufacture of artificial aggregate greatly increases the cost of the material. Natural "bank run" sand and gravel typically sells for a fraction of a dollar per ton at the pit, but even the nearby consumer frequently pays several times as much for the delivered product. If sand and gravel must be hauled in from a distance of 50 or more miles, the cost to the consumer is further increased by at least $1.00 per ton. The cost of major construction, in which the amount of aggregate used may approach thirty thousand to forty thousand tons, is thus significantly increased. The Los Angeles metropolitan area requires an estimated 75,000,000 tons of aggregate for highway construction alone in a five-year period. The dollar cost of building an artificial urban landscape can be great indeed!

Cities on certain sites usually are blessed with sufficient natural aggregate: cities along major rivers, particularly those that once carried glacial meltwaters; on coasts, where materials can usually be obtained from beaches, stream deltas, and weakly consolidated coastal plain sediments; and at the foot of mountains, where commonly alluvial fans and other stream-laid deposits supply aggregate. In all these advantageous situations problems may still arise, because cities often expand onto the well-drained and frequently flat areas underlain by sand and gravel that are the source of natural aggregate. As the need for aggregate becomes greater, such areas are no longer available for mineral exploitation. Meanwhile, the suburban fringes of the city may become and remain pockmarked from the extraction of aggregate. (Other problems associated with mining in and around cities are discussed in Chapter 6.)

Environmental Feedback in the City

The natural processes that work upon the surface of the earth continually remake our physical environment, although most of the effects upon the landscape appear slowly from man's temporal perspective. Even natural events that man views as catastrophic — such as earthquakes, landslides, and volcanic eruptions — are relatively trivial in the broader context of the earth's size and geologic time. But in the city the impact of these events is accentuated and even accelerated, because most of man's works are relatively unstable extensions and distortions of topography. What are relatively simple problems of slope instability or subsidence in the countryside become costly nuisances, or even disasters, in the city. While earth tremors merely crack the farmland soils, they may topple large buildings in the CBD. There are, in other words, feedback mechanisms whereby the works of man magnify the effects of natural processes. Fortunately, major disasters from natural causes occur only infrequently, although the frequency may be increasing owing to the intensification of man-made environmental changes.

The most obvious and destructive environmental repercussions are those caused by processes over which man has essentially no control — violent events like earthquakes, volcanic eruptions, and tidal waves. These phenomena tend to be regionally concentrated, and urban man cannot escape them except by avoiding affected areas. But man is not about to reduce his exposure to earthquakes, for example, by evacuating the lands that rim the Pacific Ocean and Mediterranean Sea!

Given the reality that cities evolve wherever man can make a living, it is still possible to reduce greatly the probabilities of earthquake-caused damage and death. One common sense solution would be the prevention of urban construction over and adjacent to known fault lines. Such actions would, of course, require the rezoning of large urbanized tracts lying on such faults, notably certain parts of California. The impact of an earthquake is dependent on other factors, too, including strength and depth of the earthquake shock, distance from its epicenter, strength and type of construction, and the substrate on which structures stand. The importance of such factors is discussed in Chapters 6 and 7, but it is worth noting here that buildings can be designed to withstand seismic shock — particularly if they are anchored on firm bedrock.

As if nature does not provide enough seismic risk, man apparently is willing now to fill the void: the problem of waste disposal has recently been linked to earthquake activity. A concept of liquid waste disposal that is frequently cited as a solution to urban waste problems has recently been tested at the Rocky Mountain Arsenal, on the outskirts of Denver, Colorado. The process involves the injection of undesirable liquids into deep reservoir rocks, some 12,000 feet below the surface. In an area that had not reported an earthquake for over eighty years, more than 700 small earthquakes occurred within four years after the test program was initiated in 1962. Geologists have suggested that deep-seated instability and slippage occurs along fractures where waste fluids have been injected. The correlation between periods of water injection and earthquake occurrence is impressive (see Figure 2.6). Although fluid injections were halted in 1966, earthquakes have continued and have become even more severe in the Denver area.

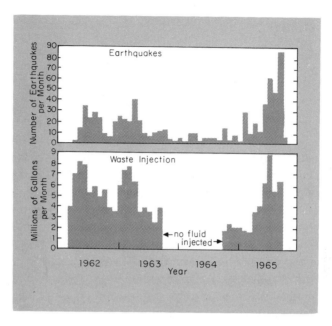

Figure 2.6. Relation between earthquake frequency and waste injection at Rocky Mountain Arsenal, near Denver, Colorado. (After Evans 1966.)

It is interesting to note, however, that although the Denver situation clearly pinpoints a problem connected with this means of liquid waste disposal, it also suggests a way of releasing stress along fault zones by means of a series of minor, nondamaging earthquakes. Perhaps fluid injection can be utilized to prevent the build-up of the major stresses that result in catastrophic earthquakes.

Subsidence is another major environmental response to urban activities. It most commonly occurs in association with heavy structural loads, withdrawal of groundwater and other underground fluids, subsurface construction, and alteration of the surface mantle (these problems are discussed in Chapter 6). The Wilmington oil and gas field in the Long Beach, California, area is a classical example. From 1937 through 1962, 913 million barrels of oil, 484 million barrels of water, and 832 billion cubic feet of gas were extracted from the underlying sediments to a depth of 6,000 feet (Poland and Davis 1969). Subsidence began in 1937, and by 1962 much of the heavily urbanized area above had subsided a minimum of 2 feet and as much as 27 feet (Figure 2.7). The

Figure 2.7. Subsidence of land, Long Beach area, California. Withdrawal of oil, gas, and water from the ground beneath had led, by 1962, to a maximum subsidence of 27 feet. (Courtesy of Long Beach Harbor Department.)

cost of repairing damaged structures and equipment exceeded $100 million by 1962. Salt water is now being injected into the ground to counteract the subsidence; it will be interesting to follow the impact of this practice on this earthquake-sensitive region.

Finally, it should be recognized that the same natural features that favor settlement and commerce may eventually prove the undoing of the city they nourished. Bruges, Belgium, is an oft-cited example of this process. In the thirteenth and fourteenth centuries, Bruges was one of the most prosperous commercial cities of northern Europe, supported by a thriving textile industry and excellent access to the sea. In the late fifteenth century, the economy of the city declined when the Estuary of Zwyn began to fill with silt and an emerging coastal plain increased Bruges' distance from the sea (Figure 2.8). The construction of new land by natural processes so altered the city's situation that Bruges never regained its commercial emminence.

Whereas Bruges has suffered the vagaries of an emerging coast-

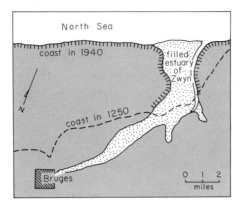

Figure 2.8. Migration of the North Sea coastline and estuarine silting near Bruges, Belgium.
(After Taylor 1949.)

line and filling deltas, waterlocked Venice is experiencing the opposite
topographic fate. The island sites of Venice were originally selected
for their isolation and defensive position, when the Veneti fled the
mainland in the seventh century to escape northern invaders. Built on
piles driven into island mud flats, the city grew to prominence as a
port and cultural center. Today the city is seriously threatened by its
environment. Venice is slowly sinking owing to a combination of
water-saturated foundations, compression and addition of sediments,
excessive artificial loading, and rise of the water level.

Climatological hazards in cities bear considerable relationship to
topography. Problems of smog, haze, and air pollutants are primarily
treated in Chapters 3 and 4, but it is worth noting here that conditions
most favorable to smog occurrence often are promoted by a city's
topographic arrangement. Valley floors and basins are natural sinks in
which fog and smog can form under certain meteorological conditions.
Because smog occurs in stable air, it tends to persist in the low-lying
areas until major changes in weather conditions diffuse it. It is no
comfort that the primary producers of urban pollutants — heavy industry and highways — usually locate in valley bottoms. Little wonder
that hilltops, where one can partially escape the noxious haze, are
becoming increasingly desirable as residential sites.

THE CITY AND THE LAND

Every city has its own character, a flavor mixed one part each from the mood and style of its inhabitants, the economic functions it performs, the patterns of its architecture and streets, and the landscape on which it is nurtured. Man may hold tentative dominance over the land, but the land remains inevitably — and often delightfully — present in the city of man. Although man remolds and destroys it, obscures and hides it, the land will not disappear. It invades the city as blocks of limestone or marble slabs and shows its face where man cuts roads or digs foundations. But best of all the land helps define the city. Try to imagine San Francisco without its very special arrangement of hills and shorelines. Or Athens without the Acropolis, Budapest without the river, Naples without the sea. Topography does indeed contribute to the city's character, and in so doing, it gives man pleasure. But although the land enhances man's life and man's works, most significantly it reminds even the most isolated urban dweller that his city, as impressive as it may be, is only skin deep.

REFERENCES

Burgess, Ernest. 1925. The growth of the city: An introduction to a research project. In *The city*, ed. Robert E. Park, Ernest W. Burgess, and Robert D. McKensie, pp. 47–62. Chicago: Univ. of Chicago Press.

Evans, D. M. 1966. The Denver area earthquakes and the Rocky Mountain Arsenal disposal well. *The Mountain Geologist* 3(1):23–36.

Flawn, P. T. 1970. *Environmental geology: Conservation, land-use planning, and resource management.* New York: Harper and Row.

Hawkes, Jacquetta. 1951. *A land.* New York: Random House.

Hoyt, Homer. 1939. *The structure and growth of residential neighborhoods in American cities.* Washington, D.C.: Federal Housing Administration.

Kaye, Clifford A. 1968. Geology and our cities. *New York Acad. Sci. Trans. Ser. 2* 30(8):1045–1051.

Mangin, W. 1967. Squatter settlements. *Sci. Amer.* Oct.: 21–29.

Marcus, Melvin G., and Buckley H. Robbins. 1970. Habitat and resources. In *Geography in an urban age*, ed. High School Geography Project, Unit 7. New York: Macmillan.

Passonneau, J. R., and R. S. Wurman. 1966. *Urban atlas: 20 American cities,* Cambridge, Mass.: M.I.T. Press.

Poland, J. F., and E. H. Davis. 1969. Land subsidence due to the withdrawal of fluids. *Reviews in Engineering Geology* 2:187–269.

Schuberth, Christopher J. 1968. *The geology of New York City and environs.* Garden City, N. Y.: Natural History Press.

Sherlock, R. L. 1922. *Man as a geological agent.* London: H. F. & G. Witherby.

Taylor, Griffith. 1949. *Urban geography: A study of site, evolution, pattern and classification of villages, towns and cities.* London: Methuen.

Thwaites, R. G., ed. 1896. *The Jesuit relations and allied documents,* vol. 48. Cleveland: Burrows Brothers.

CHAPTER 3

The Climate of the City

Reid A. Bryson and John E. Ross

If you are driving through the country, approaching a large metropolitan area, you can sense the city before the skyline climbs into view. The interstate highway widens with additional lanes. The traffic intensifies. There's a different air about it. The sky may become overcast. If snow lies on the ground, it takes on a gray tone, or may disappear. The visibility diminishes. You may be constrained from taking a deep breath. But that's getting ahead of the story. Something more fundamental than air pollution is happening.

Cities, because they are cities, have climates different from the surrounding countryside. In fact, the city reaches out and influences the region beyond the inner city — the suburbs and often the hinterlands many miles from the city. To a large extent what man has done to modify the climate in his urban places comes somewhat as a surprise to him. There probably have been crude attempts in the past to control city climate, but these mostly consisted of locating cities in favorable places. We now know that man has unwittingly changed such fundamental things as temperature, air circulation, and the heat budget. In short, the cities that man builds profoundly affect climate in the short run and almost certainly will produce significant long-term climatic effects as well.

The evidence is mounting that these climatic changes can make life unpleasant and make at least some cities, at some times, nearly uninhabitable. In this chapter we will explore the nature of these changes and their ramifications. It will become apparent that the time is at hand to begin planning and redesigning urban areas with much more attention to climatic considerations (see also Chapter 4).

DIFFERENCES IN CLIMATE BETWEEN THE CITY AND THE COUNTRYSIDE

A number of man's impacts on the land affect the climate directly or indirectly. These changes are most evident in cities, especially when contrasted with sparsely settled rural areas. Table 3.1 shows the average changes in various climatic elements caused by urbanization.

Table 3.1. Average changes in climatic elements caused by urbanization. (From Landsberg 1970.)

Element	Comparison with Rural Environment
Radiation	
global	15 to 20% less
ultraviolet, winter	30% less
ultraviolet, summer	5% less
sunshine duration	5 to 15% less
Temperature	
annual mean	0.5 to 1.0°C more
winter minima (average)	1 to 2°C more
heating degree days	10% less
Contaminants	
condensation nuclei and particulates	10 times more
gaseous admixtures	5 to 25 times more
Wind speed	
annual mean	20 to 30% less
extreme gusts	10 to 20% less
calms	5 to 20% more
Precipitation	
totals	5 to 10% more
days with less than 5 mm	10% more
snowfall	5% less
Cloudiness	
cover	5 to 10% more
fog, winter	100% more
fog, summer	30% more
Relative humidity	
winter	2% less
summer	8% less

Urbanization alters the city climate in various ways. First, urbanization changes the physical surface of the land, notably by constructing many buildings and paving much of the ground, in the process waterproofing the land, increasing its thermal admittance, and increasing its roughness and hence its effects on wind. Second, urban man and his activities produce climatically important amounts of heat in several ways. Third, by their functions cities introduce great quantities of fine particles into the air. This section examines how urban man has changed his environment in these climatically significant ways.

Changes in the Physical Surface

Waterproofing

In most cities man has waterproofed about 50 percent of the surface (see Chapter 5). Roofs, streets, and parking lots increase the runoff of even a gentle rain, and drain systems are required to transport the runoff away from settled areas quickly and efficiently; otherwise every minor storm would bring a barrage of phone calls because of filled basements and flooded underpasses. Thus we put gutters on roofs and along streets, and we build storm sewers as the waterproofed areas increase the runoff. Contrast this with the situation in rural areas, where much more water soaks into the soil, eventually to return to the atmosphere by evapotranspiration or to seep slowly away in the groundwater.

This waterproofing involves a hydrologic change with climatic consequences. Since in the city rapid runoff leaves paved surfaces dry most of the time between rainfalls, less moisture is available for evaporation than in the countryside. This is significant because the evaporation process removes heat from the air (approximately 600 calories for every gram of water evaporated) and hence has a cooling effect at the earth's surface. Paved and roofed city surfaces simply do not have this mode of heat loss.

Thermal Admittance

The city has higher *thermal admittance* than the surrounding countryside. To understand this, let us look first at a rural field covered with grass. The ground receives heat during the day and cools off at night, but vegetation acts as an insulating blanket (in large part by trapping still air, through which heat moves slowly). The flow of heat both into and out of the soil therefore is reduced. During the day, the grass blanket keeps heat from flowing into the ground as rapidly as it otherwise would, so there is less heat stored in the soil. This would leave more at the surface to heat the air, except that evapotranspiration from the vegetation helps to lower temperatures. At night, the temperature at the top of the grass drops owing to reradiation back to the atmosphere, but the insulating blanket prevents considerable heat flow from the soil below. In short, the vegetation (when growing) tends to reduce surface temperatures during both day and night.

In contrast, the city, with its acres of concrete, has high thermal conductivity and heat capacity. Heat flows easily into the concrete during the day and is stored. At night, as the surface cools, there is a flow of heat upward to balance the surface loss. The effect of this is to maintain relatively higher temperatures at the surface. Thus the city, with high thermal admittance, stores more heat during the day and lets out more at night. For these reasons, night temperature in the city a few inches over concrete may be 10° or 15°F warmer than temperature over rural fields (see Figure 3.1).

Roughness

In cities man has also altered the roughness of the earth's surface. This (aerodynamic) roughness modifies the movement of the air at

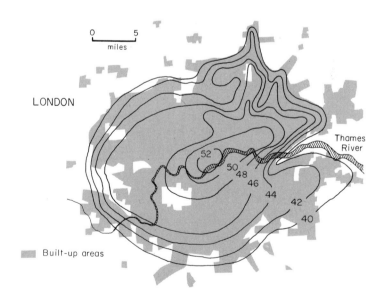

Figure 3.1. Distribution of minimum temperatures in London, May 14, 1959, in degrees Fahrenheit. (After Chandler 1965.)

the surface. What happens depends primarily upon the smaller features, such as trees, bushes, houses, less upon the spaces between them. The city, in most situations, is rough compared to the open countryside (see Figure 3.2).

Increased surface roughness affects the wind structure and causes a major adjustment in the vertical wind profile so that wind speeds near the surface are reduced. The structural features of cities, because they interfere with laminar flow, also increase the number of local eddies and thus increase the turbulence. The decrease of wind speed over cities is poorly documented. Reasonable interpretations of available records suggest that wind speed in cities is about 25 percent less than in rural areas. This is not unreasonable in the light of measurable increases in aerodynamic roughness.

Experiments show that the aerodynamic roughness is proportional to the height of the buildings (h) squared times their width (w) and inversely proportional to the size of the lot the building occupies, that is, to the square of the average distance between buildings (D):

$$Z_0 = \frac{1}{2} \frac{h^2 w}{D^2}$$

This roughness length Z may be 5 cm in the countryside and 1000 cm

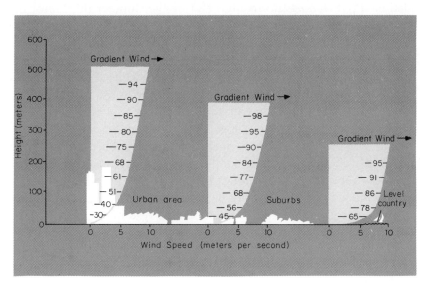

Figure 3.2. Effect of terrain roughness on the wind speed profile. With decreasing roughness, the height of the affected wind layer decreases and the profile becomes steeper. (After Singer and Smith 1970.)

in the city. Given these figures, the reduction of wind in the city at 30 m above the ground may be 80 percent or more. This reduction proportionately lengthens the time required for the wind to flush air pollutants from the city. At greater heights the reduction of the wind speed is much less.

Heat Production

Not only has man, through his urban constructions, dramatically affected the exchange of energy and moisture within the system by altering the physical qualities and materials of the earth's surface, he also has become a primary source of heat production within the system. The heat man produces has led to even more radical changes in the heat balance than result from construction. These changes are manifested in many ways, ranging from the heat release of fossil fuel combustion to that of the human metabolism.

In the mid and high latitudes during winter, the major source of heat in many cities is the production of heat by the city itself, not the heat from the sun. The heat produced by industrial activities and house heating are the important sources. On Manhattan Island, for example, one study indicates that during January the amount of heat produced from combustion only is 2½ times greater than that of the solar energy reaching the ground. During the summer this factor drops to 1/6.

All the heat produced to warm a house eventually diffuses to the outdoors. The poorer the insulation of the house, the more heat is produced to maintain a given temperature inside. If house walls were perfectly insulated, just human presence in the house would produce more than enough heat, and air-conditioning would be necessary in winter to keep the rooms from getting too warm.

A typical automobile, operating in a city, burns about three gallons of fuel per hour. The combustion in most automobile engines produces about the same amount of heat as the typical home furnace in winter; indeed one could easily heat a house with an automobile running in the garage given the appropriate exhaust system and heat exchanger. All this heat is added to the city's heat system.

Human beings themselves are another contributor to the city's heat budget. A man produces heat at a rate of between 100 and 300 watts depending on his activities — a person produces about 100 watts at rest and about 200–300 watts while working. Some heavy work produces even more. That's not insignificant with 10 million people in a city. In crowds, the heat generated is equal to summer sunshine.

The net contributions of combustion, heating, and metabolism can produce an impressive adjustment of the earth's heat budget in urban places and urban areas. One estimate indicates that in the year 2000 the Boston-to-Washington megapolis will have 56 million people living within an area of 30,000 square kilometers. The human heat source will be about 65 calories per square centimeter per day, about a sixth of the amount that the surface receives from the sun.

Turbidity: Particles in the Air

In addition to alterations of the physical surface and variation in heat production, a third factor distinguishing the city from the country-side is a difference in combustion and properties of the atmosphere. The measure of dust, smoke, and other particulate matter in the air is referred to as *turbidity*. All air is turbid to some degree. Nature con-tributes dust from sparsely vegetated land and volcanic eruption, for example, but man has greatly increased the turbidity by his agriculture, fuel combustion, industrial emissions, and other activities. Studies of atmospheric turbidity in different environments reveal striking varia-tions in particulate content. One set of measurements, made about 30 years ago, showed that typical country air had 4 particles of dust per cubic millimeter, while city parks typically had 4 times that amount (16–17 particles mm^{-3}) and a business section had 10 times more particles than the parks (190 particles mm^{-3}). An industrial area held up to 4,000 particles mm^{-3} – 1,000 times what the typical country air contained. Chapter 4 demonstrates that, in general, turbidity has worsened during the ensuing three decades.

Atmospheric dust has a number of effects. Among these is inter-ference with solar radiation by the suspended particles. Although this interference affects the whole spectrum, it is most pronounced in the short wavelengths, resulting in a reduction of about 15 percent of total direct radiation over most major cities. This reduction is generally greater in winter and less in summer. In winter, ultraviolet penetration is reduced by 30 percent on the average, and there are occasions when no ultraviolet radiation is received at the ground in some large cities. Simultaneous measurements taken at the surface and from a tall steeple have shown that this extinction takes place in a very shallow layer.

Also as a result of air pollution and associated high turbidity, visibilities are lower and occurrences of fog are greater in the city than in the country. Fog is more frequent because water vapor readily condenses on many of the atmospheric particulates introduced by man. Fog occurs from two to five times as often in the city as in the surrounding rural areas.

Data from Detroit Municipal Airport (6 miles from downtown) and Wayne County Airport (17 miles from downtown) illustrate this nicely. During conditions conducive to formation of city smogs, visibilities of less than 1 mile averaged 149 hours per year at Detroit Municipal Airport, whereas the rural site averaged only 89 hours. Smoke was listed as the cause of these low visibilities in 49 of the observations at Municipal Airport and in 4 of those at Wayne County.

When shallow temperature inversions — layers of air in which the temperature increases upward — are present, the accumulation of particulates can cause 80 or 90 percent reduction of the visual range in cities as compared with the range for the general environment low in contaminants. The haze effect is accentuated by the formation of water droplets around hygroscopic nuclei. This occurs in spite of the fact that relative humidities near the ground are generally lower in cities than in the countryside owing to higher temperatures and reduced evaporation.

Recent reports indicate that the visibility in many urban locations has improved during the last two decades. The better visibilities of major cities in the United States have been associated with local efforts at air pollution abatement and the substitution of oil and gas for soft coal in heat production. Possibly the migration of industry to surrounding satellite towns has also had an effect.

Recent clean-up campaigns, using smokeless fuels, have lessened the concentration of particulates, and hence of fog and of the attenuation of light. In London, for example, winter sunshine has increased by 70 percent in the last decade, and winter visibilities have improved by a factor of three since improvements were introduced. Similar results have been obtained in the "Golden Triangle" of Pittsburgh, where a major pollution abatement program helped rejuvenate the core of the city, where previously smog and other pollutants were significantly contributing to urban decay.

THE URBAN HEAT ISLAND

Every place on the earth's surface experiences an interchange of heat through time. This exchange, which is called the heat balance, varies diurnally, seasonally, and annually. It is dependent on the transfer of heat to and from the earth's surface by radiational, conductive, and convectional processes. The manner in which these processes operate is significantly affected in the city by the three factors discussed earlier: (1) changes in the physical surface, (2) heat production, and (3) turbidity. Thus, man's activities, in conjunction with natural energy flow, produce a rather special heat balance in urban places. This is manifested primarily in what has been called the *urban heat island.*

The urban heat balance has a profound effect that can be seen visibly in most cities: a characteristic circulation of air. To visualize this typical circulation, think of the city as a warm island surrounded by cooler countryside. The urban heating leads to increased buoyancy of the air over the city and to a city-induced wind field that dominates when regional weather patterns are too weak to displace the mass of urban air.

The Climatic Dome

A city and its surrounding countryside can, as has been mentioned, be compared to an island and its surrounding sea. Theories explaining sea breezes on islands fit the circulation of the air over cities. The surface of an island becomes hotter in the daytime than does the surface of the sea. This is in part caused by evaporation differences. The city, like the island, has less evaporation than the surrounding countryside because there is less water available. As warm air rises over either kind of island, cool air is drawn in from all sides.

There is, however, an important difference between islands and cities. The thermal admittance of the sea is higher than that of the island. In contrast, the thermal admittance of a city is higher than the surrounding countryside. Thus an island has a sea breeze (or onshore wind) during the day and a land breeze (or offshore wind) at night, whereas a city tends to have a "sea" breeze (cool air moving toward the urban island) both day and night.

Circulation within the Dome

Why does the city generate air circulation like an island? The earth's heat is generated by the sun. Of the sunlight that reaches the surface, some is reflected. The remainder is absorbed and stored in the surface materials to be emitted as outgoing heat radiation, to heat the air directly by conduction and convection, or to evaporate water. In the country, especially in summer, much of the available energy is used for evaporation. In a city, with its waterproofed surfaces and storm drains, much of the precipitation has been removed and little remains to evaporate. More energy is available to heat the air.

In the country, less heat is stored beneath the surface for night-time release than in the dense artificial materials of the city. Thus more heat is used for evaporation during the day in the country, and less is stored and available to keep the temperature up at night. The concrete, asphalt, and brick of the city, however, are efficient reservoirs from which the heat stored during the day flows back to the surface to warm the air at night.

In addition to these differences, the city adds large amounts of heat produced by commercial and domestic consumption of fossil fuel, the use of electricity, and even the metabolism of the inhabitants. All of these factors tend to make the air in the city warmer than that in the country. The buoyant warm air rises, the cool country air flows into the city under the warm air, and a characteristic urban circulation pattern develops.

A plan view of a city shows that there is a low pressure area in the city and an inflow of air from the countryside into the low pressure area. The inflow does not accelerate because the buoyant lift of rising warm air is balanced by friction due to the aerodynamic roughness of the city.

A sea breeze does not usually develop on an island that is less than about 10 kilometers (6.2 miles) across. Given this information, one would not expect a similar air circulation pattern to develop over cities less than about 6 miles in diameter. City-driven wind circulation does, however, tend to develop in somewhat smaller, compact cities on plains; it is less clear over complex, large cities and urban areas. The plan (or configuration) of the city also plays an important role in the development of wind circulation, and this is true of islands as well.

Several urban studies have considered the effect of city size on the magnitude of the heat island. During this century most major metropolitan areas in the United States have been both expanding and warming. The amount of warming correlates with city growth rate. As the heat island expands and intensifies, stronger and stronger regional winds are needed to overcome it and dissipate the heat beyond the city. Although the heat island effect is most pronounced on calm, clear nights, it is evident in long-term climatic values.

Temperatures within the City

One of the problems of defining the urban heat island in the past has been the lack of appropriate weather data. Meteorological observations are usually taken at weather bureau stations located in the CBD and at municipal airports. Because airport sites are often chosen for microclimatic features favorable to aviation and because the transect between city center and airport may be characterized by unusual topography, the comparison of temperatures within most cities is biased.

To remove some of these uncertainties, it is necessary to observe atmospheric changes as a city grows. The new town of Columbia, Maryland, provided such an opportunity, and a study was initiated three years ago. The results so far support earlier findings and have refined them. It was found that even a single block of buildings will start the process of heat island formation. This was demonstrated by using air and infrared surface temperature measurements in conjunction with ground observations. A heat reservoir was identified for a paved court enclosed by low-level structures and surrounded by vegetation. On clear and relatively calm evenings, a heat island developed in the court — fed by heat stored in the daytime under the court's asphalt parking space and within the building walls.

Within the city there are surprising temperature variations, due in part to the terrain but also sharply affected by the internal arrangement. Madison, Wisconsin, provides some interesting winter examples. There often is a spot to spot variation within the city of up to 20°F, and ranges as great as 37°F have been measured. One street intersection at the bottom of a long gentle slope on the west side of the town is typically the coldest place in the city because of cold air drainage. In winter the warmest spot in town is next to Madison General Hospital, which sits on a slight mound. There the cold air is drained off, the traffic is heavy, and the large building walls radiate heat.

Heavily traveled streets in most cities are 2° or 3° warmer than

side streets in winter. The areas around stop lights are usually 2° or
3° warmer than the areas between stop lights — not because of the lights
but because cars idle there.

At night there is a tendency for heavily wooded parts of town
to be warmer near the ground because heat is trapped there by the
tree canopy. In contrast, open terrain, such as golf courses, typically is
colder.

Cities also tend to have longer frost-free periods. Downtown
Chicago has a mean frost-free period of 197 days. All of the counties
surrounding Chicago have a mean frost-free period of between 160 and
170 days — a difference of about 30 days. One must go several hundred
miles south to Tennessee to find a frost-free period as long as that of
downtown Chicago. At Munich, Germany, with its smaller annual
temperature range and warmer cool-season temperatures than Chicago,
the difference in the frost-free season between the city and its surroundings is 60 days.

The Dust Dome

Dust is distributed throughout cities and serves as an excellent
tracer of air movement. On a relatively calm day the smoke and dust
generated near the edge of a city move in toward the center. In the
middle of the city the smoke tends to rise (see Figure 3.3). Although
the dust and larger smoke particles have a downward velocity of their
own, because of their mass and gravity, low-level turbulence and
the rising currents carry many of the particles upward. As the air starts
to spread outward, the vertical motion of the air decreases and the
dust tends to settle. Where the air begins to sink over the outer city, it
carries the remaining dust with it. By recirculating the same particles
and adding new material from the edge of the city, this pattern creates
a *dust dome* and concentrates particulate pollution in the inner city.

Dust domes are easily observed. In relatively flat terrain they
may stand sharply and well developed against the blue of the sky
around. Before Chicago developed extensive industrial suburbs, its dust
dome was easy to see. During World War II, observers reported a wall
of dust just west of Midway Airport (8 miles southwest of downtown
Chicago). Visibility of up to 15 miles prevailed in the countryside,
but inside the wall-like edge of the dust dome the visibility dropped to
1/2 to 3/4 mile! By contrast, the visible polluted air of Los Angeles
lies in its topographic basin like soup in a bowl.

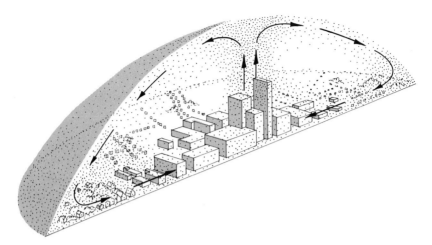

Figure 3.3. The urban dust dome – a pictorial perspective.

Gases generated in the city may follow the total circulation pattern but do not fall out as the dust does.

The vertical extent of the dust dome, and indeed the vertical transport of pollution out of the city, is limited by inversions. Often the city is a major contributor to the development of inversions. They occur when the blanket of pollutants created by the city — including particulates, water vapor, and carbon dioxide — absorb heat radiated upward from the city's surface. Because particulates also absorb sunlight, especially in the upper part of the dust dome, the inversion is intensified, and pollutants are trapped even more tightly in the city.

Local terrain may promote the development of inversions by providing topographic sinks for cold air drainage. Thus cities in basins, such as Los Angeles, California, or in valleys, such as Donora, Pennsylvania, act as receptacles for the cool air that flows into them. These conditions accentuate the temperature differential between surface and upper dome air. Because temperature inversions prohibit air from rising vertically, pollution troubles will invariably arise in locations where temperature inversions are likely to occur.

Precipitation in the City

The enormous number of condensation nuclei produced by human activities in and around cities almost certainly contributes to increased cloudiness and precipitation over cities. Also, convective uplift associated with the heat island promotes cooling of and condensation of the water vapor. Most studies indicate that the increase in precipitation in urban areas is around 10 percent (still in the realm of sampling errors), but some analyses have shown considerably larger increases. The urban area of Champaign-Urbana, Illinois, is a representative example; see Figure 3.4.

In the state of Washington there is evidence of a 30 percent increase in precipitation over an interval of four decades in some areas near pulp mills. Thundershowers in London yield 30 percent more rain than in the surrounding area. Observations in various cities (for example, Chicago) indicate increased precipitation for the days Monday through Friday as compared with values for Saturday and Sunday. These higher values parallel the increased industrial activity during the work week. The rather startling variation of urban precipitation in accordance with the pattern of the human work week is a convincing argument for a cause and effect relationship; the week is such an arbitrary subdivision of time that artificial forces must be at work. (This weekly pattern also shows up in temperatures. In New Haven, Connecticut, on Sunday the minimum temperatures differ from the countryside by only 1.2°F; during the rest of the week, the figures are 2.0° to 2.4°.)

THE PLUME BEYOND THE CITY

The city circulation described thus far only exists with light winds. The pattern changes as wind speeds increase to about 8 miles per hour or more. Then the heat and particulate matter produced by the city go downwind into the countryside rather than forming or maintaining a dome over the city. Thus, when the wind exceeds 8 miles per hour, the city spreads a plume across adjacent rural areas (see Figure 3.5). In other words, man's urban complexes are beginning to modify climate in an area far larger than the city or urban area.

The plume, carrying dust along with it, may extend hundreds of miles beyond the city. One of the authors followed a well-developed plume from Chicago toward the northwest. Taking back roads, he drove back and forth under the edge of the plume. Upon arrival in Madison, Wisconsin, 150 miles away, the plume was still clearly visible. Similarly, the dust plume from Winnipeg, Canada, sometimes reaches south to

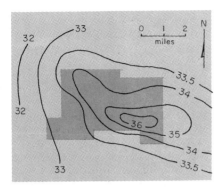

Figure 3.4. Average annual precipitation (in inches) in Champaign-Urbana, Illinois, 1949–1967. (After Changnon 1970.)

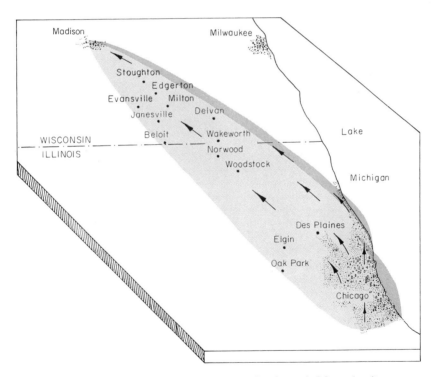

Figure 3.5. Plume of heat and pollutants extending downwind from the city.

Fargo, North Dakota. This effect is ubiquitous. Hong Kong, for example, sometimes has a severe air pollution problem produced at Canton. The air currents follow the Pearl River from Canton to the sea, a distance of about 70 miles, and their pollutants decrease visibility at the Hong Kong airport. The filtered samples show this dust to be mostly soot that comes with the air from Canton.

The effects of plumes are not restricted to pollution; precipitation and temperature may also be significantly altered. At La Porte, Indiana (30 miles downwind from the large Chicago-Gary industrial complex), the amount of precipitation and the number of days with thunderstorms and hail have increased markedly since 1925 (Changnon 1968). Furthermore, the year-to-year variation of precipitation at La Porte agrees generally with the production of steel and the number of smoke-haze days at Chicago. For small towns, a substantial increase in the number of condensation nuclei has also been noted as much as 3 kilometers downwind.

POLLUTANTS IN THE URBAN AIR

Both gases and suspended solids are dramatically present in the urban atmosphere. We have already pointed out that there is from 4 to 1,000 times more dust in the city air than in the country air. What is in the city dust? One thing is lead. Inner areas of cities typically have 3 times as much lead in the air as the suburbs. These figures are matched by the figures for lead concentration in the blood of the inhabitants. In the inner city areas of Chicago and Cincinnati, for example, the blood of the inhabitants contains 3 times more lead than the blood of suburbanites. The lead concentration in the Sumner Tunnel in Boston is 44 times the figure for the suburbs!

City air also contains roughly 10 times as many microorganisms as the surrounding countryside air. The variation in microorganism count appears to approximately parallel the number of dust particles.

Gases and chemical pollutants are also important constituents of the urban atmosphere, particularly as they combine with water droplets to form smog. Carbon monoxide in a city may average 10 to 30 parts per million (ppm); 100 ppm is rated as dangerous. Nitrogen oxides exist at 1 to 6 ppm, while hydrochloric acid occurs at 1 to 4 ppm.

Danger levels are defined as 25 and 5 ppm, respectively. Sulfur dioxide is usually present at 0.1 to 2 ppm; 3 ppm is regarded as dangerous. Sulfur dioxide is particularly dangerous in cities with a high incidence of fog because the two combine to produce a weak solution of sulfuric acid, which is injurious to health and many materials. Further, the presence of sulfuric acid in the air allows fog to form at relative humidities lower than 100 percent, thus increasing the number of fog and smog occurrences. In these cities fogs can develop at relative humidities as low as 90 percent.

Thus, although fog along the seacoast might seem romantic, the romance tends to drain out in the city. Fogs occur under conditions where the concentration of various pollutants attain a maximum and inversions are present. Fog increases the probability of damage to human health. With saturation of the air, droplets form that are capable of dissolving physical materials. The resulting aerosols are often potentially more dangerous than gases, because toxic substances are absorbed on soot particles. These insoluble particles enter the lungs, where they remain concentrated on small spots.

Fog, like precipitation, is more common in urban areas than in the countryside. For instance, in Paris mornings are foggy 41 percent of the time (October through March), whereas the suburbs and countryside experience only 28 percent and 2 percent foggy mornings, respectively. The greater incidence of fog in the city increases the dangers of urban air pollution.

Fog and pollution of course vary from city to city, but all cities experience maximum pollution when the air is stable. In London, the year 1952, when subsiding stable air and high pollution emission converged, was a disaster year. On December 1, 2, and 3 the general level of smog in London was normal. On the fourth, concentrations of sulfur dioxide and smoke increased and remained high for three or four days before dissipating. Prior to the air pollution episode the death rate in London had been relatively constant at about 250 people per day, a normal figure. During the smog, it jumped to 750 per day and continued to rise until the smog disappeared. The death rate then tapered off, but for weeks it was excessive. The number of deaths over and above the normal rate totaled about 4,000 during the period of heavy smog in London, presumably because of the smog. Statistics indicate that perhaps another 4,000 people in London eventually died because of this episode of smog.

Disasters provide colorful examples, but they do not do much to call attention to the chronic problems. These are obviously significant in human and material costs, but unfortunately reliable statistics that treat "normal" death rates as a function of the urban atmosphere have not yet been compiled. Thus, the city changes its own air chemistry as well as its climate — both with considerable expense to the city dweller's quality of life.

REFERENCES

Chandler, T.J. 1965. *The climate of London.* London: Hutchinson & Co.
Changnon, S. A., Jr. 1968. The LaPorte weather anomaly: Fact or fiction? *Bull. Amer. Meteor. Soc.* 49(1):4–11. (Reprinted in *Man's impact on environment*, ed. T. R. Detwyler, pp. 155–166. New York: McGraw-Hill, 1971.)
——— 1970. Recent studies of urban effects on precipitation in the United States. In *Urban climates,* pp. 325–341. Geneva: World Meteorological Organization, No. 254, Tech. Paper 141, Tech. Note no. 108.
Geiger, R. 1965. *The climate near the ground.* Cambridge, Mass.: Harvard Univ. Press.
Landsberg, H. E. 1956. The climate of towns. In *Man's role in changing the face of the earth,* ed. William L. Thomas, Jr., pp. 584–606. Chicago: Univ. of Chicago Press.
——— 1970. Climates and urban planning. In *Urban climates,* pp. 364–374. Geneva: World Meteorological Organization, no. 254, Tech. Paper 141, Tech. Note no. 108.
Lowry, W. P. 1967. The climate of cities. *Sci. Amer.* Aug.:15–23.
Matthews, W. H., W. W. Kellogg, and G. D. Robinson, ed. 1971. *Man's impact on the climate.* Cambridge, Mass.: M.I.T. Press.
Peterson, J. T. 1969. *The climate of cities: A survey of recent literature.* Washington, D.C.: National Air Pollution Control Administration Publ. no. AP-59. (Reprinted in *Man's impact on environment*, ed. T. R. Detwyler, pp. 131–154. New York: McGraw-Hill, 1971.)
Schaefer, V. J. 1969. The inadvertent modification of the atmosphere by air pollution. *Bull. Amer. Meteor. Soc.* 50(4):199–206.
Singer, T. A., and M. E. Smith. 1970. A summary of the recommended guide for the prediction of the dispersion of air-borne effluents (ASME). In *Urban climates,* pp. 306–324. Geneva: World Meteorological Organization, no. 254, Tech. Paper 141, Tech. Note no. 108.

CHAPTER 4

Urban Climate, Air Pollution, and Planning

Wilfrid Bach

Factors of climate and air hygiene have rarely played a decisive role in urban planning. A historical review of city planning reveals that most city sites and their plans have been determined by some combination of strategic, social, economic, and transportation considerations. If some old cities were well planned from the standpoint of air hygiene and climate, this was usually the fortuitous by-product of strategic or other considerations rather than the result of an ecology-conscious town planner.

Since the onset of the Industrial Revolution, cities have devoured their surrounding countryside at an ever increasing pace. Urban and industrial agglomerations have reached proportions that can adversely affect the weather, climate, and air quality of regional areas comparable to several states. Growth in the variety both of urban structure and of urban activities has increased the problems that result if the environment is not fully considered in urban planning.

The problems are obvious in midtown Manhattan, a mountainous desert of concrete and glass with congested traffic and smog concentrated in the city canyons. Seen from the Empire State Building, the shadows of skyscrapers disappear in the noon smog of a summer day (Figure 4.1). Although air pollution episodes do occur in the winter, photochemical smog spells — which require automobile ex-

Figure 4.1. Midtown New York in smog, June 1969. (Photograph by Wilfrid Bach.)

hausts, sunshine, and stagnating air masses for their formation — occur most often in the summer. The smog hazard to health in July 1970 was so serious that the mayor of New York almost banned traffic from the streets. Heat stroke also is a significant health hazard in cities such as New York, which can be many degrees warmer than the surrounding countryside. The hot and muggy weather of our big cities even produces psychological irritations and has been held in part responsible for aggressive behavior, riots, and other disorders.

We often are content with apparent solutions to these problems, but upon closer inspection discover that we have been deluding ourselves. Central Park, for example, has often been cited as an "oasis" of quietude and clean air in the midst of Manhattan. The fact is that one third of the park consists of a reservoir, and a large part of the remaining area has been spoiled by dissecting it with six-lane roads, favorite racing routes for New York taxi drivers. High concentrations of automobile exhausts inevitably occur in these misused recreation grounds.

Another example of poor planning is shown in Figure 4.2, which depicts urban renewal in an industrial valley in Sheffield, England, on a very clear day. Most of the back-to-back houses like those in the foreground have already been torn down. Instead of attacking the basic problem — air pollution — the planners merely resettled people within this heavily polluted valley in new high-rise apartments. The people live in the same polluted air but no longer in their own homes or in familiar neighborhood units; an increased percentage of people there now need psychiatric care.

Figure 4.2. Clearance of slums and construction of new residences in an industrial valley, Sheffield, England. The ground, typically left bare for long periods during urban renewal, is subject to severe erosion by wind and running water. (Photograph by Wilfrid Bach.)

Figure 4.3. Freeways, streets, and parking lots in downtown Cincinnati. (Photograph by Wilfrid Bach.)

The freeways, streets, and parking lots that accompany urban and suburban sprawl are another generator of pollution (see Figure 4.3). Vehicles produce concentrated pollution and high noise levels. Experience has shown that more roads do not alleviate the traffic problem; on the contrary, they favor increased traffic congestion and pollution. Moreover, highways in downtown areas typically consume open ground and parkland. And when there is no more open ground left, multilevel and multilane expressways may be cut into the ground beneath highrise apartments and hotels (see Figure 4.4).

The combustion-engine automobile is a very profitable object for the car producers and the oil companies, but its economy for the user and for society as a means of transportation is poor. The automo-

Figure 4.4. Multiple-laned freeways passing underneath buildings in Boston. (Photograph by Wilfrid Bach.)

bile is an obvious mass killer through accidents and a less evident, but nevertheless effective killer through pollution. Auto pollution and traffic congestion are major factors in making today's city an unpleasant place in which to live.

Planning should provide a means of creating functional, pleasant cities and enhancing the quality of urban life. However, the complexity of the city and the profit orientation of individuals and corporations frequently overwhelms the interest of the common citizen. Health, air pollution, climate, and noise — all of which constitute major facets of the quality of life — should receive much greater attention in city planning. This chapter discusses how these environmental variables should be incorporated in urban planning.

CLIMATIC FACTORS

The conversion of the natural landscape to the artificial city-scape has resulted in a number of well-documented adverse weather and climatic changes. Planners and architects, as the executors of the demands for more housing development and industrial growth, have a critical function in shaping the urban environment. Climatological expertise is essential in planning and siting new towns and industrial complexes, and also in renewing and relocating existing ones. The following major climatological considerations should be incorporated in any planning program.

Solar Radiation

Depending on the climatic region, solar radiation can be either beneficial or undesirable. At high latitudes both heat radiation and illumination are welcome. The urban planner can influence the amount of sunshine received by calculating the most favorable aspect toward the sun, by varying the heights of buildings, by modifying the arrangement of windows, and by changing the orientation and width of streets.

At low latitudes heat radiation and illumination should be reduced. With tall buildings and small windows on narrow streets, the planner can help keep the heat outside. It is difficult to keep the streets narrow, however, because modern traffic now requires broad streets. But the architect can avoid large glass fronts on buildings behind which the heat becomes trapped as in a greenhouse. And he can considerably reduce the expenses of air conditioning by providing reflective shades to cover the windows.

Green areas are an important tool of the urban planner because they can be used to modify the urban climate and to influence urban air quality. Specifically, trees shade the ground surface from insolation and reduce the effective radiation. According to the climatologist Helmut Landsberg, illumination (that is, the visible part of the spectrum) under a fully-leaved tree is only 25–30 percent of that received on a horizontal surface in an unshaded area. Lawn areas without trees also reduce heating of the surface by using part of the insolation for evapotranspiration and by inhibiting heat penetration into the ground.

Further, urban green areas reduce the concentration of particulate matter in the air and hence allow more solar radiation to strike the ground there. In contrast, dirty air in other parts of the city attenuates solar intensity there. These effects are clearly shown in a 1969 study by the author, in which a sun photometer was used to measure the intensity of solar radiation received over various land uses in greater Cincinnati. From the intensity and solar height, calculations were made of the turbidity coefficient. This provides an index of the amount of small suspended particles in the atmosphere. The percentage frequency of "polluted," "normal," and "clean" air over a variety of land uses is given in Figure 4.5. The industrial site experienced almost exclusively "polluted" air, whereas the city park had predominately "clean" air over the same summer period.

Solar radiation plays a vital role in the formation of photochemical smog in regions where insolation is intense — notably the subtropical west coasts of continents, including such major cities as Los Angeles; Santiago, Chile; Casablanca, Morocco; and Capetown, South Africa. In such places light energy reacts with oxides of nitrogen and certain hydrocarbons to produce *photochemical smog* (popularly

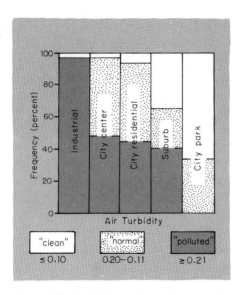

Figure 4.5. Turbidity of air over various land-use sites in greater Cincinnati, as measured by W. Bach in 1969. A turbidity value of 0.10 corresponds to a mass concentration of approximately 120 micrograms per cubic meter.

referred to as Los Angeles–type smog, because it was first noticed there). Smog commonly reduces visibility, injures plants, and irritates the eyes and mucous membranes in human beings. Automotive exhaust is the largest source of the substances that, in intense light, produce photochemical smog; in California about 60 percent of the nitrogen oxides and 75 to 85 percent of the reactive hydrocarbons come from motor vehicles. Planners in smog-prone regions should stringently control such emissions by enforcing the use of pollution control devices on vehicles, as well as work to reduce the amount and density of motor traffic.

Temperature

The heat island effect in urban places, as explained in Chapter 3, is produced by the greater heat absorption and storage in the dark urban structures and by the artificial heat generation from combustion and metabolic processes. It has been calculated that one fourth of the long-wave heat loss at night in Cincinnati is replaced by heat production within the city. In colder climates the heat island can be beneficial, reducing fuel costs, rapidly removing any snow cover, and prolonging the growing season. In warmer climates the heat island aggravates muggy and oppressive conditions.

Temperature Contrasts

The influence on a city's temperature pattern of different kinds of land use can be detected from an airplane by remote thermal sensing devices or on the ground by an automobile equipped with sensing instruments. The latter is a fast and economical method of surveying a city's temperature regimes.

Temperature contrasts within Washington, D.C., and within Sheffield, England, are shown in Table 4.1. It is clear that park areas and rural environs are slightly cooler during the day and considerably cooler during the night than the business centers, industrial zones, and dense residential areas. The average contrasts shown by 33 automobile traverses in Sheffield for summer, autumn, and winter are presented in Table 4.2. Contrasts are usually largest in winter because a snow cover over the outskirts reflects solar radiation, whereas the snow-bare city surfaces absorb solar heat. Note also how much drier the city is than the rural environs, especially at night.

Perhaps the most detailed temperature study in the United

Table 4.1. Temperature variations with urban land use in Washington, D.C., and in Sheffield, England, on a clear summer day. (Washington, D.C., data from Landsberg 1968.)

Land Use	Washington, D.C.		Sheffield, England	
	Daytime (1320 EST)	Nighttime (2200 EST)	Daytime (1459 GMT)	Nighttime (2337 GMT)
Business center	97°F	85°F	69°F	54°F
Industrial	–	–	71	56
Dense residential	96	83	70	53
Park near city center	95	84	66	46
Park near city fringe	94	78	–	–
Suburban residential	95	79	69	51
Rural environs	95	76	65	42
Contrast between land uses	3	9	6	12

States was conducted in St. Louis, Missouri, in 1952–53. The greatest temperature differences between park areas, outskirts, and downtown areas were recorded in winter. On December 16, 1952, for example, the temperature differential between downtown St. Louis and Forest Park, 5 miles to the west, was 13 °F. Within the park temperatures were 2° to 10° warmer on the edges than in the center. Summer differences are also high; in a June 9, 1953, survey the Forest Park temperature was 9° lower than the downtown temperature. St. Louis suffers excessive heat spells in summer each year that cause a number of heat stroke casualties.

Extensive three-dimensional temperature studies have been conducted in the San Francisco, San Jose, and Palo Alto region by Duckworth and Sandberg (1954). Surface traverses between downtown San Francisco and the waterfront revealed temperature differentials as high as 20 °F. Vertical soundings showed that the heat influence of the city normally extends to an altitude three times the height of the tallest city structures. Above this height the city tends to be cooler than the country. The vertical temperature profile, and hence stability conditions, is a critical factor in the accumulation of pollutants. Climatological records regarding the frequency, duration, and depth of temperature inversions should be consulted by city and industrial planners before they build homes or industrial plants in an ill-ventilated valley.

Table 4.2. Temperature and relative humidity contrasts between central Sheffield, England, and its rural environs (based on observations from 33 automobile traverses).

| | Temperature °F | | | | | | Relative Humidity (percent) | | | | | |
| | Summer | | Autumn | | Winter | | Summer | | Autumn | | Winter | |
Setting	Day	Night	Day	Night	Day	Night	Day	Night	Day	Night	Day	Night
City center	70.7	55.6	63.4	54.1	32.6	26.8	34	63	40	57	69	77
Rural Environs	65.3	42.8	59.6	42.6	22.7	12.1	47	95	47	86	77	96
Contrast	5.4	12.8	3.8	11.5	9.9	14.6	13	32	7	29	8	19

The effect of the atmosphere's vertical temperature structure on noise is finally receiving increased recognition in the planning of airports near cities. Instead of diffusing noise, inversion layers reflect it to the ground and thus contribute to the general noise level in cities.

Considerable attention should also be given to small-scale and localized temperature contrasts. Landsberg (1970a) studied temperatures in a courtyard, a lawn area, and a grove of trees in Columbia, a new town which is presently being developed in Maryland. Observations were made on a mid-summer day with a weak onshore flow of marine tropical air. Temperatures and humidities were relatively high. In the early afternoon, air temperatures over the courtyard and over the lawn were both 87°F and the wood grove was 86°F. The parking lot surface temperature was 111°F, whereas the grass surface temperature was only slightly above the air temperature. At sunset, the surface temperatures of the lawn and the wood grove were almost identical to the air temperature, while the walls and pavements in the courtyard were 3.6° to 9.0° higher. Two hours after sunset, the courtyard surface remained 3.6° to 9.0° above the falling air temperature, but the grass surface temperature had dropped 3.6° below air temperature. These observations show that after sunset an isolated building complex can produce a heat island effect which is comparable in magnitude to contrasts between city and country temperatures. These new and important findings should be considered both in future building schemes and in the planning of new towns.

Effects of Green Areas

Green areas have been used to modify city temperatures. As seen in Chapter 3, vegetational covers of land tend to stabilize temperatures and decrease extremes, whereas man-made surfaces exaggerate them.

In the summer of 1969 the author attempted to determine how small or how large a park or green area has to be to produce calm-air differences in temperature, humidity, and comfort. A small park in Cincinnati, 0.84 acres in size and consisting only of two rows of trees, some hedges, and five-yard-wide lawn plots (Figure 4.6) was instrumented for humidity, temperature, and wind. Measurements were recorded over the lawn and over the curbside on days of less than five-tenths cloud cover and when the maximum temperatures exceeded 85°F. The results are shown in Table 4.3. For the period of the investi-

Figure 4.6. A small park in downtown Cincinnati. This is the site of the meteorological measurements presented in Table 4.3. (Photograph by Wilfrid Bach.)

gation (seven days in August), conditions in the small park were more comfortable during both day and night than they were on the adjacent city streets and sidewalks. At a discomfort index (DI) of 75, for example, at least half of all people tested feel uncomfortable. At a DI of 79 hardly anybody feels comfortable. Positive values of the radiant heat exchange (R) and the convective heat exchange (C) indicate that the body gains heat from the environment; negative values mean heat is transferred from the body to the environment. At 3:00 P.M. EST, when the photograph in Figure 4.6 was taken, the people sitting near the lawn received a significant 347 Btuh less than those standing at the curbside, and also the convective heat loss was 50 Btuh greater in the park, further increasing the comfort there. Because such small green

Table 4.3. The effect of a small city park in downtown Cincinnati on some meteorological elements in summer, 1969.

The following symbols are used in the table:

TDB   is the dry bulb, or air, temperature.

TG   is the globe temperature obtained from a globe thermometer, which consists of a thermometer inserted inside a blackened copper sphere about 10–15 cm in diameter.

MRT   is the mean radiant temperature of the environment, which is calculated from globe temperature (TG), wind speed (u), and dry bulb temperature (TDB) using MRT = $[(TG + 460)^4 + 1.03 \times 10^8 u^{0.5} (TG - TDB)]^{0.25} - 460$ (Hertig and Belding 1967).

RH   is the relative humidity.

WBGT   is the wet bulb globe temperature, a comfort index developed for use by U.S. Marine Corps training centers; it is calculated from TWB (the wet bulb temperature), TG, and TDB: WBGT = 0.7 (TWB) + 0.2(TG) + 0.1(TDB).

DI   is a discomfort index developed by Thom (1959); DI = 0.4 (TDB + TWB) + 15.

R   is the radiant heat exchange; R = 17.5(MRT - 95) (Hertig and Belding 1963).

C   is the convective heat exchange; C = $0.756\, u^{0.6}$ (TDB - 95) (Hertig and Belding 1963).

Meteorological Elements	Afternoon (1430–1500 EST)			Evening (2030–2200 EST)		
	Urban Park	Urban Concrete	Difference	Urban Park	Urban Concrete	Difference
TDB (°F)	85.5	88.2	2.7[a]	80.5	80.5	0.03
TG (°F)	98.7	109.4	10.7[a]	80.5	82.0	1.4
MRT (°F)	121.8	141.7	19.8	82.6	84.4	3.7[b]
RH (%)	40.6	38.5	2.1	53.3	50.5	2.7
WBGT (°F)	75.9	79.2	3.3[a]	71.9	72.4	0.3
DI	76.4	78.0	1.6[a]	74.5	74.6	0.1
R (Btuh)	470	817	347[a]	−251	−185	−66[b]
C (Btuh)	−162	−112	−50[a]	−158	−179	−21

[a]Significant at the 5% level (Student's t-test).
[b]Significant at the 1% level (Student's t-test).

areas have such an unexpectedly large effect, the ample use of their beneficial influence should become an integral part of comprehensive planning.

Ventilation

Wind speed is one of the most important climatic elements in urban planning, because human comfort and the dispersion of air pollutants are largely dependent on it. On the one hand, winds that are too strong cause a funnel effect in canyon-like streets, and this may concentrate air pollutants locally by lifting street dust and fumigating emissions from elevated sources. On the other hand, if the winds are too light, the air may stagnate and raise concentrations of pollutants.

The ideal urban ventilation system would prevent the funneling effect and favor the "country" breeze — a local wind that is produced by the city's heat island and that draws into the warmest part of the city relatively cleaner and cooler air from nearby country, suburban, and green areas. Such desirable winds might be achieved by a properly arranged system of green areas cutting through the entire built-up area; the green areas would further serve to remove some of the pollutants circulated in the urban dust dome.

One of the rules planners appear to have adopted is to construct industrial plants downwind, not upwind, of residential areas. Such a rule may have deleterious effects if light winds from the nonprevailing directions are accompanied by stagnation conditions with high air pollution potential. If the prevailing winds are strong and provide adequate dispersion of pollutants, a plant site in the prevailing wind direction would be preferable.

Local air circulation is of great importance in urban planning. In hilly urban terrain, downslope winds may bring valley residences relatively clean and cool air during oppressive summer nights. In the cold season, however, this topographic situation may lead to the accumulation of a sea of cold air with attendant frost hazard. Also, daytime upslope winds may transport valley pollution to adjacent hillsides. Nonetheless, many slope locations are excellent residential sites, because commonly they are above the valley inversion, have good air drainage with reduced frost hazards, are protected from strong winds, and enjoy greater amounts of sunshine.

Sea and lake breezes usually have a tempering effect on weather extremes in coastal cities. A cool sea breeze is very welcome in hot summer weather. In daytime sea breezes may displace pollutants inland, and at nighttime land breezes transport them seaward again. Pollutants may be repeatedly transported back and forth under a shallow inversion, as sometimes happens in Los Angeles, for instance.

The interaction of wind speed, green areas, and air pollution is interesting. In general, green areas influence ventilation through their shape, width, roughness and permeability, and their thermal stratification. Kühn (1959) found that the local reduction of wind speed by green areas causes suspended particulates to settle out more easily.

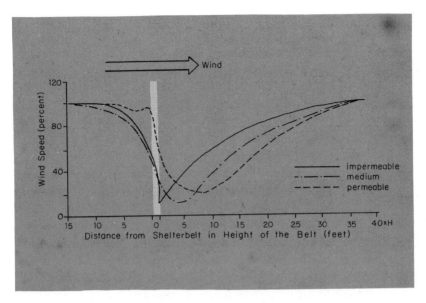

Figure 4.7. Effects on wind speed of shelterbelts having different degrees of permeability. (After Panfilov in van Eimern 1964.)

Leaves increase turbulence in the air stream and thus cause particulate pollutants to impact more easily on the vegetation, facilitating their removal from the air. Dense evergreens may act as a wall rather than a baffle, causing the air stream to pass over them. In such cases pollutants settle a certain distance downwind behind the evergreens, rather than filter out in the vegetation. Trunks and branches of deciduous trees significantly reduce wind velocities even after leaves have fallen. In an area of Nashville, Tennessee, with well-spaced, large deciduous trees (such as a long-established residential neighborhood), the wind speed increases by 25 percent after defoliation. Areas devoid of trees have velocities 40 percent greater than those in the areas of leaved trees. Figure 4.7 illustrates the reduction in wind speed behind obstacles with different degrees of permeability.

AIR POLLUTION FACTORS

In the past, happenstance has primarily governed the development of most cities. The result has been urbanization and industrialization with today's immense air pollution problems. Imaginative and insightful approaches are now needed that lead to controlled planning and eventual pollution prevention. The two major pollution species, namely, particulate and gaseous pollutants, are discussed here in order to demonstrate the potential for air pollution control by the proper application of planning measures.

Particulate Pollutants

The influence of planning measures on controlling particulate air pollution in a city can best be shown by comparing pollution levels inside and outside green areas. Green spaces have long been known to filter out dust, soot, and fly ash. Every aquatic or vegetated open space, park, or garden reduces the amount of dust in the air. For example, only 2.5 acres of beech woods are capable of extracting about four tons of dust per year from the atmosphere and incorporating it into the humus layer. A lawn is able to collect three to six times as much dust as an equally large piece of smooth glass.

Studies of Hyde Park in London reveal that this green area of only 1 square mile reduces smoke concentration by an average 27 percent. Under stable atmospheric conditions, when pollution tends to spread uniformly within a shallow mixing layer, the cleansing effect of Hyde Park regarding smoke pollution is reduced to an average of 17 percent. A 600-foot-wide green belt can reduce the dust count by as much as 75 percent (Landsberg 1947). Several studies show that coniferous trees are more effective than deciduous trees in filtering out particulate pollutants; they are, however, more easily damaged, especially by gaseous pollutants.

A dense coniferous forest can reduce the concentration of ragweed pollen by 80 percent (Neuberger and others 1967). Laboratory experiments also show the relative filtering effects of various types of vegetation. Coniferous species such as white pine and red spruce reduce particulate matter by 20 to 50 percent, whereas broad-leaved species such as box-elder and black cherry reduce the particulate pollution by less than 20 percent.

Russian studies also have shown the extent to which park areas can reduce particulate air pollution. "Sanitary clearance zones" built around factories cleanse the air; gardens and parks in the vicinity of factories can lower the local dust content in the air by 40 percent or more (Sokolovskii and others 1966).

Which tree genera exert the greatest filtering effect? Measure-

ments of the weight of dust per unit area of leaf surface (g/m²) indicate
that the best vegetative dust filters in descending order are: lilac (2.33),
maple (1.11), linden (0.61), and poplar (0.26) (Dokutschajeva 1959).
The subsequent removal of dust from leaf surfaces by rain is of great
importance, because it guarantees a continuing filtering process by
the leaves, without damaging the plant.

The author has conducted extensive studies in the Cincinnati
area to learn more about relations between the variation of particulate
(or mass) concentration and urban land use. Figure 4.8 shows the

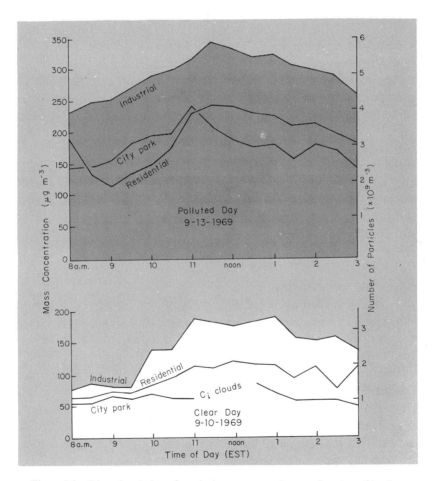

Figure 4.8. Diurnal variation of particulate concentration as a function of land use,
Cincinnati, Ohio. Data were obtained by measuring solar attenuation using a sun
photometer and by applying light scattering theory (see Bach 1969).

diurnal variation of mass concentration and numbers of aerosols for a
"polluted" day and for a "clean" day in three different areas of
Cincinnati. The high concentrations on the "polluted" day were favored
by stagnating air masses, light winds, and fog. The relatively low concentrations on the "clean" day were recorded under unstable, nearly
cloudless conditions with gusty 1 to 10 mph winds. From a planning
point of view it is important to note that air over the city park and residential sites has considerably lower concentrations of suspended particulates than air over the industrial site. Concentrations over the
industrial site on a "clean" day were as high as those over the park and
residential sites on a "polluted" day.

In another study using a mobile sampling method, the author
sought to determine quantitatively how far an urban dust dome (or haze
layer) extends over its neighboring region. Starting at the geographic
midpoint of the Cincinnati metropolitan area, six investigators fanned
out simultaneously in six different directions, each recording solar attenuation at one-mile intervals for 24 miles. From the calculated mass
concentration values and on-the-spot observations, the extent of the
urban dust dome was delineated (see Figure 4.9). On this calm and polluted day (September 12, 1969), the haze layer was concentrated over
the industrialized and most densely built-up areas. Under these stagnating conditions the cleansing effect of green spaces and rivers on the
air is pronounced. Such areas have relatively clean air because they do
not emit pollutants and because they cleanse the air by filtering and
impaction.

Gaseous Pollutants

The influence of planning measures on modifying gaseous pollutant levels has not been investigated in the same detail as have measures
for controlling particulate pollution. Of the numerous gases expelled
into the air by man's urban activities, the most important (because
of organic or material damage that they do) include carbon monoxide
(primarily from automobiles), sulfur dioxide (mainly from combustion
of coal and oil), nitrogen oxides (mostly from automobiles), and various
organic gases (from various sources, including automobiles). The best
way to control gaseous pollutants is to regulate them at their sources,
before they are emitted into the atmosphere, because planning procedures after emission are less effective than in the case of particulates.
Green areas do, however, reduce concentrations of certain gases, as
Table 4.4 and the research discussed below indicate. The important

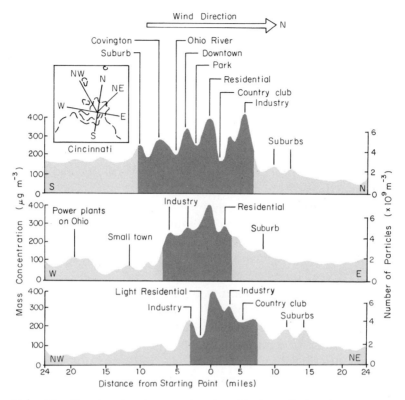

Figure 4.9. The urban dust dome as a function of land use, Cincinnati. The heavily shaded areas mark the extent of the dust dome on September 12, 1969, a calm, polluted day.

Table 4.4. Reduction of selected gaseous pollutants by forest vegetation (managed as a green "sanitary clearance zone"). (After Kalyuzhnyi and others 1960.)

Pollutant	Concentration of Pollutant (mg/m³)			
	1000 m from Source	1500 m from Source, No Green Zone	1500 m from Source, with 500 m Green Zone	Percent Reduction Attributed to Green Area
Sulfur dioxide	0.27	0.14	0.08	22
Hydrogen sulfide	0.07	0.03	0.025	7
Nitrogen oxides	0.22	0.13	0.07	27

effects of gaseous pollutants on vegetation — the other side of green area–air pollution relations — are discussed in Chapter 9.

Sulphur dioxide concentration in a Leningrad park was found by Litvinov (1955) to be only half of that in an adjacent open area. Kalyuzhnyi and others (1960) found that during the leaf-bearing season the air in sanitary clearance zones and parks contained 24.2 percent less sulphur than air monitored over neighboring streets.

Carbon monoxide levels were sampled in two residential blocks by Baikov and Feldman (1966). The residential study area was free of industrial pollution. One residential block was shielded from the street by a dense stand of trees and bushes 10 m wide and up to 6 m high. During the sampling period the wind was blowing from the street towards the houses at one to nine mph. At the sidewalk, 22 m from the edge of the road, carbon monoxide was reduced by 44 percent, and at a balcony on the fourth floor, 30 m from the edge of the road, this gas was reduced by 54 percent.

Increased combustion of fossil fuels has increased the carbon dioxide concentration in cities. In photosynthesis plants use carbon dioxide and give off oxygen. Whether the carbon dioxide assimilation by vegetation is of significance has been debated by Kühn (1959), who assumes that three acres of wooded area can only absorb as much carbon dioxide as is produced by four people through breathing, heating, and cooking.

IMPACT OF HEAT AND HUMIDITY ON HUMAN HEALTH

It has been shown that different types of urban land use produce modifications in climate and air hygiene; it follows that they also influence human health. It is beyond the scope of this chapter to consider the long-term, chronic effects on health caused by air pollutants or unsanitary slum conditions. Two short-term effects of thoughtless planning are instead considered: comfort and deaths due to summer heat waves.

Of the many existing comfort indices, *sultriness* is selected for discussion because it is related to excessive heat and its value can easily be obtained from dry and wet bulb temperature readings. A vapor pressure of 14.08 mm of mercury defines the minimum value of sultri-

Table 4.5. Sultriness in different parts of greater Cincinnati during July through October, 1968.

| Urban Setting | Occurrence of Sultriness (percent) | | | |
	Morning	Noon	Evening	Average
City Center	42.9	60.0	66.7	56.9
City Park	69.2	85.7	58.4	68.8
Industrial	47.0	94.1	100.0	79.6
Suburban	73.4	81.6	77.5	77.2

Note: Data represent 90 percent of possible readings.

ness. The occurrence of summer sultriness in greater Cincinnati is shown in Table 4.5. The city center usually has the highest temperatures, but it is also much drier than other land-use areas and therefore registers the least sultriness. The industrial site is the most sultry, particularly at noon and in the evening, when greenhouse conditions trap long-wave radiation and additional water vapor enters the air from cooling towers. City parks and suburban sites have intermediate values of sultriness because lower temperatures there are compensated for by higher humidity (from vapor evaporated by the vegetation). It is obvious that green areas can be used by planners to filter out pollutants and also to lower temperatures and thus provide a more comfortable urban climate.

Extended exposure to high summer temperatures can cause death by bringing on heat stroke and by contributing to heart disease. Heat waves causing hundreds — and at times thousands — of excess deaths in big cities occur periodically in summer. For example, the heat wave of July 1966, which covered the eastern United States, has been blamed for more than 1,100 deaths each in New York City and in the state of Illinois. More than 500 casualties in St. Louis were attributed to the heat. A closer examination of the distribution of the deaths in St. Louis showed that the death rate within the city was 5 1/2 times greater than that of suburban areas. These excess deaths, however, only occurred when temperatures rose above the critical value of 90 °F. At 91 °F, 11 people died; at 95 °F 73 people died. In this critical temperature range it is significant to human health that park and suburban areas are 5 °F or more cooler than the densely built-up and industrial quarters of the city (see Tables 4.1 and 4.2).

Several studies have shown that heat waves usually cause deaths after an exposure of 24 hours or more. This suggests that extended exposure to heat, and the inability to escape heat when night temperatures remain high, is more critical than spectacular daytime temperatures as a cause of high casualty rates. Green areas, trees, window shades, and air conditioning are major planning and architectural measures that can be applied to avoid deaths from excess heat.

PLANNING MEASURES

Green Areas

The use of green areas is a major planning technique by which city planners and landscape architects can prevent or reduce adverse effects of climate. Green areas in cities include (for purpose of definition) parks, woodlots, cemeteries, scenic areas, recreation grounds and playgrounds, golf courses, institutional grounds, plazas, lawns, gardens, greenhouses, agricultural land, bare land, and water bodies. The average land use in five large American cities shows that about 30 percent of the total city area is residential (see Table 4.6). The next largest share (26 percent) is reserved for open space, primarily green areas as broadly defined above. Streets cover more than 20 percent of the city area. Community facilities and industrial and commercial land share approximately 20 percent.

Cincinnati is an example of a city that has a large proportion of open space (25.3 percent). Fortunately these open areas are distributed fairly well over the city (see Figure 4.10). About 40 percent of the open area consists of parks, playgrounds, and golf courses for recreational purposes. The remaining 60 percent is undeveloped land, that is, bare land or woodlot. This may be used for future urban development.

The importance of green areas in urban planning can be summarized as follows: A park-like area consisting of grass and sparse stands of trees appears to be the best means of avoiding temperature and moisture extremes, and yet maintaining a certain amount of ventilation. Green areas also help to prevent flooding by reducing the rate of runoff. In order to provide solitude, clean air, and accessible recreation, green areas should be dispersed throughout an urban area and legally protected.

Table 4.6. Various uses of urban land, as percentage of total area (averaged for New York, Philadelphia, Washington, D.C., Cincinnati, and Chicago).

Land Use	Percent of Total Area
Residential	29.8
Commercial	2.7
Industrial	6.9
Community facilities	8.2
Streets	23.5
Open Space	26.0
Other	2.9

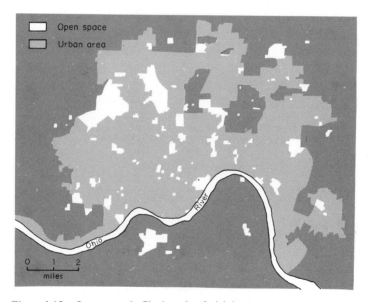

Figure 4.10. Open space in Cincinnati and vicinity.

The impact of noise is discussed in Chapter 8; therefore, noise protection qualities of green areas are only mentioned here. Green areas and buffer strips of shrubs and trees can insulate residential areas from noisy factories and highways. Whether deciduous or coniferous trees should be planted must be decided in each specific case. Generally, deciduous trees are more resistent to pollution damage, whereas coniferous plants are more effective in filtering out noise and pollution.

Slum Clearance

Elimination or reduction of adverse pollution and climatic conditions can be one of the beneficial results of slum clearance and urban renewal. The urban renewal area in Sheffield, England, shown in Figure 4.2, though on the whole poorly planned, does incorporate one major improvement: the multistory residences have no polluting, open fireplaces, but are instead connected to a central heating system. It is unfortunate that these new buildings were erected over the location of the former slums in the vicinity of a heavily industrialized valley.

Slum clearance and urban renewal can, however, be applied more imaginatively, as is exemplified by the planning and development of some new and satellite towns. Instead of rebuilding houses in the crowded and polluted slum areas, many urban planners are developing park cities. The plan for the new town of Nürnberg-West in Germany, for instance, provides greenbelts and parks that surround the residential area and protect it from air pollution and noise. Traffic in the residential area is reduced because no arterial routes are permitted, and parking is prohibited in streets near the houses. Parking is restricted to lots separated from the living areas. This plan has produced more favorable climatic conditions in the residential area.

Traffic Sanitation

Streets in major United States cities consume more than 20 percent of the city area (see Table 4.6). In downtown areas, streets and parking lots occupy almost 50 percent of the available space. Construction of more roads and highways has resulted in more traffic accidents, more traffic congestion, greater pollution, and higher noise levels, instead of the predicted alleviation of traffic. Constructions such as expressways through and underneath buildings have created a continuous source of gas and noise pollution. Many of the roads leading into downtown areas terminate in multilevel, underground parking lots beneath multistory office, hotel, and apartment buildings; the result is toxic levels of pollution for the dwellers.

Pollution is, of course, only one of the unfortunate by-products of our automobile-oriented transportation systems. Town planners must abandon their old formula: more automobiles, more roads. This concept is economically, culturally, and aesthetically destroying downtown areas. Different solutions are needed. One successful method — proven in a number of cities to move people quickly, safely, and with minimum noise and pollution — is the underground rapid transit system. London, for example, is comprehensively covered by a net of subways (which run frequently and on time) that provides by far the fastest and most convenient means to get from one place to another. Subways in Montreal run on rubber wheels and have stabilizers, which make them quiet, comfortable, and convenient. In contrast, subways in New York, Philadelphia, and Chicago are dirty and noisy. This sorry state, fostered by a one-sided transportation policy favoring private automobiles, encourages continued automobile usage and consequent pollution.

Although the construction of rapid transit systems is expensive, the long-term benefits outweigh the costs. In Germany, a proposal is being seriously considered that would provide free public transportation as an incentive for commuters to leave their cars at home, and thus reduce the dangerous levels of automobile pollution. It is revealing, however, that just such a program failed in Chicago on a pilot basis. And when, during a particularly serious smog period (July 1970), the mayor of New York tried to persuade drivers to use the public transit system in an attempt to hold pollution accumulations below the danger level, he had little success; a worse episode may force the mayor to *forbid* all private vehicle traffic. These examples show that the traffic crisis is already upon us, and that only drastic measures can cure the choking patient: the city.

Summary recommendations

The development of new towns or redevelopment of existing urban places requires careful study of climatic and air hygiene conditions. Only in a few cases, such as the construction of the new communities of Columbia in Maryland and Kitimat in British Columbia, has a climatologist been consulted.

The selection of sites for new industrial plants should include meteorological studies, such as tracer and diffusion experiments. In addition, climatological data should be obtained on the frequency, duration, and depth of inversion layers, the mixing depth, and ventilation conditions. Effective stack height calculations also are valuable. A careful evaluation of the meteorologic, topographic, and engineering factors involved can avoid hazardous pollution accumulations and subsequent costly modifications.

The planning of airport locations should consider fog frequency and visibility conditions, prevailing wind direction, the depth of inversion layers, and adjacent land uses to reduce pollution and noise hazards (see Chapter 8).

Residential areas should, from a climatological standpoint, be located on hills and ridges rather than in narrow valleys so that they can enjoy sunshine and clean air above the polluted inversion layer. Furthermore, green areas should separate residential areas from industrial and commercial zones.

Park areas should have no through automobile traffic. Numerous park entrances with ample parking facilities should be provided. The green areas of parks will moderate adverse climatic and air hygiene effects by cooling oppressive summer days, reducing gusty winds, and screening air pollutants. Park areas should retain their original function as recreational areas or refuges of solitude and fresh air where man can escape from his daily worries and pressures.

Expressways and other major roads should be enclosed by earth walls with shrubs to contain and filter air pollution and noise (see Figure 4.11). Downtown streets can be climatically and aesthetically improved by planting trees and flower beds (see Figure 9.6). All surface parking lots should have rows of trees to prevent overheating of cars and to reduce gasoline loss through evaporation. Moderation of the urban heat island would also result.

Shopping areas should be segregated from automobile traffic. Downtown shopping areas should be off limits to private vehicular traffic. This plan was suggested for New York during the July 1970 smog period and has been successfully accomplished for a short period in Tokyo, with a 40 percent increase in retail sales.

In summary, the role of climatology should be significant in urban planning, although it has often been overlooked by the planners,

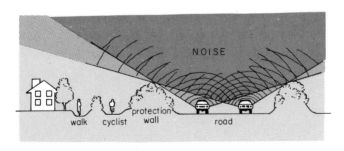

Figure 4.11. Road design with protection from noise and air pollution. (After Reichow 1966).

builders, and politicians who make the major decisions concerning urban growth. The climatologist should participate jointly with experts from other environmental disciplines in the complex process of constructive urban development.

REFERENCES

Bach, W. 1969. Solar radiation and atmospheric turbidity. Report prepared for the Kettering Laboratory, Univ. of Cincinnati, Cincinnati.
——— 1971. Seven steps to better living on the urban heat island. *Landscape architecture* 141:136–138.
——— 1972. *Atmospheric pollution.* New York: McGraw-Hill.
Bach, W., and W. Patterson. 1969. Heat budget studies in greater Cincinnati. *Proc. Assoc. Amer. Geogr.* 1:7–11.
Baikov, B. K., and Yu. G. Feldman. 1966. Effect of the planning of streets and residential blocks on the pollution of air by exhaust gases. *Hyg. and Sanit.* 31:315–319.
Beryushev, K. G. 1967. The provision of parks and open spaces in cities. *Hyg. and Sanit.* 32:25–28.
Bridger, C. A., and L. A. Hefland. 1968. Mortality from heat during July 1966 in Illinois. *Intern. Jour. Biometeorology* 12:51–70.
Clarke, J. F., and W. Bach. 1971. Comparison of the comfort conditions in different urban and suburban microenvironments. *Intern. Jour. Biometeorology* 15(1):41–54.
Dokutschajeva, V. F. 1959. Die Rolle von Baumanpflanzungen die der Entstaubung der Luft. (The role of tree plantations in filtering particles from the air). *Jour. Hyg. Epid. Microbiol. Immunol.* (Prague) 3:329–338.
Duckworth, F. S., and J. S. Sandberg. 1954. The effect of cities upon horizontal and vertical temperature gradients. *Bull. Amer. Meteor. Soc.* 35:198–207.
Eimern, J. van, R. Karsehon, L. A. Razumova, and G. W. Robertson. 1964. *Windbreaks and shelterbelts.* Geneva: World Meteorological Organization, no. 147, Tech. Paper 70, Tech. Note no. 59.
Frederick, R. H. 1961. A study of the effect of tree leaves on wind movement. *Monthly Weather Review* 89:39–44.
Hansbrough, J. R. 1967. Air quality and forestry. In *Agriculture and the quality of our environment,* ed. N. C. Brady, pp. 45–55. Washington, D.C.: American Association for the Advancement of Science, Publ. 85.
Hertig, B. A., and H. S. Belding. 1963. Temperature: Its measurement and control in science and industry. In *Evaluation and control of heat hazards,* ed. American Institute of Physics, pp. 347–355. New York: Reinhold Publ. Corp.

Kalyuzhnyi, D. N., Ya. I. Kostovetskii, S. A. Davydov, and M. B. Aksel'rod. 1960. Effectiveness of sanitary clearance zones between industrial enterprises and residential quarters. In *Survey of U.S.S.R. literature on air pollution and related occupational diseases,* trans. B. S. Levine, vol. 4, pp. 179–183. Washington, D.C.: U.S. Dept. of Commerce.

Kühn, E. 1959. Planning and the city's climate. *Landscape* 8(3):21–23.

Landsberg, H. E. 1947. Microclimatology. *Architectural Forum* March: 114–119.

—— 1968. *Physical climatology.* DuBois, Pa.: Gray Publ. Co.

—— 1970a. Micrometeorological temperature differentiation through urbanization. In *Urban climates,* pp. 129–136. Geneva: World Meteorological Organization, no. 254, Tech. Paper 141, Tech. Note no. 108.

—— 1970b. Climates and urban planning. In *Urban climates,* pp. 364–374. Geneva: World Meteorological Organization, no. 254, Tech. Paper 141, Tech. Note no. 108.

Litvinou, N. N. 1955. Urban planning and construction. *Roy. Soc. Health Jour.* 75:629–631.

Neuberger, H., C. L. Hosler, and W. C. Kocmond. 1967. Vegetation as aerosol filter. *Biometeorology* (Proc. 3rd Intern. Congr. Biometeorology) 2:693–702.

Reichow, H. B. 1966. Stäbauliche Massnahem im Dienste der Lärmbekämpfung und der Reinhaltung der Luft. *Ztsch. Präventivmed.* (Zurich) 11(6):642–659.

Sokolovskii, M. S., Zh. L. Gabinova, B. V. Popov, and L. F. Kachor. 1966. Sanitary protection of Moscow atmospheric air. In *Survey of U.S.S.R. literature on air pollution and related occupational diseases,* trans. B. S. Levine, vol. 14. Springfield, Va.: U.S. Dept. of Commerce.

Stanford Univ. Aerosol Laboratory and R. M. Parsons Co., 1952–53. Behavior of aerosol clouds within cities. *Jt. Quart. Reports.* no. 2, Oct.-Dec. 1952 (AD 7261); no. 3 Jan.-March 1953 (AD 31 509); no. 4 April-June 1953 (AD 31 508); no. 5 July-Sept. 1953 (AD 31 507); no. 6, vol. 1, Oct.-Dec. 1953 (AD 31 510); no. 6, vol. 2, Oct.-Dec. 1953 (AD 31 711).

Thom, E. C. 1959. The discomfort index. *Weatherwise* 12(2):57–60.

Wainwright, C. W. K., and M. J. G. Wilson. 1962. Atmospheric pollution in a London park. *Intern. Jour. Air Water Polln.* 6:377–347.

CHAPTER 5

Water and the City

John C. Schaake, Jr.

On July 23, 1962, the most intense storm of the summer struck the Baltimore area. At the height of the storm 10,000 customers were without electric power, and 6,000 telephones were knocked out. A 28-year-old mother of two young children was driving home from shopping when her car was swept into swollen Moores Run and carried downstream. Her body was found in the stream near the car. The car was wrecked, with even the tires torn off by the violence of the flood waters.

This accident is similar to many tragedies that happen during storms and floods in urban areas. This particular incident occurred at a remote stream crossing on a narrow road. The culvert under the road was not adequate to carry the flood flows. Moores Run frequently flows over the road during storms, but this was the first time anyone was killed.

In another accident, a young boy was drowned while wading in a flooded street. Beneath this street a major storm drain was flowing under pressure, causing the water to flow upward into the street through a manhole. The flooding attracted a group of children, and one of them happened to be near the open manhole when the flood peak passed in the drain below the street. The sudden rush of water back into the manhole carried the boy down into the drain.

Both of these accidents could have been prevented if the flooding conditions that occurred could have been foreseen or prevented.

In each case, the engineering works involved were constructed years ago when designers were not as aware of hydrologic problems in the city as they are today. Furthermore, increasing urbanization has increased the magnitude of floods and other water problems. As more people move into urban areas, these areas grow in size and the population density of once rural areas greatly increases. This city growth changes the processes that govern the occurrence and movement of water.

In this chapter, some of the important topics relating to the occurrence and use of water in the city are presented. The first section discusses how man has altered the hydrologic cycle in the city, including facets of its flood hydrology, sediment production, changes in water quality, water treatment and removal. The next section looks at urban man's water demands and needs and how these may be satisfied by controlling surface runoff and by withdrawing water from underground. The final part discusses the important topic of urban water management for the future, including aesthetic, cultural, and environmental considerations.

THE URBAN WATERSHED

The concept of the hydrologic cycle has long provided the basic model whereby the occurrence, movement, and storage of water are studied and explained. The most common presentation explains the cycle in sequential terms: Water evaporates from ocean surfaces, is transported over the continents as vapor, condenses to form clouds, and falls to the land surface as precipitation; the precipitation, in turn, eventually works its way back to the oceans as stream runoff or groundwater. This is, of course, an oversimplification. Water does not move in a purely circular path from the oceans to the land and back again. In fact, only an astonishingly small proportion of the earth's total water supply falls as precipitation each year (.031 percent) — and only about one fourth of that amount falls on land. Yet this water is the essential source of moisture for plants and soil, streamflow, and replenishment of groundwater supplies. Furthermore, more than half of this water does not return directly to the oceans via stream and groundwater, but rather is evaporated back into the atmosphere.

In the United States the average total water supply is 1.2 trillion gallons per day — the average daily discharge of streams. Total water use in 1960 was about 270 billion gallons per day, or 22 percent of the total supply. But *consumption* of water (that is, the amount of water not returned after use) was only about 61 billion gallons daily, or 5 percent of the total supply. How can this be squared with claims of a water shortage and a water crisis? One answer is the pollution of water. The United States uses 95 percent of its aquatic assets as a conveyor belt for sending waste products out to sea; the pattern is similar in Europe and other highly developed areas.

Much of this transformation of quality occurs in urbanized areas, where man not only has injected pollutants into the water supply but also, through his activities and physical works, has altered the flood hydrology, sediment production, and drainage characteristics of the watershed.

Floods in the City

In general, urbanization increases the magnitude of floods and reduces the average interval between floods that exceed a given magnitude. Four principal processes work to cause this phenomenon, although there is only one principal effect downstream: increased flood damages. Of course, urban development may proceed in small steps, and the hydrologic effects of any one step may seem insignificant at the time; but the aggregate effects of all urban land development drastically change the physical condition of the land surface and drainage ways.

Causes of Increased Floods

The four major mechanisms that increase the flood potential of an urban water catchment are:

1. increasing the percentage of impervious surfaces, which tends to increase the total volume of storm runoff and reduce the amount of water that infiltrates into the ground (see Figure 5.1 and the discussion of waterproofing in Chapter 3);
2. paving, straightening, or otherwise "improving" stream channels, all of which reduce the time lag between rainfall and channeled runoff;
3. landscaping and subdivision of the land into building sites,

Figure 5.1. Urban development waterproofs the land surface. In this aerial view of Wheaton, Maryland, roofs and pavement have made most of the surface impervious to water. Such constructions also strongly influence the heat regime, as discussed in Chapters 3 and 4. (Courtesy of U.S. Department of Agriculture.)

which usually shorten the distances over which water flows before reaching a drainage way and thereby reduce the time lag between rainfall and channeled runoff;

4. filling in and human settlement of flood plains, which reduce the space available for storing flood waters in the valley bottom so that water is forced to rise and flow more rapidly.

Natural Flood Frequency

Natural stream channels are formed as the result of complex, time-varying processes of erosion and deposition of soil particles. These processes act to form a stream channel bounded on each side by a *flood plain*. The stream channel, typically, has a flow capacity adequate to carry the flood flows that occur, on the average, once in every two years. The shape and capacity of the stream channel is determined primarily by events that occur only a few times each year.

The largest flood that occurs in a given year is called the annual flood. The magnitude of the annual flood varies from year to year in a random fashion. Together, all of the annual floods may be described in terms of a probability distribution of annual floods. The mean of this distribution is called the *mean annual flood*. As a rule of thumb, the capacity of a stream channel is usually adequate to carry within its banks the mean annual flood.

The concept of the mean annual flood, indicating a magnitude rather rarely achieved, should not be confused with the concept of the average annual streamflow, which is exceeded during about 90 days each year. The annual flow is simply the mean of all of the instantaneous rates of flow that occur throughout the year. Like the annual flood, the annual flow in any year is a random phenomenon, describable as a probability distribution. The mean of this distribution is the *mean annual streamflow*. The fact that this rate usually is exceeded on one out of four days each year emphasizes the variable and uncertain nature of streamflow.

Infrequently the flood plain will be inundated to depths that result in damage to property, both structures and their contents, and sometimes in loss of life through drowning, automobile accidents, people being buried alive by mud, or through physical exertion during and after the flood. On an average of about once in 50 years, as a rule of thumb, the flood plain may be inundated to a depth equal to the depth of the stream channel below the top of its banks. This event is called a 50-year flood. The term derives from the general term N-year flood, which refers to the height or discharge of a stream that can be expected, on the basis of records of the stream's past performance, to be equaled or exceeded on the average of about once in N years (but not at regular intervals of exactly N years); the reciprocal of the recurrence interval defines the probability of the event occurring in any one year. The quantitative probability of a 50-year flood occurring in any one year is thus 1/50, or 0.02, and the probability of it not occurring is 0.98. The probability of a 50-year flood not occurring in any given number of years (N years) is 0.98^N; thus, the probability of at least one 50-year flood occurring in an N-year period is $1 - 0.98^N$. For N equal to 10 years, this means that the chance of a 50-year flood occurring at least once during the next 10 years is $1 - 0.98^{10}$, or 0.184.

Urban Flood Frequency

As a drainage basin urbanizes, the probability distributions of the annual floods and of the annual streamflows are affected. The social and economic repercussions of changes in the flood hydrology generally are much more important than those of changes in the annual stream-flow distribution.

In order to measure directly the influence of urbanization on peak flood flows, it would be necessary to have long historical records of flood events before and after the area developed. Records that could give statistically reliable results seldom exist, so it is necessary to assess the effects of urbanization by less direct means. One promising indirect approach is to use mathematical, computer simulation models to simulate the behavior of a catchment in response to storm rainfall. Such models offer the opportunity to estimate the magnitude of a flood that would occur from the same storm on a certain catchment for assumed different degrees of urban development. One of the better known simulation models is the Stanford Watershed Model; this model has been used by S. D. James to study the increase in flood magnitudes caused by urbanization. He analyzed runoff from a 44-square-mile basin near Sacramento, California, 12 square miles of which had been urbanized over the period of record. James correlated historical measurements of rainfall and runoff with changes in urban development, such as percent of impervious area and percent of area served by storm sewerage. By operating the simulation model with values for different combinations of impervious area and sewered area, the effect of urbanization on the mean annual flood was estimated. James originally presented this figure in terms of the actual discharge, in cubic feet per second; but hydrologist L. B. Leopold has expressed this information as the ratio of discharge before and after urbanization; see Figure 5.2. Qualitatively, this figure suggests that urbanization can increase the mean annual flood as much as sixfold in this particular drainage

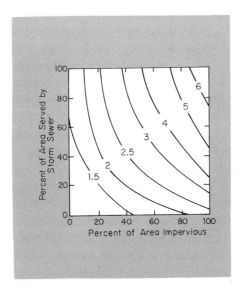

Figure 5.2. Effect of urbanization as measured by percent of storm sewers, on mean annual flood for a one-square-mile drainage area. Values on curves are ratios of discharge after urbanization to discharge before urbanization. (After Leopold 1968.)

basin. Leopold also calculated the effect of increased sewerage on flood frequency, with the results shown in Figure 5.3.

Another urban runoff model developed by the author to assess the influence of drainage basin shape and drainage density (that is, the ratio of the total length of drainage channels to the catchment area) on the peak runoff rate indicates that drainage density has a pronounced effect on the peak runoff rate, but that the shape of the area has no significant effect.

A study of data assessing the effects of urbanization on the occurrence of overbank flows in Brandywine Creek, Pennsylvania, shows that the stream will leave its bank five to six times more often after complete urbanization than it did in its natural state.

Production and Movement of Sediment

Urban sediment yields have physical, biological, aesthetic, and economic impacts downstream. Physical changes result from the depo-

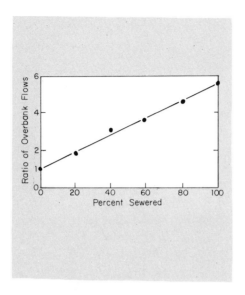

Figure 5.3. Effect of urbanization on flood
frequency for a one-square-mile drainage area.
Increase in number of flows per year equal to
or exceeding original channel capacity as ratio
to number of overbank flows before urbanization, as measured by percent of sewers. (After
Leopold 1968.)

sition of sediment in flat reaches of streams, in reservoirs, and in estuaries. Sediments may cause ecological harm by covering plants and
animals on stream bottoms. Increased turbidity reduces light transmission and may change the composition of fish populations. Studies of
a tributary of the Columbia River, for example, suggest that sediment
from highway construction reduced the number and weight of large
game fish by 94 percent in a period of two years. An estimate of the
economic consequences of sediment discharge is given in Table 5.1;
however, most of the values affected by sediment cannot be precisely
evaluated in economic terms. The aesthetic and recreational values lost
because of uncontrolled erosion and sediment loads may greatly exceed
the economic costs of exerting reasonable control over construction
practices.

Sediments eroded from urbanizing or developing areas in the
eastern United States range from 1,000 to more than 100,000 tons per

Table 5.1. Estimated costs of sediment damage. (From Wolman and Schick 1967.)

Location of Sediment	Unit Cost or Value	Method of Estimation
Reservoir	$100/acre-ft	Cost of storage of water: range $60 to $145 per acre-ft
	$0.03/yr/acre-ft	Annual cost assuming rate of depletion of storage, Liberty Reservoir, Patapsco R., 0.03%/yr sedimentation at prevailing rates
	$1/yr/acre-ft	Annual cost assuming rate of depletion of storage, Liberty Reservoir, 1%/yr; urbanization with extremely high sediment yield of 80,000 t/sq mi
Reservoir	$4000/acre-ft	Present value of storage per acre-ft (Liberty Reservoir)
Reservoir	$22,000 to $78,000/yr	Loss of reservoir use: alternative sources and emergency pumping, Worcester, Mass.
Reservoir	$2/yd^3	Dredging of small lake (Lake Barcroft, Va.)
	$1.25/yd^3	Dredging of small reservoir (Tollgate, Md.)
Reservoir	Estimated	Recreation: dependent upon % loss capacity, turbidity, etc. at $1.00/visitor/day
Estuary	$0.60 to $1.25/yd^3	Dredging: Baltimore Harbor – much dependent on disposal
	$0.19	Dredging: Anacostia Area – much dependent on disposal
Channel	$0.80/yd^3	Removal of sediment: spoil placed adjacent to channel
	$1.20/yd^3	Removal of sediment: spoil removed
Channel	Value unknown	Increase in flood damage due to channel obstruction
Channel	Value unknown	Deposition of sediment during floods
Channel	Value unknown	Fish kill, substitution of less desirable species, or recreation time lost due to poor fishing
Channel	Variable	Increased costs of water treatment, $23,400/yr in treatment of 180 mgd (Washington, D.C.)
Riparian lands	Damage equivalent	Legal award for damages equal to cost of restoration (if less than diminution in value) plus value of loss of use

square mile per year according to a study by geographer M. G. Wolman. The largest yields of sediment are derived from areas under construction where men have cleared the land surfaces, thereby exposing the bare soil to erosion (see Chapter 6 for a discussion of soil factors influencing sedimentation).

Before examining some factors that contribute to sediment yields from urban areas, it is important to observe that there is a natural, variable *background* level of sediment produced by every drainage basin. The lowest background levels are for woodland areas or areas that may once have been farmed, but now are overgrown with brush. Typically these areas are found on the urban fringe, and the amount of sediment produced from them is likely to be less than at any time in their recent history. Also, they commonly are areas that will soon be developed for urban use. In evaluating the sediment characteristics of a particular area, it is first necessary to establish the background level. Then the degree to which sediment loads have increased can be determined. Sediment yields from very small areas of land under construction may exceed 20,000 to 40,000 times the amount eroded from farms and woodlands in an equivalent period of time.

Annual sediment production for a number of urbanized and rural areas is shown in Figure 5.4. The data indicate that sediment yields from developing areas depend upon the proportion of the total area under development at any one time. At the upper left of the figure are two points that represent sediment yields in excess of 100,000 tons per square mile per year. These two points (as well as several others) represent areas that are almost completely undergoing development. Partial development (for example, the Little Falls Branch basin) produces intermediate sediment yields whereas agricultural land (for example, Watts Branch basin) has the lowest sediment loss. In summary, sediment yields from basins partially under development may range from 2 to 10 times the yields from natural areas, whereas yields from areas completely under development may range from 20 to 200 times the yields from natural areas.

It is apparent that sediment production is indirectly influenced by population growth and economic development, because most of the sediment from urban areas results from the construction of buildings and highways. For the Baltimore and Washington metropolitan areas, annual sediment production is estimated to be of the order of one to two tons per person increase in population, depending on the density of land development.

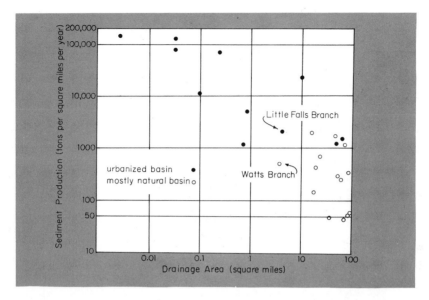

Figure 5.4. Annual sediment production per square mile for urbanized and natural areas. (After Leopold 1968.)

Not all of the sediments from a construction site are carried downstream with the water that originally eroded and transported the material. Accordingly, deposits of sediments are found downstream of construction sites along streams and rivers as well as in numerous small alluvial fans at the base of sloping, eroded hillsides. But the increased runoff that typically follows urban development commonly carries much sediment farther downstream eventually. For instance, approximately one third of the material removed from an industrial area near Cockeysville, Maryland, was present in a one-mile reach of stream (Oregon Branch) immediately downstream, whereas in a small tributary to this same stream no sediment remained from a nearby highway construction project that had been completed seven years earlier.

The amount of sediment being transported in a stream at any time depends on the rate of flow in the stream (and to some extent on the type of catchment being drained). Most sediment is carried by high flows. Of the sediment carried annually by Brandywine Creek, about 54 percent is carried by flows that occur, on the average, only three days each year. The relation between rate of stream flow and sediment yield is called a *sediment rating curve*. Typical curves for two streams located 10 miles apart — one urban, the other rural — are shown

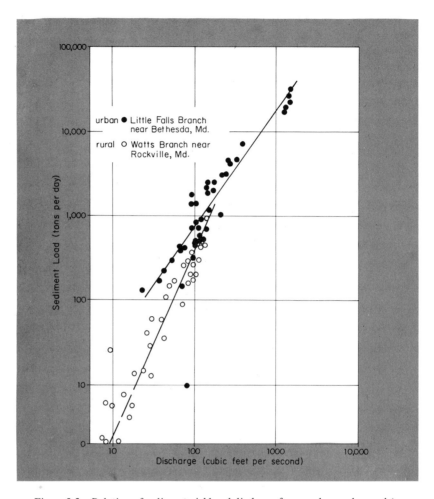

Figure 5.5.   Relation of sediment yield and discharge for an urban and a rural (un-urbanized) area. (After Leopold 1968.)

in Figure 5.5. Although the rating curves are not very different from each other, there is a larger total yield of sediment from the urban area each year. The greater annual sediment yield from the city is caused by the increase in the peak runoff rates following urban development, as discussed earlier. In the sample of storms used to prepare Figure 5.5, the Little Falls Branch (4.1 square miles, urbanized) data include discharges ranging from 20 to 1500 cubic feet per second (cfs) whereas the Watts Branch (3.7 square miles, rural) data include flow from 7 to only 150 cfs.

Changes in Water Quality and Temperature of Streams

Urbanization affects water quality and water temperature as well as flooding and sedimentation. Industrial and domestic waste from hundreds of thousands of septic tanks and cesspools drains into shallow groundwater reservoirs, which in turn run into streams. Obviously the quality of water in such streams is altered.

To study the effects of urbanization on streams, the U.S. Geological Survey, in cooperation with the Nassau County, New York, Department of Public Roads, compared five Long Island streams — three in urbanized southern Nassau County and two in natural, undeveloped areas of Suffolk County. Analyses of the two Suffolk County streams indicate low concentrations of most chemical constituents, placing the water well within the quality limits established for drinking water by the United States Public Health Service. The dissolved solids content of the urbanized Nassau County streams is higher: the average nitrate content is about 14 times greater; detergent content is 9 to18 times greater; and average amount of dissolved solids is 3 to 4 times greater. Similarly, studies of Sharon Creek on the San Francisco Peninsula by J. R. Crippen indicate that the outflow of dissolved solids was 10 times more than if the basin had remained in its natural state.

The effects of urbanization on the temperature of these same five Long Island streams was studied by Edward J. Pluhowski (1970). Because most Long Island streams possess a small capacity for heat storage, they respond markedly and quickly to heat input from solar energy and storm runoff — both of which are factors strongly affected by urban development. Urbanization generally results in the introduction of ponds and lakes along streams, the clearing of vegetation from stream banks, an increase in storm runoff to streams, and a reduction in the amount of inflowing groundwater. Consequently, urban streams are much warmer in summer and somewhat cooler in winter than are their rural counterparts. Man's modifications in Nassau County have raised average stream temperatures in summer by as much as 5° to 8°C (up to 10°C on days of high solar input). During periods of heavy rainfall, street runoff has raised the temperature of urban Nassau County streams as much as 8.5°C. Winter temperatures average 1.5° to 3°C cooler. This is, in part, because (1) in winter urban surface runoff is often colder than the groundwater that flows into streams and (2) streams unprotected by vegetation lose heat to the cold winter atmosphere.

It is feasible to reduce the degree of these urban effects, by such measures as leaving or planting vegetation along streams and installing multiple outlets from ponds (at different depths) to regulate downstream temperatures. Other alternative engineering controls also can be employed to influence water quality; but their costs, which often are substantial, must be weighed against environmental and other benefits.

The environmental effects of stream warming (and to a lesser extent of chemical changes) due to urbanization are poorly known. Such effects should nevertheless concern us, both because of unknown dangers and because urban areas continue to grow. The magnitude of temperature changes reported by Pluhowski for Long Island is of the same order as the magnitude of changes caused by waste heat discharge from electric power plants. Biologists are just beginning to study the effects of such waste heat discharge on aquatic ecosystems.

Drainage and Sewage Disposal

The history of constructing systems for removing water from cities dates back to ancient Rome and Nippur. These early systems were constructed primarily to drain storm water runoff and were built in natural drainage channels. The systems terminated in the nearest river or estuary, and it was forbidden to use them for sanitary waste disposal — a practice continuing until the nineteenth century. Except for clandestine dumping of domestic wastes in the sewerage systems, the only waters flowing in these early sewers were intermittent storm runoff and the continuous flow of groundwater seepage.

Since sanitary wastes could not be put in the sewers, they were disposed of in a variety of inadequate ways. Privies were used, but their contents frequently oozed through the basement walls of the occupied apartments beside them. In other places, wastes were simply heaped on the ground or placed in pits in the centers of courtyards; some courtyards were covered with filth up to the doorways of the houses.

Problems of Combined Sewers

Ultimately, the solution to these foul conditions was to use the existing storm drains, thereby creating a system of so-called *combined* sewers. Although it had been appropriate to discharge storm waters through these sewers into rivers and lakes, the addition of the sanitary wastes created serious new problems. The organic waste load decomposed after entering the water body, exhausted the dissolved oxygen, and produced anerobic conditions that are accompanied by the offensive odors of hydrogen sulfide and other putrid matter. During the mid-nineteenth century, a period known as the Great Sanitary Awakening, men such as England's Sir Edwin Chadwick led a crusade to build sewage treatment facilities. They proposed the construction of separate sewerage systems for storm water and sanitary sewage. For existing combined sewers, they recommended the construction of *interceptor* sewers that would drain to sewage treatment plants.

Many cities in the United States have combined sewerage systems. In 1964 the U.S. Public Health Service estimated that 1,943 communities serving 59 million people had combined sewerage systems. Included among these are some of the larger cities, such as New York, Philadelphia, Boston, Detroit, and Washington, D.C. Today, combined sewage systems remain one of the chief sources of water pollution in cities. When it rains, the rate of storm runoff may be about 100 times the average rate of the dry weather flow in the system. Economical sewage treatment plants cannot be designed to treat water at such high rates of flow; one solution is to have cities with combined sewerage systems construct storage facilities to detain excess flow until its constituent wastes can be properly treated. But in most cases no such facilities have been built.

The required capacity of an interceptor sewer is typically determined on the basis of projected future dry weather flows from the area served. An overflow structure must be provided at the point along the combined sewer where the interceptor connection is made. The storm runoff in excess of the interceptor sewer capacity must be discharged to the receiving water body through an overflow facility. In most systems, the capacity of the interceptor sewer is exceeded whenever it rains. Thus almost every time it rains, a polluted mixture of storm runoff and sanitary sewage is discharged to the receiving water. A typical overflow structure is illustrated in Figure 5.6.

The Boston Example

The extent of the pollution problem from combined sewers depends on the physical configuration of the particular system and on the hydrology of the area. The drainage and sewerage system of Boston is used as a case example in this section to elucidate the complexities involved in the removal of water and waste in a metropolitan area.

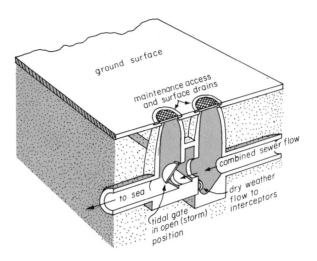

Figure 5.6. Schematic diagram of a combined sewer overflow structure.

In the Boston area the sewage system is partly a combined system and partly a separate system. Figure 5.7 shows the locations of known combined sewer overflows from the Boston main drainage system, a combined sewerage system. The system is designed so that the interceptor sewers carry the sanitary wastes either to the Deer Island treatment plant or to the Nut Island treatment plant, where the wastes undergo primary waste treatment before they are released into Boston Harbor. The Metropolitan District Commission (MDC) builds and operates the interceptor sewers and the treatment plants. The individual towns (about 40 are served by the MDC) build and operate their own collection systems.

Primary waste treatment consists of removing the suspended solid materials by screening, sedimentation, and floatation. Primary treatment typically requires from one to three hours; the solid materials form a sludge that is treated in digesters where the organic material undergoes anerobic decomposition. The typical outputs, then, of the primary treatment process are (1) a liquid effluent that still contains more than half of the dissolved and suspended organic material from the raw waste and (2) the solid waste from the sludge digesters. In Boston, the primary effluent is chlorinated to kill the pathogenic bacteria and then released to the harbor through a system of offshore

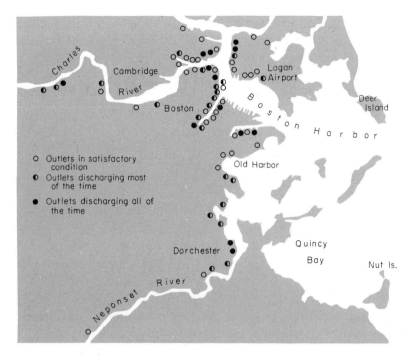

Figure 5.7. Location and condition of combined sewer overflows in the Boston main drainage system. (After Schaake 1970.)

outfall pipes. Sludge disposal is a relatively expensive part of waste treatment, so inexpensive alternatives always seem attractive. In this case the treated sludge simply is dumped (on the outgoing tide) into the harbor.

Although a substantial amount of organic matter enters the harbor in the form of primary effluent — the treated sludges and over-flows from combined sewers — the dissolved oxygen levels in the harbor are not reduced significantly below saturation concentrations. This is mainly because the ten-foot tidal range provides enough dilution of the wastes during each tidal cycle to prevent high concentrations of biochemical oxygen demand (BOD).

Because Boston Harbor, except for a small part known as the Inner Harbor, is used for recreational activities such as boating and swimming, bacteria are the most serious pollutant. A main source of these bacteria are the combined sewer overflows, which are estimated to occur five or six times a month during the summer — provided that the overflow structures function properly! Tidal conditions at Boston require that tide gates be installed between the harbor and the interceptor connections so that the harbor water will not flow into the interceptor system during high tide. For a variety of administrative reasons, these tide gates have not been well maintained, and many overflows do not have effective tide gates. As a result, the tides wash back and forth in the sewage system during each tidal cycle, and sewerage spills into the harbor more frequently than it should. Additionally, the salt water enters the interceptor system and flows to the treatment plant. The interceptor system does not have the capacity to carry both sanitary wastes and salt water from the malfunctioning tide gates, so some polluted wastes must flow into the harbor. Thus even in dry weather sewage may overflow at properly functioning tide gates because other tide gates malfunction. Finally, salt water has an adverse effect on the treatment plant operation because the bacteria that are responsible for the anerobic decomposition of the sludges function poorly in a saline environment. Because the major function of the treatment plants is to treat the primary sludges, malfunctioning tide gates can render the treatment plants almost totally ineffective.

To improve water quality in the harbor the MDC has undertaken a program to replace or rebuild the malfunctioning tide gates, and the agency is considering chlorinating the storm water overflows at critical locations during the summer months. By 1972 the tide gate program should be finished, and chlorinators will be operating at some locations.

Controlling Sewerage and Storm Runoff

There is a variety of alternatives for controlling the discharge of combined sewers into receiving waters. The Federal Water Pollution Control Act authorizes grants and contracts to assist in the development of projects that demonstrate new or improved methods. The grants pay up to 75 percent of the project cost. By 1969, some 80 projects had been initiated.

One ingenious scheme, adopted by the Minneapolis–St. Paul Sanitary District, provides storage of combined wastes inside of the combined system. This method uses inflatable dams, automatic gates, remote sensors, and a digital computer to store storm runoff in below-capacity sectors of trunk and interceptor sewers. Another method of control is the use of storm water holding tanks, which have been widely employed in Europe. The Metropolitan District Commission in Cambridge, Massachusetts, has just constructed a holding tank designed to protect the Charles River. It will provide chlorination and ten-minute sedimentation for large storms. Longer detention times (for better treatment) will be provided for smaller storms that will not overflow the holding tank. Open ponds and lagoons also may be utilized as holding facilities; however, algae in the effluent of these ponds can constitute an operational problem.

A recent systems study of storm runoff problems in the new town of Columbia, Maryland, examined the use of many small reservoirs dispersed throughout an urban community to control pollution by storm water. Water collected and stored in these reservoirs was to be treated to drinkable quality and released for use in the community. By using storm water for water supply, part of the cost of pollution control is offset. Additional benefits include erosion control, reduction of peak runoff rates, and provision of recreation.

The notion of storing urban runoff for control and treatment is fundamental to most of the effective alternatives that have been proposed thus far. William F. Bauer, one of the authors of the Chicago Deep Tunnel concept, is a prominent advocate of the creative use of storage in urban areas. He has advocated four basic rules for engineers and planners to use in searching for the best possible urban drainage and flood control systems.

1. The first step in the planning of a drainage or flood control system for an urban area is to allocate space for the temporary storage of flood waters. That these waters will occupy space somewhere in the watershed is an inescapable fact.

2. Transportation of water from one point to another — by means of sewers, pumping stations, channels, spillways, diversion structures, and similar engineering projects — has value only to the extent that such transportation effectively allocates storage by moving water between different zones within the system. Such transportation is usually expensive and it does not reduce the volume of storage required; it can merely change the location of the storage space.

3. Multipurpose use of public open space and recreational areas should be considered in the planning and engineering of urban drain-

age systems to provide space for the temporary storage of flood waters.

4. Building codes should be an integral part of the planning and operation of any urban drainage system, particularly insofar as they control the building of damageable structures in zones that should be used for the temporary storage of flood waters.

The role of storage is not always considered when urban water resource systems are conceived and designed. Engineers have usually perceived the role of the storm drainage system as being to take the storm water falling within the land boundaries of the system off the land surface and carry it to some predetermined location, usually a nearby river or lake. For many years engineers have designed systems to meet this narrow goal without regard for possible external effects in the community. The range of effects resulting from the failure to incorporate storage areas in urban drainage systems is impressive, as we have seen in the preceding sections on floods and sedimentation. They include an increase in the frequency of flooding; reduction of ground-water recharge, which lowers flow during dry periods; and increased soil erosion due to higher flow velocities.

The future is not promising. Already there is some evidence that the quality of urban runoff is too poor to be permitted to enter some receiving waters without prior treatment. Unfortunately, not much is known about the quality of urban runoff at this time, although one study was conducted by the Public Health Service in Cincinnati, Ohio. Extensive measurements were made of a 27-acre urban area sewered with separate storm and sewage systems. During dry periods the flow in the storm sewer was provided by groundwater seepage; the water was clean, clear, and of high quality. During storms the quality was poor. The annual waste load of suspended solids averaged 140 percent more than expected for the sanitary sewage discharge from such an area. Ratios of storm water to other raw sewage constituents indicate that during storms the actual instantaneous concentration of pollutants in urban runoff may equal or exceed the concentrations of the same pollutants in sanitary sewage. Bacterial tests of the runoff revealed that much of the water is contaminated and unsuitable for contact recreational use. This situation, unfortunately, has become more common than not in urban areas and is placing serious constraints on recreational, consumptive, and other uses of the water resource.

MAN BRINGS WATER TO THE CITY

Municipalities supply water for a large variety of uses — residential, commercial, industrial, public, and others. Some industries supply their own water, but future freshwater needs of industries are expected to be supplied from publicly controlled sources because (1) the nation's water resources are highly interrelated; (2) efficient management of these resources is increasingly needed; (3) as the best sources are tapped, costs of development of additional water increase; and (4) large-scale development produces economies of scale.

The Demand for Water

Residential uses of water may be classified into domestic, or household, use and sprinkling use, and the flows for these uses can be traced (see Figure 5.8). Water used in the household for drinking, cooking, bathing, and so forth, is returned to sewers after use. When the natural supply of water to lawns by precipitation is deemed inadequate (whether such a threat is real or not), much residential water is used to irrigate lawns. Such irrigation water is lost by evapotranspiration, not returned to sewers. The single most important factor influencing the amount of water used in a residential area is the number of homes. Three other major factors are economic level of the consumer, climate, and whether water consumption is metered or on a flat rate basis. The economic level of the consumer is believed to effect water use for two reasons. First, more affluent consumers tend to have more appliances that use water; and second, more affluent consumers are likely to have larger lots with larger lawn areas. A study of water use in 23 communities revealed the relationship between economic level and water use that is illustrated in Figure 5.9. Hence, one can see that water *demand* is not the same as water *needs;* rather, water demand and use commonly greatly exceed the minimal amounts actually required.

Commercial and industrial water demands are influenced by the level of economic activity in these sectors of the economy. The problem of estimating future water needs in any particular sector of industry or commerce is very complex because the level of economic activity in a given sector depends on the level of economic activity in all other

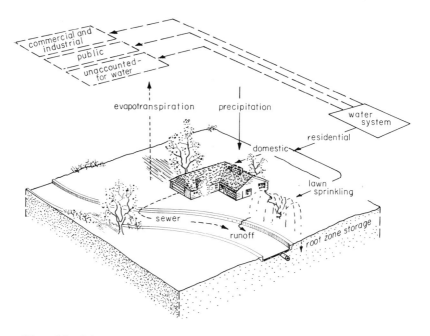

Figure 5.8. Schematic diagram of residential water use, in gallons per day per dwelling unit. (After Linaweaver 1965.)

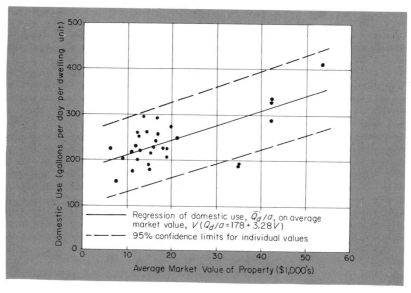

Figure 5.9. Relationship between domestic (household) water use and average market value of residential property. (After Linaweaver 1965.)

sectors. One approach to this problem that gives consistent results with regard to economic theory is to use a simplified model of the economy, known as an input-output model, as a basis for estimating water needs. This kind of model was used by the U. S. Army Corps of Engineers to estimate water demands in 50 different geological areas and in each of 39 economic sectors in the North Atlantic region of the United States. Projections of Gross National Product are used together with information on the distribution of consumer preferences for sectoral outputs, the amounts of the outputs from each sector needed to produce a dollar's worth of output in every other sector, and the amount of water of a given quality needed to produce a dollar's worth of output in each sector.

Present practice in estimating municipal water demands does not explicitly take into account the fundamental economic principles involving the relationship between supply, demand, and price. In a study of the impact of price on residential water demand, Howe and Linaweaver (1967) found that (1) domestic demands are relatively inelastic with respect to price; (2) sprinkling demands are elastic with respect to price, but less so in the west than in the east; and (3) maximum day sprinkling demands (which control the design of major system components such as treatment plants and transmission mains) are inelastic in the west but relatively elastic in the east. The significance of these findings for the design of urban water systems is as follows. The price of water usually is determined by municipal water managers on the basis of the cost of providing the service. Often, the price is established by dividing the total cost by the quantity supplied, which makes the price equal to the average cost. However, the resulting price influences the demand, which in turn alters the need for the supply and thus alters the average cost. Ideally, the economic demand function for water and the pricing policy for setting water rates should be taken into account to achieve an economical, efficient use of all resources. However, more must be learned about the demand functions before this approach can be employed.

Cities obtain their water from either or both of two basic sources: (1) surface supplies, water running off the surface of the land as streams or temporarily stored as lakes and ponds; and (2) groundwater, water stored or slowly flowing within the ground. The limitations and consequences of using these water supplies are discussed below.

Controlling Runoff to Meet Urban Needs

Many cities and towns in the United States and throughout the world take their water supplies from surface water sources such as streams and lakes. As the present trend of migration from rural areas to urban areas continues, and as total water use continues to increase with the increase in population and per capita income, demands for municipal water will continue to increase. However, the total average supply of water in any part of the world remains about constant (although the amount of water available in any year and how this amount is distributed through the year fluctuate somewhat). Thus, in order to meet the future needs for water, society must manage this resource carefully, taking into account the natural hydrologic uncertainty in the amount of water available at any time (also see Chapter 7).

There are many aspects to the problem of water management, and one of the important technical factors is the *storage-yield relation*, discussed in detail later. This relation must be considered whenever municipal water needs exceed the minimum natural flow at the source of supply. In such cases, reservoirs — such as natural lakes or man-made impoundments — must be used to store water during wet seasons for subsequent dry season use.

Fluctuations in Water Demand

In the United States, the early cities in the east first took their water from the nearest surface watercourse. As the cities grew, the drainage basins that supplied water became urbanized and the quality of the water was degraded. Nonetheless, the demand for water increased and new sources were sought. Recognizing the large future demand for water, many cities selected new water sources in areas unlikely to be urbanized that would yield abundant quantities of high quality water. For example, New York City developed several upland sources in the Catskill Mountains and others in the Pocono Mountains. Boston developed Quabbin Reservoir on the Swift River, a tributary of the Connecticut River more than 40 miles west of the city. The water from both of these municipal supplies is so pure that chlorination is the only treatment needed (to kill any harmful bacteria that may enter the system). Most large American cities now draw water from several sources; however, the problem of assessing the total water supply from several sources is so complex that discussion is limited to the case in which all water is supplied from a single source. It is difficult both to describe how big a reservoir should be constructed and to determine the yield that may be expected from a given reservoir after it is built.

Municipal water requirements vary during the year, generally being greatest in the early summer and least during the winter. The chief causes of this variation include outdoor use of water for lawn irrigation, car washing, and swimming pools, periods of high evapotranspiration, and periods of low rainfall. A typical seasonal pattern of water use in a small California community is shown in Figure 5.10. There are also fluctuations in water use within each day. Peak use occurs in the morning and evening, with slight use during the middle of the night. The daily use pattern is different in summer and winter (see Figure 5.11).

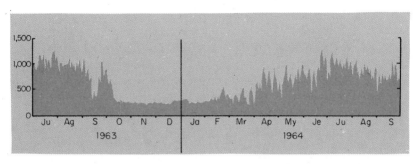

Figure 5.10. Seasonal pattern of water use in Creekside Acres, East Bay Municipal Utility District, California. (After Linaweaver 1965.)

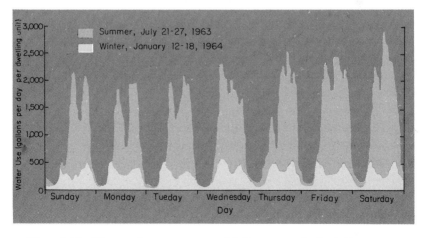

Figure 5.11. Winter and summer pattern of daily water use in Creekside Acres, California. (After Linaweaver 1965.)

Fluctuations in Natural Water Supply

Just as urban water demands are not uniform during the year,
streams do not flow uniformly through time. In the eastern part of the
United States, the spring months usually are wet and the late summer
months usually are dry. Figure 5.12 shows how the average monthly
precipitation and runoff for the Potomac River Basin vary during the
year. Notice that although precipitation over this particular basin
is almost uniform throughout the year, the runoff has a marked seasonal
pattern.

The Storage-Yield Relation

Because of these fluctuations in the use and supply of water, and
particularly because during some periods of the year the need for
water exceeds the supply of water, reservoirs must be built. The supply
function of a reservoir is to store water in the wet seasons for use during
the dry seasons. Some reservoirs also are built to store water during
wet years for use during subsequent dry years; such reservoirs are said to
contain *over-year storage* in addition to the *seasonal storage* they
always provide.

The maximum amount of water that can be withdrawn, in the
long run, from a very large reservoir at a given site is the average annual
runoff at that site. In practice the long-term withdrawal from a reservoir is less than the long-term average streamflow into the reservoir,
because streamflow variations prohibit accurate prediction of required
storage volumes. The total amount of water that can be withdrawn
from a reservoir is known as the *yield* of the reservoir. The yield may be
measured in terms of an average rate, taken as a constant rate throughout the year, or it may be measured in terms of a yearly total volume
that can be withdrawn unevenly during the year. In the example that
follows, the yield is measured as a proportion of the average annual
streamflow rate, and the yield is assumed to be constant throughout the
year.

With every estimate of yield from a given reservoir for any
future year there is an associated level of risk that the yield cannot be
met, because of the aforementioned uncertainties. The storage-yield
relation must take this risk into account. The relationship is a three-way
one between (1) the volume of storage provided by a given reservoir,
(2) the yield of withdrawals that can be taken in a given temporal
distribution through a year, and (3) the risk that the yield cannot be
met in a given year because of random climatic factors.

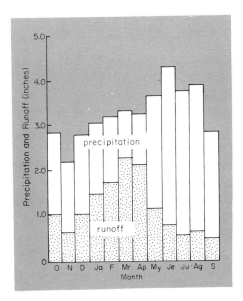

Figure 5.12. Average monthly precipitation and runoff in the Potomac River Basin above Point of Rocks, Maryland (1933–1943). (After Maryland Department of Geology 1944.)

A typical graphical representation of the storage-yield relation appears in Figure 5.13 (see also the discussion of water supply risk in Chapter 7). The storage-yield relation is actually a whole family of probability curves, not just a single curve; thus, each of the four curves shown in Figure 5.13 represents a given level of risk that the actual yield will be less than the desired yield. The level of risk is represented by the parameter a; where, for example, $a = 0.01$, there is a 0.01 chance of failing to get the given yield in any year after the corresponding reservoir volume has been built. The storage-yield curves in this figure have been estimated by simulating the streamflow of the Gunpowder River, Maryland. The average annual runoff rate in the river is 257 million gallons per day (mgd) — equivalent to a total volume of 284,000 acre feet. According to the storage-yield relation, a reservoir volume of 0.6 x 284,000 = 170,000 acre feet would yield an average flow rate of 0.81 x 257 = 208 mgd at a risk level of $a = 0.01$. Also, the same reservoir volume could yield somewhat more water, 0.86 x 257 = 221 mgd at the higher risk level $a = 0.05$ or as much as 0.90 x 257 = 231 mgd at the higher risk level of $a = 0.10$. In other words, there is considerable risk in planning to take more than about 200 mgd of

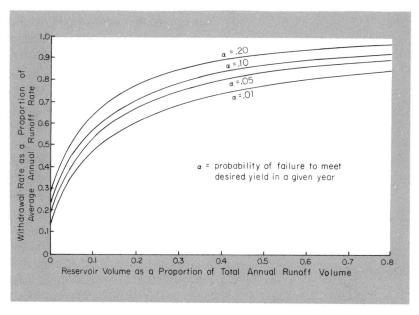

Figure 5.13. The storage-yield relation for the Gunpowder River, Maryland.

the average 257 mgd that enter the reservoir. The required storage, to achieve a given yield at a given level of risk, results from two principal factors. First, part of the required storage is needed to store water from the wet seasons for use in the dry seasons. Second, the remaining part of the required storage is needed to allow for the random variations that may occur from month to month during the dry seasons.

The Gunpowder River has a drainage area of 303 square miles and is a major source of water for the Baltimore metropolitan area. The average month-to-month variations of streamflow in the Gunpowder River are shown in Figure 5.14. The actual flow in any month, however, is a random variable that is distributed according to some statistical distribution. Since this is a real river, it is impossible to know precisely the statistical distribution that the observed streamflow data have come from, although it is possible to estimate this distribution from historical observations. Indeed, a source of uncertainty about the yield from a reservoir is the uncertainty in our knowledge of the true mean monthly streamflow. In this case, the average monthly streamflows are averages from the period 1883 through 1963.

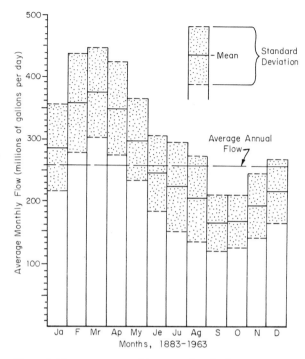

Figure 5.14. Average monthly streamflow in the
Gunpowder River, Maryland (1883–1963).

Thus the storage-yield relation has several valuable uses. It may
be used to determine how much yield can be obtained from a given
reservoir at a given level of risk. Alternatively, it may be used to evaluate the level of risk one must assume if a given withdrawal is made from
a given size of reservoir. Finally, this relation can indicate how large
to build a reservoir to obtain a given yield at a given risk level.

Withdrawal of Water from the Ground

Groundwater is a major water supply source for many cities.
One fifth of the largest 100 cities in the United States used exclusively
groundwater for public water supply as of 1962. Another 14 cities
relied upon a combination of groundwater and surface water supplies
(Durfor and Becker, 1964). As of 1955, K. A. MacKichan (1957)
of the U. S. Geological Survey reported that 19 percent of the total
national water use was supplied by groundwater. The largest single use

of groundwater, 65 percent, was for irrigation, and 91 percent of that water was pumped in the 17 western states. Thus, although many cities rely heavily on groundwater supplies, they do not account for the majority of water withdrawn in the nation.

Groundwater is withdrawn through wells from a variety of geological formations. The most common are deposits of sand and gravel and consolidated sediments such as sandstone and limestone. The porous material from which the groundwater is taken is called an *aquifer.* An aquifer performs two hydrologic functions: it stores the groundwater until it is withdrawn and it provides the underground conduit for groundwater flow.

In bringing water to the city, the main concern is how much water can be taken from any particular groundwater location. Where should wells be drilled? How deep should they be? How close together should they be? Should some of the water be returned to the ground after use? Answers to these questions depend upon the spatial configuration of the aquifers and their relation to adjacent and impervious formations and upon the hydrology of the region.

Groundwater aquifers may be described or characterized in many ways, one of which is illustrated in Figure 5.15. They have inputs (that is, sources) of water, and they have outputs (that is, sinks) where groundwater is withdrawn from (or seeps out of) the aquifer. Together the inputs, outputs, and groundwater storage are in a state of dynamic equilibrium.

Inputs to a groundwater system occur as follows: (1) by percolation where the aquifer outcrops at the surface; (2) by percolation downward from an overlying formation; (3) by leakage from a stream

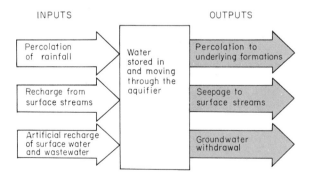

Figure 5.15. Elements of a groundwater system.

that intersects the aquifer; or (4) through recharge basins that are constructed to increase recharge from surface waters. For example, there are more than 800 recharge basins in Suffolk and Nassau counties on Long Island, New York. Storm runoff is diverted to these basins, which are designed for a recharge rate of 11 gallons per square foot per day. One of the larger recharge basins is 11 feet deep, holds 3.7 million cubic feet and has an average recharge rate of 23 gallons per day per square foot. Periodical maintenance is required to prevent the basin from becoming plugged with street washings.

The outputs from an aquifer include seepage into streams, seepage into underlying pervious formations, and groundwater withdrawals by man.

Continuing urbanization has led to increased demands for fresh water that historically have often been satisfied with groundwater supplies. In rural areas of Long Island, for example, water is withdrawn through shallow wells and then partially returned to the ground through cesspools, leaching fields, diffusion wells, and agricultural irrigation. In urban areas on the western third of the island, water is withdrawn from public wells and in part returned through cesspools and leaching fields. This means of waste disposal has, however, caused significant contamination of groundwater near the surface. To obtain uncontaminated water, deeper wells have been developed and additional sewering has been installed. Unfortunately, both of these practices may cause a problem known as *saltwater intrusion.* Normally, fresh groundwater extends seaward some distance under coasts because fresh water, being slightly less dense than salt water, floats as a body in salt water and pushes it outward. If wells withdraw more fresh groundwater than is replaced from the surface, the underground interface between fresh and salt water moves landward — the phenomenon of saltwater intrusion. One of the earliest instances of saltwater intrusion on the Atlantic coast of the United States was noted on Long Island. Studies have shown that large subsurface bodies of salt water are present in the coastal regions of the aquifers underlying southeastern Queens and southwestern Nassau counties. To the east of this area, Brooklyn (which once took its supply from the ground), has been underlain by intruded salt water since 1930.

A modeling study of the Long Island aquifer system was undertaken at the Massachusetts Institute of Technology to examine the flow of fresh and salt water in the ground under various conditions

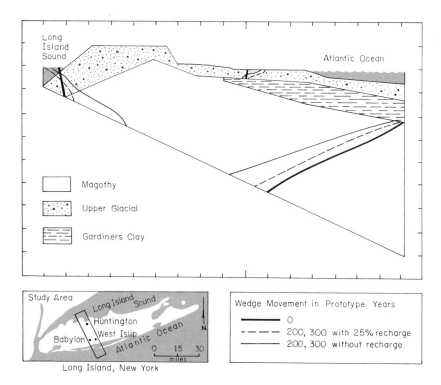

Figure 5.16. Simulated saltwater intrusion, Long Island, New York. Over a 300-year period saltwater encroachment will be significant if there is no recharge. A 25 percent recharge rate will almost arrest intrusion. (After Collins and Gelhar 1970.)

(Collins and Gelhar, 1970). Three major geologic formations underlie the study area — the Upper Glacial, Magothy, and Gardiners Clay (see Figure 5.16). Groundwater development schemes using wells near the surface to withdraw water from the Upper Glacial formation or deep wells to withdraw water from the Magothy formation were studied. The simulated rate of withdrawal was approximately equal to the long-term input of percolating surface water from rainfall.

Exemplary results of the simulation are illustrated in Figure 5.16. The diagram shows how the body of salt water (called the *saltwater wedge*) may move under different water management schemes. The greatest changes occur where there is no recharge of the withdrawn groundwater taken from deep wells in the Magothy formation. This condition would occur if the island were completely sewered and none of the treated water were returned to the ground. In such a case, the north shore wedge eventually would intrude to the center of the island. The motion of the saltwater wedge, however, would be very slow. Typically, the simulated wedge advanced landward at 0.004 miles per year during its first 100 years of movement. This advancement can be arrested if only 25 per cent of the withdrawal is replaced by recharge at the surface (see dashed line in Figure 5.16).

One of the most important results of this study is the conclusion that groundwater changes occur very slowly. It may take 50, 100, or more years for important changes to occur. This means that the effects of today's activities will not be apparent for many years, and it may take decades to detect the consequences of present contamination of groundwater sources. Conversely, it is important to recognize that there is no quick way to correct past mistakes.

In some cases, however, salt water can intrude at rapid rates because of urbanization processes. Miami, Florida, is an excellent case in point. In only a few decades, the Miami metropolitan area has spread along the entire Biscayne Bay coastline and many miles inland on low-lying terrain (see Figure 5.17). The regional water table is only a few feet below the surface, and because the area is underlain by a highly permeable aquifer, groundwater moves at a relatively fast rate. Salt water already occurred in the aquifer when the area was sparsely settled at the turn of the century, but it was confined to small areas adjacent to the bay. Efforts to drain and reclaim land for the rapidly growing urban area led to the construction of sea level canals that penetrated several miles inland. Salt water subsequently flowed into the aquifer (Wait and Callahan 1965, p. 14). Reliance on residential wells in the suburbs also enhanced saltwater intrusion by drawing down the freshwater table. As Figure 5.17 shows, by the 1950's saltwater encroachment had become a major threat to groundwater resources in the Miami region.

Another potential hazard to the quality of groundwater supplies that has recently been recognized is the percolation of salt used to deice roads during winter storms. For example, the town of Burlington, Massachusetts, experienced increasing concentrations of chlorides in its water supply. The state Board of Health safety standard is 250 parts per million (ppm), but tests of the town's supply in July 1970, revealed a chloride level of 272 ppm. The community responded by

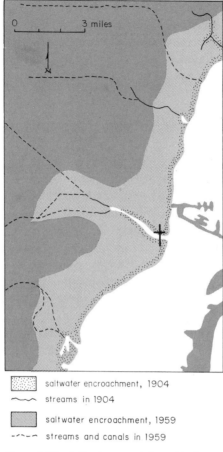

saltwater encroachment, 1904

streams in 1904

saltwater encroachment, 1959

streams and canals in 1959

Figure 5.17. Saltwater encroachment in the
Miami area, Florida. (After Wait and Callahan
1965.)

banning the use of salt on roads, but the state predicted that there
would be no substantial change for at least five years. By July 1971,
however, the chloride level had dropped to 175 ppm. The town is
fortunate in view of the slow responses of most groundwater systems,
and the ban on road salt has been continued. To avoid Burlington's
experience, the nearby city of Concord has enacted a ban on road salts,
and other communities are expected to take similar action.

URBAN WATER MANAGEMENT FOR THE FUTURE

The purpose of managing water is to provide the water that people need and want. As we have seen, these requirements and demands are growing, especially in cities. Hence, it is important to consider how urban water should be managed in the future. Today there are many agencies at all levels of government — local and regional, state and federal — whose concern is water. Each agency typically has some defined range of responsibility, usually pertaining to a specific function, such as water supply, sewage treatment, drainage, flood control, recreation, or harbor development. There are construction agencies, operating agencies, control agencies, and budgeting agencies. As a result of this *institutionalization* of water management, many engineers and managers have become *socialized* to perceive urban water problems in terms of these specific functions and institutions. This approach tends to preclude development of alternatives for water management that involve different functions or that require cooperation between different political bodies, even at the same level of government.

As population and per capita income grow, the demands for urban water services also will increase. Because the total quantity of available water is fixed and the capacity of the environment to assimilate wastes is limited, we need to explore new management alternatives such as water reuse, changing industrial processes, flood plain zoning, dual water systems, and efficiencies provided by automated control of water operations. Nonstructural alternatives such as effluent charges, zoning, and automatic operational control will need to be considered as substitutes and supplements for the limited range of structural alternatives now usually thought to be required.

In planning for the future a single super-agency for urban water management appears to be unlikely in the United States. The attitude toward local government functions seems to be to give the citizen as much access to his government as possible. Accordingly, the functions are assigned to the lowest and smallest governmental entities apparently qualified to perform them, with assignment of area-wide functions to metropolitan agencies. In order for an agency to exist, the need for its function must clearly be perceived. Historically, crisis situations have provoked the clearest perception of society's needs in America, which helps to explain why so many special-purpose agencies have been created. We need to see that the solution to one crisis may lead only to another, that crises are symptoms of problems rather than causes, and that a more rational approach to perceiving needs may be required.

Accompanying the requirement for a more rational approach for perceiving needs is a requirement for a more rational strategy for designing institutions to cope with these needs. On the one hand, we want institutions to be directly responsible to the people served by them. On the other hand, we see that many institutions are required to manage urban water resources. Presently our needs are met not by a single institution but by a system of interdependent institutions. Further institutions must be planned to function well together, to be responsible to the people served by them, and to consider a range of alternative approaches for satisfying the needs they are intended to fulfill.

REFERENCES

Ardis, D. V., K. J. Ducker, and A. T. Lenz. 1969. Storm drainage practices of thirty-two cities. *Jour. Hydraulics Division, Am. Soc. Civ. Engin.* 95(HY1):383–408.

Bauer, W. J. 1962. Economics of urban drainage design. *Jour. Hydraulics Division, Am. Soc. Civ. Engin.* 88(HY6):93–114.

Carter, R. W. 1961. *Magnitude and frequency of floods in suburban areas.* U.S. Geological Survey Prof. Paper 424B. Washington, D.C.: Govt. Printing Office.

Carter, R. W., and D. M. Thomas. 1968. Flood frequency in metropolitan areas. In *Proc. 4th Amer. Water Resources Conf.* (New York), pp. 56–67.

Collins, M. A. and L. W. Gelhar. 1970. *Groundwater/Hydrology of the Long Island aquifer system.* M.I.T. Laboratory Report 121. Cambridge, Mass.: M.I.T.

Durfor, C. N. and E. Becker. 1964. *Public water supplies of the 100 largest cities in the United States, 1962.* Geological Survey Water Supply Paper 1812. Washington, D.C.: Govt. Printing Office.

Fair, G. M., and J. C. Geyer. 1966. *Water and waste-water engineering,* vol. 1. New York: John Wiley and Sons.

Grava, S. 1969. *Urban planning aspects of water pollution control.* New York: Columbia Univ. Press.

Howe, C. W., and F. P. Linaweaver, Jr. 1967. The impact of price on residential water demand and its relation to system design and price structure. *Water Resources Research* 3(1):13–32.

James, S. Douglas. 1965. Using a digital computer to estimate the effects of urban development on flood peaks. *Water Resources Research* 1(2):223–234.

Jones, D. E. 1967. Urban hydrology: A redirection. *Civ. Engin.* 48(8):58–62.

Leopold, Luna B. 1968. *Hydrology for urban land planning: A guidebook on the hydrologic effects of urban land use.* U.S. Geological Survey Circular 554. Washington, D.C.: Govt. Printing Office.

Linaweaver, F. P., Jr. 1965. *Report II, phase two, residential water use project.* Baltimore: Johns Hopkins Univ.

MacKichan, K. A. 1957. Estimated use of water in the United States, 1955. *Jour. Amer. Water Works Assoc.* 49:369–391.

Malloy, C. W., and J. J. Boland. 1970. A systems study of storm runoff problems in a new town. *Water Resources Bull.* 6(6):980–989.

Maryland Dept. of Geology. 1944. *Mine and Water Resources Bull.* 1. Baltimore.

Pluhowski, E. J. 1970. *Urbanization and its effect on the temperature of the streams on Long Island, New York.* U.S. Geological Survey Prof. Paper 627-D. Washington, D.C.: Govt. Printing Office.

Schaake, J. C., Jr. 1970. *Mathematical programming applications to water quality planning for the Boston Harbor region.* Urban Systems Laboratory Report TR–70–33. Cambridge, Mass.: M.I.T.

Wait, R. L. and J. T. Callahan. 1965. Relations of fresh and salty ground water along the southeastern U. S. Atlantic coast. *Ground Water* 3(4):3–17.

Weibel, S. R., R. J. Anderson, and R. L. Woodward. 1964. Urban land runoff as a factor in stream pollution. *Jour. Water Poll. Control Federation* 36(7):914–924.

Wolman, M. G. and A. P. Schick. 1967. Effect of construction of fluvial sediment, urban and suburban areas of Maryland. *Water Resources Research* 3(2):451–464.

CHAPTER 6

Soil and the City

Donald H. Gray

Man as a rule must found his dwellings and structures on the surface of the ground; cities floating on water or suspended in air are still a pipe dream. Furthermore, most of our cities are founded on soil — all the unconsolidated earth material above solid bedrock — even though bedrock provides a superior foundation. Many soils are unsuitable as foundation materials, and the disturbance of some soils may have serious consequences for man and environment. Given the dependency of man on soils, on the one hand, and the limitations of the relationship, on the other, it seems reasonable to assume that soils would be given careful consideration in locating cities and planning their development. However, historically this has not been the case. By and large people have disregarded soil in deciding where to settle and build.

If soils had been considered, Mexico City would never have been built where it is now — on an old lake bed underlain by soft, compressible volcanic clays. Nor would we have festooned steep, landslide-prone hillsides with houses and roads, as we have done with abandon in the hills overlooking Los Angeles and San Francisco Bay. Nor would we have permitted all the ill-planned housing developments across the nation that have contributed to vast amounts of soil erosion and sedimentation in our streams. In short, urban development is characterized by failure to recognize ground conditions and to assess the impact of soil disturbance.

This chapter explores the nature and extent of cities' impact on soils, the influence of problem soils on urban functions, and some repercussions resulting from our misuse of soils. The chapter closes with a discussion of conflicting uses of soils and the need for rationally surveying and evaluating soils in regional and urban planning. Throughout this discussion the term *soil* is meant to encompass all the unconsolidated earth material above bedrock — a definition commonly used by the geologist and the engineer. Urban interactions with soils run far deeper than the roots of most plants, the earth material around which is defined as soil by the farmer and the pedologist.

THE IMPACT OF URBANIZATION ON SOIL

Cities are nodes of maximum alteration by man of environment to suit his needs, and his reworking of the ground through urbanization is no exception. Urban man has changed the shape, distribution, and quality of soil in numerous ways. These include (1) the consumption of great expanses of agricultural land by covering it with metropolitan structures; (2) the excavation of mineral materials (such as sand and gravel) from the earth to supply urban construction demands; (3) the erosion and sedimentation of soil; (4) the conscious remolding of the land by cutting and filling; (5) the filling of depressions with solid wastes; (6) the contamination of the ground, and water in it, by injecting liquid wastes; and (7) the desiccation of the soil both by making the surface impervious and by pumping of groundwater. Thus, problems of the soil are no longer just rural problems, which traditionally have been emphasized; soil problems now are shifting to urban areas and proliferating there.

Consumption of Agricultural Land

Many United States counties that formerly were rural are becoming urban almost overnight, as more and more land is cleared and otherwise disturbed for roads, houses, and shopping centers. At the present time, more than 4,000 acres of agricultural land are being converted *daily* to other uses — this is equivalent to urbanizing an area the size of Delaware *each year*! Much of this converted land is prime agricultural soil. Running counter to this trend is a yearly increase of two to three million domestic consumers of food. These opposing trends, if they continue, are irreconcilable. The processes of urbanization probably destroy much of the future agricultural utility of the converted lands. Commonly the fertile topsoil is scraped off, buried, or covered by pavement. The extent to which this withdrawal of land from agriculture is reversible is unknown: the feasibility of growing crops on land reclaimed from pavement and parking lots, for example, is virtually unstudied.

Mining Related to Urban Growth

Urban growth requires great quantities of earth materials for construction, and a high proportion of the sand, gravel, and stone that a city uses is mined locally (see Table 6.1). The low unit value of such materials weighs against long-distance transport unless they are unavailable near their point of use. As a consequence, mines and pits pock the earth in the environs of cities (see Figure 6.1). Sand and gravel mines, which are concentrated near cities, account for 26 percent of the 3.2 million acres (5,000 sq mi) that have been disturbed by surface mining in the United States through 1964 (U.S. Dept. of Interior 1967).

Mining can influence urban functions in a variety of ways. It is interesting, for instance, that the catacombs of Rome, which have a length of 550 miles, originally were excavated as quarries. Similarly,

Table 6.1. Examples of surface mining concentrated in and near urban areas in the United States. (After Risser and Major 1967.)

	Urban Area	1964 Tonnage (millions)	Percent of State Tonnage	Percent of State Area
Sand and gravel	Chicago Metropolitan Area (6 counties)	12.6	41.6	6.6
	Los Angeles County	26.2	23.2	2.6
	Los Angeles Metropolitan Area (3 counties)	39.2	34.7	8.2
	Detroit Metropolitan Area (5 counties)	18.7	36.0	5.7
	Suburban Long Island (2 counties)	10.6	27.0	2.5
	Denver Metropolitan Area (5 counties)	6.3	30.1	3.5
Stone (crushed and broken)	Cook County (Chicago), Ill.	12.2	31.6	1.7
	Dade County (Miami), Fla.	10.2	32.3	3.7

Figure 6.1. Extensive metropolitan sand and gravel pits, Woodbridge, New Jersey. (Courtesy of Aero Service Corporation, Division of Litton Industries.)

13 million cubic yards of earth — four times the volume of the Great Pyramid — were mined from the catacombs of Paris (Legget 1962, p. 776). In extreme cases, mining may force the relocation of towns and cities (for example, Asbestos, Quebec — see Ross 1967).

Accelerated Erosion and Sedimentation

Man's use of the land has increased rates of soil erosion to such an extent that they now far exceed rates of the past before man was an erosional factor. It is estimated that 24 billion tons of material are now moved annually by rivers to the earth's oceans — two and one-half times the rate before man's intervention (Judson 1968).

In the United States, man-abetted erosion strips nearly four billion tons of sediment from the land each year, of which three billion tons are deposited in flood plains, river channels, lakes, and reservoirs; the remaining one billion tons are carried to the oceans (Schwab and others 1966; Powell and others 1970). The generalized distribution of erosion by geographic region in the United States is more or less known, but the relative contributions according to land use (agricultural, natural, urban, and so forth) are not. Severely gullied farmlands in the South and Midwest are grim reminders of the fact that agricultural practices have tended (especially in the past) to accelerate erosion. The U. S. Soil Conservation Service, which originally had a mandate to deal with rural problems, increasingly directs its efforts to urban areas. Furthermore, some urban counties and municipalities have recently adopted soil conservation and sediment control ordinances.

Current research shows that sediment yields in areas undergoing suburban development can be as much as 5 to 500 times greater than in rural areas (Powell and others 1970, p. 3). A report published in 1963 by the Interstate Commission on the Potomac River Basin estimated that sediment from urban developments in the Potomac Basin ran as high as 50 times that yielded from agricultural lands. In some urbanizing areas along the Potomac, the sediment yield was as much as 39 tons and more per acre per year. Most agricultural experts consider 1 to 2 tons per acre annually a maximum permissible sediment yield from croplands (Schwab and others 1966). (See Chapter 5, pp. 103–108, for further discussion of the relation of sediment production to degree of urban development.)

Erosion involves both the detachment and transportation of soil particles. The factors affecting stream transport of sediments are presented in Chapter 5 (pp. 107–108). Mention of soil erodibility is appropriate here. The soils most susceptible to erosion are loose, cohesionless soils of relatively small particle size. Fine sands and silts without much clay fall into this category. Erosion is enhanced further by a decrease in forces that bind soil particles together. For example, removal of surface vegetation (a usual preliminary to new construction and development) results in a loss of cohesion between soil particles and also exposes the soil directly to the erosive force of raindrops.

Erosion by overland flow is favored by an increase in the amount and velocity of runoff water, just as it is in streams. Overland runoff is increased by waterproofing the surface (for example, by paving streets and by building parking lots), compacting the ground surface (as in the cases of fills and embankments), and clearing surface vegetation. The first two factors act by reducing infiltration of surface water and the third by decreasing interception and transpiration.

The consequences of uncontrolled erosion and sedimentation are disturbing (see Figures 6.2–6.4). Most of us are familiar with the loss of agricultural productivity that results from farmland erosion. The loss of productivity is particularly acute if the topsoil, which is richest in organic matter, is less than six inches thick. Along with the topsoil are washed out many inorganic nutrients that are adsorbed on the soil particles. As a consequence, erosion may result not only in stream turbidity and sedimentation, but also in depletion of the terrestrial nutrient pool and overloading of the aquatic one. This nutrient enrichment of lakes and streams is part of the eutrophication that has caused the demise of Lake Erie and other waters.

Thus, repercussions of urban soil erosion may be felt far beyond the city. The end result of erosion, of course, is eventual sedimentation – apparent in silt-clogged streams and lakes (Figure 6.5). Of the four billion tons of sediment eroded in the United States each year, an estimated one and a half billion tons ends up in the nation's reservoirs. This represents an annual loss of nearly one million acre-feet of reservoir storage capacity. Some 380 million cubic yards of sediment are dredged annually from harbors and waterways to keep them navigable. The cost for this alone is about $125 million annually.

Cutting and Filling

Grading of the land is discussed in Chapter 2 (pp. 41–43), so the topic is only mentioned here. Man has become a potent geomorpho-

Figure 6.2. Erosion associated with new construction and lack of suitable ground cover, Ann Arbor, Michigan. (Photograph by Donald Gray.)

Figure 6.3. Erosion of disturbed and highly susceptible soil. Seeding of temporary vegetation would have helped control erosion resulting from construction activities. (Courtesy of Soil Conservation Service, U.S. Department of Agriculture.)

Figure 6.4. Gully in an unpaved street coming from an urban renewal project. Roofs and paved surfaces in the apartment complex in the background have accelerated overland flow, but there are no storm sewers – so erosion results. (Courtesy of Soil Conservation Service, U.S. Department of Agriculture.)

Figure 6.5. A silt-clogged marsh – a condition produced by excessive erosion from a nearby housing development. (Courtesy of Soil Conservation Service, U.S. Department of Agriculture.)

logic agent in his purposeful landscape sculpturing. Generally, the purpose of cutting and filling is to create ground conditions suitable for structural foundations. Earth materials commonly are excavated from high places and transported to low-lying places. Cutting in southern California has reduced peaks as much as 100 to 200 feet and filling has elevated valley bottoms as much as 300 to 400 feet. The volumes and weights moved may be tremendous. In the course of private construction in Los Angeles County alone, 133 million cubic yards of earth were moved from July 1, 1960, to May 1, 1966 (Scullin 1966, p. 230).

Fills should be compacted and tested for stability under the supervision of a soils engineer (in which case they are termed *controlled fills*). Uncontrolled fills may settle, or collapse downslope, severely damaging structures founded on or below them.

Filling with Solid Wastes

In addition to the accelerating grading of earth material occurring in urban areas by erosion and sedimentation and by excavation and filling, modern cities draw in tremendous amounts of various substances that they discard eventually as refuse. *Refuse* is the discarded solid waste material resulting from normal community activities – including garbage, rubbish, ashes, street refuse, dead plant and animal matter, and solid industrial wastes (see Table 6.2). Urban areas in the United States generate more than 200 million tons of refuse per year (National Academy of Engineering and National Academy of Sciences 1970).

Man introduces most of this refuse – intentionally or inadvertently – into the soil. Incineration, composting, and hog-feeding consume only about 10 percent of the solid wastes. The remaining 90 percent is deposited in the nation's 90,000 recognized land-disposal sites, of which only some 12,000 are subject to a degree of local control. Of the latter, only 6 percent meet the minimum requirements of "sanitary landfills": daily cover, no open burning, and no water pollution problems (National Academy of Engineering and National Academy of Sciences 1970).

Too often urban refuse is dumped on nearby sites where competing land uses are minimal but where there are environmental dangers. Flood plains are close to the water table and are subject to periodic erosion, and refuse dumped there promotes contamination of water. Dumping refuse on areas served by shallow bedrock wells also leads to water contamination.

Table **6.2.** Sample municipal refuse composition, United States. The composition has changed greatly during the past 30 years; garbage (organics) has declined from 65 percent to only 12 percent of total weight. A relative increase in combustible material has increased the heating value of refuse about 1,000 Btu's per pound, increasing the economic incentive for incineration. (From Kaiser 1967.)

Physical	Weight (percent)	Rough Chemical	Weight (percent)
Miscellaneous paper	25	Moisture	28.0
Newspaper	14	Carbon	25.0
Garbage	12	Hydrogen	3.3
Glass, ceramics, stones	10	Oxygen	21.1
Grass and dirt	10	Nitrogen	0.5
Metallics	8	Sulfur	0.1
Cardboard	7	Glass, ceramics, etc.	9.3
Wood	7	Metals	7.2
Textiles	3	Ash, other	5.5
Plastic film	2		
Leather, molded plastics, rubber	2		

Frequently a goal of refuse landfilling is to create level, dry land from depressions and wetlands for urban expansion. Solid wastes may be used to fill the gashes produced by surface mining that are prevalent near cities. An innovation is progressing on the flat terrain of Virginia Beach, Virginia. There the three-year production of refuse from the municipality's 170,000 inhabitants is being used to construct a hill 60 feet high. The mound is being sculptured as an amphitheater and coasting ramp for soap box derbys (Marx 1971, p. 125).

The problem of refuse "sedimentation" in and around cities has ancient roots that have long been recognized. More than a century ago, the pioneer environmentalist George Perkins Marsh, in his classic *Man and Nature*, observed:

The soil near cities, the street sweepings of which are spread upon the ground as manure, is perceptibly raised by them and by other effects of human industry, and in spite of all efforts to remove the waste, the level of the ground on which large towns stand is constantly elevated. The present streets of Rome are twenty feet above those of the ancient city. The Appian way between Rome and Albano, when cleared out a few years ago, was found buried four or five feet deep, and the fields along the road were elevated nearly or quite as much (1864; pp. 458–459 in edition of 1965).

Rome is not unique. London's surface, too, has risen by the accumulation of waste over centuries – an average of 11 feet in the central city. The rain of dust from the air, most of which is of human origin, is an important contribution. In English industrial areas atmospheric deposition may exceed 395 metric tons per square kilometer per year, whereas on the urban fringe and in open countryside amounts decline to 132 mt/km²/yr and 70 mt/km²/yr, respectively (Brown 1970).

Soil Contamination by Wastes

The soil is used purposely as a receptacle for a great variety of liquid, as well as solid, wastes, and it inadvertently receives many others (see Flawn 1970, pp. 145–162). The repercussion of deep-well injection of liquids into the bedrock substratum beneath Denver has been mentioned in Chapter 2 (see Figure 2.6). Several examples of soil contamination by wastes are cited here to illustrate the point that urban activities may radically alter some qualities of urban soil that man depends upon. Very small amounts of certain wastes may have adverse effects. Contaminated soil can lead to contaminated water supplies (see Chapter 5 for further discussions of water quality), to sickly vegetation, and even to human health problems.

Groundwater may be contaminated in a variety of ways, but the introduction of contaminants via the soil from refuse dumps and landfills and subsurface sewage disposal systems is notable. In many urban fringe areas, municipal sewers are not provided, and sewage is disposed of by individual treatment (septic) tanks and seepage fields. High residential density, improper location of septic tanks and seepage sites, and certain soil properties may present hazards to water and health. Soil permeability is especially important. On one hand, soils through which waste water percolates more slowly than 1 inch per hour are inadequate absorbers. On the other hand, soils that permit percolation faster than 12 inches per hour commonly allow groundwater contamination. Generally, seepage sites should be at least 100 feet from any water supply well, 50 feet from surface waters such as streams, and 25 feet from the foundations of buildings.

Groundwater contamination from individual sewage disposal systems has occurred in many metropolitan areas – Chicago, Minneapolis–St. Paul, and Suffolk County, New York, for instance. In the early 1960's one tenth of the 6.5 million inhabitants of metropolitan

Chicago were served by approximately 162,000 individual sewage disposal systems. Open dumps and landfill, used to dispose of 9,000,000 cubic yards of domestic refuse yearly, are additional proven sources of groundwater contamination in this region — where 1.6 million people obtain their water supplies from the ground (Hackett 1965).

Concentrated vehicular traffic in cities has contaminated soils and vegetation with lead, cadmium, nickel, and zinc. The contamination is related to the composition of gasoline, motor oil, and tires, and the deposition of the residues of these materials. The concentrations in soil of these metals increase with proximity to roads, with traffic volume, and with nearness to the ground surface (see Table 6.3). Lead in surface soil near busy streets and highways may reach concentrations of more than 2,400 parts per million (ppm) — about 100 to 1,000 times its natural content. Contamination extends as far as 1,000 feet downwind from roadways, although much of it is concentrated within 100 feet. Even the city's least affected areas — parklands — are markedly contaminated relative to surrounding rural areas. For example, in 12 representative soils from parks in Edinburgh, Scotland, lead and

Table 6.3. Concentrations of cadmium, nickel, lead, and zinc in roadside soil and grass, as a function of distance from traffic and depth in the ground. Data are averages from duplicate sampling and analysis of materials from west of Highway U.S. 1, near Plant Industry Station, Beltsville, Md. Traffic density was 20,000 vehicles per day in the year of the sampling (1966). (From Lagerwerff and Specht 1970.)

Metal	Meters from Road	Grass	0-5	5-10	10-15
			(mg per kg dry weight, or ppm)		
Cadmium	8	0.95	1.45	0.76	0.54
	16	0.73	0.40	0.38	0.28
	32	0.50	0.22	0.20	0.20
Nickel	8	5.0	4.7	1.0	0.81
	16	3.8	2.4	0.90	0.60
	32	2.8	2.2	0.62	0.59
Lead	8	68.2	522	460	416
	16	47.5	378	260	104
	32	26.3	164	108	69
Zinc	8	32.0	172	94	72
	16	28.5	66	48	42
	32	27.3	54	46	42

Soil Layer, cm below Surface

zinc averaged 5.33 and 16.0 ppm, respectively, in contrast to concentrations of 0.36 and 4.6 ppm in the same number of samples from the nearby countryside (Purves and MacKenzie 1969).

What are the consequences of soil contamination by such metals? Cadmium is the most hazardous to human health. Doses of this metal approximating those currently found in many cities have been related to cardiovascular disease. Lead also is a well-known poison; its threat to health in the urban environment is often suggested but not yet defined in detail. Accumulations of lead in the upper layers of soil may cause a decline in the quality of shallow-rooted crops, especially grasses. The normal content of lead in the ash of plant food products ranges from 2 to 20 ppm, but in Canandaigua, New York, the ash of homegrown vegetables from gardens generally less than 50 feet from the street averaged 115 ppm lead and ranged to 700 ppm (Cannon and Bowles 1962).

Road salt, applied for deicing, is another soil contaminant associated with streets and highways that has deleterious effects on roadside vegetation (see Chapter 9).

Desiccation of the Ground

Urban development greatly reduces the amount of water supplied to the soil by precipitation. The waterproofing of city surfaces increases both the amount and immediacy of runoff. Hence, the ground has little chance to absorb moisture. The pumping of groundwater supplies has drastically lowered the water table under most cities, thereby removing one source of moisture even for deep-rooted plants, namely, water rising in the soil by capillarity from the water table. Many of the artificial surfaces laid down by man also are impervious to air, which (like moisture) normally is exchanged between atmosphere and soil pore spaces.

Soil air and soil moisture are vital to the growth of soil microorganisms and plant roots. Soils, and thus trees, in city parks usually have sufficient water and exchanged air, but those along streets commonly do not. Trees there may be retarded or killed (see Chapter 9). This situation along streets is exacerbated by the accumulation of road salt, which reduces the ability of plants to absorb soil water.

Though desiccation is the rule, soils in certain urban areas receive excess water by the hand of man. The irrigation of lawns, religiously practiced in nearly every American suburb, is the prime example. Consequences, in addition to consumption of gigantic quantities of water, include contamination of groundwater with fertilizers and pesticides, and sometimes landslides.

THE INFLUENCE OF PROBLEM SOILS ON URBAN FUNCTIONS

The soil-city relationship is two-sided, and we now turn to discussing (1) the kinds of soils that inherently are bad risks when it comes to founding roads or structures on them and (2) the constraints that such "problem soils" place on various urban activities.

Kinds of Problem Soils and Ground Conditions

It is important to recognize soil types and soil conditions that are inherently poor and to make due allowances for them in planning urban developments. In many instances the best land use decision may be to leave these soils alone and let the land remain in its natural state. In other cases, remedial or soil stabilization measures can be attempted in order to accommodate development.

Before discussing problem soils, it is worth considering the major soil components and their significant properties. These are summarized in Table 6.4, which classifies soils into six main components, the most important of which are gravels, sands, silts, and clays. In nature soils rarely occur in such well-defined size ranges; more often soils are mixtures that reflect the properties of their various constituents.

Most problem soils are in a broad class of soils referred to as *transported*, or *sedimentary*, soils. These include aeolian, lacustrine, glacial, fluvial, marine, and alluvial deposits. Unfortunately, it is this class of soils that we mostly choose to build upon. Sedimentary soils usually bear some imprint of their transporting agent or depositional environment. Thus, glacial till is very poorly sorted by particle size; loess is a well sorted, silt-size material; and dune sand is well sorted and relatively free of fines.

The other broad class of soils is the *residual* soils — those that are formed in place by weathering of bedrock. These have a reputation for being more stable and less troublesome than transported soils. However, this assessment may simply reflect fewer encounters and less experience with these soils in engineering practice.

The major kinds of problem soils and problem ground con-

Table 6.4. Soil texture and engineering properties. (After Wagner 1957.)

Soil Component (and symbol)	Grain Size Range	Significant Engineering Properties
Cobbles and boulders	Average particle diameter larger than 6 inches	Boulders and cobbles are very stable components, used for fills and to stabilize slopes (riprap). Because of size and weight, their occurrence in natural deposits tends to improve the stability of foundations. Angularity of particles increases stability.
Gravel (G)	Particles 2.00–76.2 mm diameter	Gravel and sand have essentially the same engineering properties, differing mainly in degree. They are easy to compact, little affected by moisture, not subject to frost action. Gravels generally are more perviously stable, resistant to erosion and piping, than are sands. Well-graded sands and gravels generally are less pervious and more stable than those that are poorly graded. Finer, uniform sand approaches the characteristics of silt.
Sand (S)	Particles .074–2.00 mm diameter	
Silt (M)	Particles .002–.074 mm diameter and slightly plastic or nonplastic regardless of moisture; little or no strength when air dried	Silt is inherently unstable, particularly when moist, with a tendency to become quick when saturated. It is relatively impervious, difficult to compact, highly susceptible to frost heave, easily erodible and subject to piping and boiling.
Clay (C)	Particles smaller than .002 mm diameter and exhibiting plastic properties within a certain range of moisture; considerable strength when air dried	Clay is distinguished by its cohesive strength, which increases as moisture decreases. The permeability is very low; difficult to compact when wet and impossible to drain by ordinary means; resistant to erosion and piping when compacted; not susceptible to frost heave; subject to expansion and shrinkage with changes in moisture. The properties are influenced by the size, shape, and mineral composition of particles.
Organic matter (O)	Organic matter of various sizes and in various stages of decomposition	Organic matter, even in moderate amounts, increases the compressibility and reduces the stability of the fine-grained soils. It may decay, causing voids, or by chemical alteration change the properties of a soil; hence organic soils are not desirable for engineering uses.

ditions, discussed below are quick clays, expansive soils, varved clays, loose and saturated silts and sands, permafrost, collapsing soils, and organic soils. *Quick clays* are highly sensitive marine or glacial lake clays that have a metastable structure – they tend to lose all their shear strength when they are remolded or disturbed, even though their un-disturbed strength may be quite high. Quick clays are common in Scandinavia and the St. Lawrence valley of Canada. Landslides may occur in hillsides composed of quick clays with slopes as low as 10 per-cent. Clearly, extensive construction in quick clay slopes should be avoided. (Refer to Kerr 1963 and Crawford and Eden 1967 for further discussion of quick clays and problems relating to their use.)

Expansive soils will both heave and expand when subjected to seasonal variations in moisture. They usually contain significant amounts of the swelling clay mineral, montmorillonite. Swelling clays are preva-lent in the so-called adobe soils of the arid southwestern United States. Expansive soils pose a particular problem in road and canal construc-tion. Water that seeps under the pavement causes swelling of clay soils and, in turn, heaving and buckling of the road. Construction of build-ings on expansive soils requires either control of ground moisture, soil stabilization treatments with lime, or special foundations (see Holtz and Gibbs 1956).

Varved clays are lacustrine deposits consisting of alternating layers of silt and clay. Varved clays often combine the worst features of silts and clays – high compressibility and low strength. Varved clays sometimes pose difficult problems in the construction of buildings (Milligan, Soderman; and others 1962).

When loose, saturated silts and sands are subjected to shock or vibration, as by earthquakes, explosions, or the pounding of traffic, a phenomenon known as *liquefaction* commonly occurs. The vibration induces compaction of highly porous granular soils that are not cemented. Liquefaction results in a temporary but substantial loss of shear strength, causing subsidence of the ground surface as the soil particles pack into a denser arrangement. Liquefaction probably con-tributed heavily to the widespread destruction in the Anchorage, Alaska, and Niigata, Japan, earthquakes (Seed and Idriss 1967; Seed and Wilson 1967). Figure 6.6 illustrates typical damage caused by soil liquefaction during the Niigata earthquake. Silts also are subject to other problems, the most notorious being the tendency to frost heave in cold climates. Ice lenses that develop in silty soils under certain conditions can

Figure 6.6. Settlement and tilting of buildings resulting from the Niigata earthquake. (Photograph by Joseph Penzien.)

exert damaging pressure on pavements, structures, and retaining walls. Silts need not be saturated in order to be frost susceptible, but freezing ground temperatures and a nearby water table are necessary conditions.

Permafrost, or perennially frozen ground, is a ground condition that poses special problems for many of man's engineering activities. Few people realize the geographic extent of permafrost; it underlies 20 percent of the world's land area, including about 50 percent of both Canada and the U.S.S.R. and 85 percent of Alaska (Ferrians and others 1969). These are areas where urban settlement is accelerating. The major industrial cities built in the permafrost regions of the U.S.S.R. demonstrate that the deleterious effects of frozen ground can be overcome at a technological and economic price. Permafrost in bedrock or well-drained coarse-grained sediments presents few construction problems. However, where there is permafrost in saturated silts or clays, thawing produces soupy, unstable ground. The soil then may subside or flow laterally, or, upon refreezing, heave – all processes that can destroy structures. For example, heated buildings at Barrow, Alaska, have been observed to settle differentially as much as 20 inches in three

Figure 6.7. Building in Alaska damaged by thawing of underlying permafrost. The structure, located at mile 278.5 of the Richardson Highway, is situated on ice-rich permafrost in fine-grained silts and sands. The porch did not sink as much as the rest of the building because it was unheated. The building was constructed in 1951 and had to be razed in 1965. (Photograph by T. L. Péwé, May 29, 1962.)

to four years; when the buildings were no longer heated the ground under them refroze and heaved them upward at least one foot within a year (Ferrians and others 1969). Figure 6.7 shows an Alaskan building damaged by these processes. On ice-rich permafrost even unheated structures — piles, roads, railroads, airfields, pipelines, dams, utility lines — may cause the ground to melt by changing the reflectance, and hence the heat exchange, of the surface. The structures then may heave differentially during the winter. Corte (1969) has reviewed the relations between engineering and frost phenomena.

Soil collapse and resulting land subsidence — as great as 15 feet — is observed in certain soils, most notably in deposits of loess, when water is added in large amounts. The structure of soil subject to collapse is open, and before collapse such soil always has been less than 100 percent saturated. The major soil constituents are bulky particles of silt, sand, or gravel, or any of their combinations, with slight or no clay present. Water in tension is the general binding agent. Both Lofgren (1969) and Dudley (1970) have reviewed the causes and problems of collapsing soils.

Most organic soils, typified by peat, present serious problems to human activities because of their high water content, low bulk density, and slight bearing strength. When loaded by construction or drained, peat may lose as much as 90 percent of its volume. The amount of ground subsidence can be dramatic: one quarter of a million acres in the delta at the confluence of the Sacramento and San Joaquin rivers in California have sunk more than 10 feet since drainage began a hundred years ago.

Suitability Criteria for Various Urban Uses of Soils

The aforementioned soils and soil conditions clearly have inherent drawbacks for most urban uses. The vast majority of other soils normally present no serious obstacle to urban use. However, certain soil characteristics may be preferred or required for some urban activities that present special demands on their substratum. Each of the major uses of soil by a city may be limited, economically if not technologically, by different specific soil qualities. The major urban uses of soil that are briefly discussed here are as foundations for buildings, as embankments or structural fill material, as supports or subbases for roadways, and as subgrades in which to place underground utilities and subways. (Chapter 9 relates soil qualities to the growth of plants in the urban environment.)

Building Foundations and Structural Fills

The essentials of a good foundation are that it not settle excessively and that it not collapse into the ground. If the surface or near surface soils do not have these essential qualities, it sometimes is possible to achieve the same objectives by resorting to pile foundations. Piles are structural columns that transfer the surface loads to a soil horizon at a depth that has an adequate bearing capacity. Piles, however, are expensive, and therefore a preferable alternative is to found a building on footings resting on or near the surface.

Bearing capacities and settlement characteristics of any given soil can be estimated quite precisely on the basis of engineering soil tests and theories of soil mechanics. Simple experience has shown which soils are generally suitable or unsuitable as foundation soils. Several systems of soil classification that reflect bearing capacities and settlement characteristics have been proposed. The system most widely used in soil mechanics and engineering practice is the Unified Classification System, which is described in most soil mechanics textbooks (see, for example, Lambe and Whitman 1969). In this system the soils are classified on the basis of their grain size distribution and plasticity characteristics. Soils are identified and classified by a two-letter symbol designation in which the first symbol identifies the soils as basically a gravel (G), sand (S), silt (M), clay (C), or organic soil (O), as summarized in Table 6.4. The second symbol indicates whether the soil is well or poorly graded (W or P); silty, sandy, or clayey (M, S, or C); and of high or low plasticity (H or L).

Table 6.5 is a classification and engineering use chart for soils based on the Unified Classification System. As can be seen in the table, well-graded gravels and sands make the best foundations, whereas silts, clayey soils, and organic deposits are undesirable. The same criteria generally apply for structural fills and embankments. In the case of high embankments, drainage characteristics of the soil can be important.

Road Subbases and Subgrades

The bearing capacity requirement for roads usually is less stringent than that for buildings because vehicular loads are usually not as great as those of buildings. Other considerations are important, however, particularly susceptibility to frost action, drainage characteristics, and volume stability under seasonal moisture variations. The weight of pavement is usually not sufficient to prevent vigorous heaving and expansion in the subbase and subgrade. Silts and silty soils are notoriously susceptible to frost heaving and are highly undesirable as road subbases or subgrades unless stabilized. Table 6.5 indicates the desirability of various soil types for road subbases or fills.

Tunnels

The main problem in underground tunneling is water. Another problem that is sometimes encountered in soft clays is that of "squeezing." Underground construction technology has advanced to the stage where it can effectively contend with these and associated problems. Nevertheless, problems should be avoided by careful selection of tunnel routes whenever possible. In addition, it is important to minimize surface effects of underground tunneling operations, such as subsidence. Subsidence can occur as a result of dewatering operations conducted in excavations or as a result of "squeezing" of tunnel walls in soft clay prior to installation of shoring.

Repercussions from Unwise Use of Soils

Landslides from Clearing or Building on Unstable Slopes

The factors contributing to instability of earth slopes are outlined in Table 6.6. It is clear from this table that a number of man-made disturbances associated with urbanization can result in slope failures. Triggering actions include cutting and filling for residential hillside developments, vibrations from machinery, and alteration in hillside hydrology (for example, from lawn watering, leaking mains, and septic tank drain fields). Removal of hillside vegetation, particularly trees and woody vegetation, also can cause accelerated erosion and land-sliding, as discussed by Gray (1970).

The impact of hillside developments on slope stability in the Los Angeles area has been described by Schoustra and Lake (1969). They noted that serious property damage and loss of life occurred in hillside developments during the January 1969 rains. The most common type of damage – for both natural slopes and fill and cut slopes – consisted of shallow slumps and mud flows. Their main conclusion and recom-mendation was a call for better engineered developments – better compaction efficiency, adequate grading ordinances, and wider terraces. It could be argued that the real need was simply to prohibit intensive development on steep, slide-susceptible slopes.

Some examples of slope instability problems in urban areas are illustrated in Figures 6.8–6.10. Extensive residential development atop the bluffs shown in Figure 6.8 probably is incompatible with the stability of the bluffs.

Ground Subsidence

Settlement of the ground surface can occur for a variety of reasons. If differential settlement occurs, it may cause considerable distress to structures founded on the surface. Settlement usually is asso-ciated with compressible clays of high void ratio that are subjected to surface loads. Externally imposed loads are not the only source of settlement. Consolidation and settlement also may occur as a result of fluid withdrawal from the ground. Mexico City and Long Beach, Cali-fornia, provide good examples of large-scale subsidence caused by pump-ing. Parts of Mexico City have settled as much as 30 feet because of lowering of the water table beneath the city. Subsidence also can occur as a result of underground mining operations, and is often a problem in limestone areas that are underlain by sinkholes, caverns, and solution channels.

Swelling clays that are subjected to either seasonal or artificial moisture variations may settle or heave. Ground settlement also is associated with the phenomenon of "soil liquefaction," which some-times accompanies earthquakes. Volume change of both types occurs

Table 6.5. Urban engineering use of soils (dashes indicate unsuitability). (After Wagner 1957.)

Unified Soil Classification Symbol	Typical Names of Soil Groups	Important Properties				Relative Desirability for Various Uses					
		Permeability when Compacted	Shearing Strength when Compacted and Saturated	Compressibility when Compacted and Saturated	Workability as a Construction Material	Foundations		Roadways			
						Seepage Important	Seepage not Important	Fills		Frost Heave Possible	Surfacing
								Frost Heave not Possible	Frost Heave Possible		
GW	Well-graded gravels, gravel-sand mixtures, little or no fines	pervious	excellent	negligible	excellent	—	1	1	1	1	3
GP	Poorly graded gravels, gravel-sand mixtures, little or no fines	very pervious	good	negligible	good	—	3	3	3	3	—
GM	Silty gravels, poorly graded gravel-sand-silt mixtures	semipervious to impervious	good	negligible	good	1	4	4	4	9	5
GC	Clayey gravels, poorly graded gravel-sand-clay mixtures	impervious	good to fair	very low	good	2	6	5	5	5	1
SW	Well-graded sands, gravelly sands, little or no fines	pervious	excellent	negligible	excellent	—	2	2	2	2	4
SP	Poorly graded sands, gravelly sands, little or no fines	pervious	good	very low	fair	—	5	6	4	4	—
SM	Silty sands, poorly graded sand-silt mixtures	semipervious to impervious	good	low	fair	3	7	8	8	10	6
SC	Clayey sands, poorly graded sand-clay mixtures	impervious	good to fair	low	good	4	8	7	6	6	2
ML	Inorganic silts and very fine sands, rock flour, silty or clayey fine sands with slight plasticity	semipervious to impervious	fair	medium	fair	6	9	10	6	11	—

CL	Inorganic clays of low to medium plasticity, gravelly clays, sandy clays, silty clays, lean clays	impervious	fair	medium	good to fair	5	10	9	7	7
OL	Organic silts and organic silt-clays of low plasticity	semipervious to impervious	poor	medium	fair	7	11	11	12	—
MH	Inorganic silts, micaceous or diatomaceous fine sandy or silty soils, elastic silts	semipervious to impervious	fair to poor	high	poor	8	12	12	13	—
CH	Inorganic clays of high plasticity, fat clays	impervious	poor	high	poor	9	13	13	8	—
OH	Organic clays of medium to high plasticity	impervious	poor	high	poor	10	14	14	14	—
Pt	Peat and other highly organic soils	—	—	—	—	—	—	—	—	—

Table 6.6. Factors contributing to instability of earth slopes. (After Varnes 1958).

Factors that Contribute to High Shear Stress	*Factors that Contribute to Low Shear Strength*

A. Removal of Lateral Support
  1. Erosion – bank cutting by streams and rivers
  2. Human agencies – cuts, canals, pits, etc.
B. Surcharge
  1. Natural agencies – wt of snow, ice, and rainwater
  2. Human agencies – fills, buildings, etc.
C. Transitory Earth Stresses – Earthquakes
D. Regional Tilting
E. Removal of Underlying Support
  1. Subaerial weathering – solutioning by groundwater
  2. Subterranean erosion – piping
  3. Human agencies – mining
F. Lateral Pressures
  1. Water in vertical cracks
  2. Freezing water in cracks
  3. Swelling
  4. Root wedging
	A. Initial State
	  1. Composition – inherently weak materials
	  2. Texture – loose soils, metastable grain structures
	  3. Gross structure – faults, jointing, bedding planes, varving, etc.
	B. Changes Due to Weathering and Other Physico-chemical Reactions
	  1. Frost action and thermal expansion
	  2. Hydration of clay minerals
	  3. Drying and cracking
	  4. Leaching
	C. Changes in Intergranular Forces Due to Pore Water
	  1. Buoyancy in saturated state
	  2. Loss in capillary tension upon saturation
	  3. Seepage pressure of percolating ground water
	D. Changes in Structure
	  1. Fissuring of preconsolidated clays due to release of lateral restraint
	  2. Grain structure collapse upon disturbance

Figure 6.8. Slope failures at Pacific Palisades, California. Repeated slides have removed chunks of the bluffs. (Courtesy of Los Angeles Department of Building and Safety.)

only in certain kinds of soils, as discussed previously. It also is important to remember that many settlement phenomena are associated with changes in the groundwater regime. Any urban development that alters the position of the water table (as by pumping for water supplies, by altering drainage, or by injection) may cause a change in elevation of the ground surface.

Earthquake Damage: Variations Related to Surficial Geology
Certain soils are inherently bad earthquake risks. Loose, saturated alluvial deposits are perhaps the worst because they tend to "liquefy" under dynamic or shock loading. Soft and sensitive clays also are subject to earthquake hazard. A surprising amount of development and construction takes place atop these soils in spite of their potential

Figure 6.9. Destruction of hillside home by mudslide, Los Angeles, California. (Courtesy of Los Angeles Department of Building and Safety.)

instability during earthquakes. A major controversy now surrounds the construction of housing developments built on top of fill placed over the mud flats and soft bay sediments of San Francisco Bay. This region is adjacent to a major fault system and is seismically active.

Disregard for subsoil conditions and related potential earthquake hazards is perhaps best illustrated by the case of Anchorage, Alaska. In 1964 this area was struck by a severe earthquake that destroyed many homes, largely as a result of excessive ground movements and slippage during the quake. Four years earlier, the U.S. Geological Survey had said that much of Anchorage was built over layers of unstable ground. The astonishing fact is that in spite of all this Alaskans have moved right back and rebuilt on the same sites. They have even done so in areas declared ineligible for federally supported reconstruc-

Figure 6.10. Bedding slide in soft, shale slope surcharged with fill, Encino District, Los Angeles. (Courtesy of Los Angeles Department of Building and Safety.)

tion because of the unstable nature of the underlying soil. In the area of one slide (L Street), new buildings have been built on the slide itself, and an apartment house and a luxury hotel have been built nearby, all with private financing. Apparently the old adage, "once bitten, twice shy," does not hold in the case of the type of soil on which we found our cities.

Earthquake damage to structures and buildings can be mitigated to a large extent by careful structural design that takes into account likely ground motions and accelerations. Dynamic response characteristics of a building are crucial; therefore, in determining the degree of damage likely to result. This fact notwithstanding, it is still the surficial geology and local soil conditions that largely control the ground motions and displacements beneath buildings. A striking example of the influence of surficial geology in an earthquake is shown in Figure 6.11.

Figure 6.11. Severe earthquake damage to buildings situated on water-saturated alluvium; earthquake of 1966, Varto, Turkey. Here 12 of 14 buildings situated on old river channel deposits collapsed, whereas buildings on an adjacent dry bench did not. (Courtesy of U.S. Geological Survey, R. E. Wallace, photographer.)

SOILS AND PLANNING

Regional Planning

The uncontrolled urban sprawl that has engulfed the landscape since the end of World War II has been created with little regard for many values of the landscape or for the hazards that attend its misuse. Urban planners, administrators, and legislators as well as earth scientists have become increasingly aware of the need for information concerning the environment and resources of rapidly urbanizing regions.

We have seen in this chapter some of the consequences of disregarding the assets and liabilities of land resources. It should be self-evident that earth science information is critical in the planning process.

Unfortunately, such information is not always available, and the information that is available often is presented in forms that are virtually unintelligible to the planner or to those not trained in the earth sciences. Although the earth sciences are relatively old and have had a tremendous impact on the search for and development of mineral, water, and fuel resources, they have been employed sparingly in land use planning and development.

Soil problems associated with urbanization and regional development can be avoided in several ways. The most important and effective way is by adhering to rational land use policies. This requires that planners determine the type of land use (for example, natural area, recreation site, residential construction, or industrial use) best suited to a given region on the basis of its surficial geology and topography. Land-use decisions made on a local basis may be fragmented and are often inappropriate when considered on a regional scale. For example, minimization of earthquake hazard in a region cannot be achieved soley in a local context; the fault pattern of the entire region must be analyzed. The same holds true for landslide activity. Extraction of locally concentrated mineral resources, including cement, lime, and sand and gravel essential for building and construction in the entire region, should be coordinated through regional planning and meshed with other demands for the sites where these materials occur.

The San Francisco Bay Region Environment and Resources Planning Study — a Prototype Effort

The San Francisco Bay Region Environment and Resources Planning Study is investigating the physical environment and resources of that region and their significance for urban and regional planning. The study (being conducted cooperatively by the U.S. Department of Housing and Urban Development and the U.S. Geological Survey) relies heavily on work in geology, soil mechanics, geophysics, hydrology, and cartography and applies these disciplines to improve regional and urban planning and decision making.

The project is a pilot study and experimental in nature. The innovative aspects include the type of physical data collected, the way in which the data are synthesized, the formats in which the data are presented, and the lines of communication that are designed to help society gain optimum benefits from the physical environment.

The San Francisco Bay region was selected as a study site for several reasons. Few urbanizing areas must contend with a greater variety of environmental factors. Land and water assets, including the bay itself, have great economic, aesthetic, and climatic importance. Here too are encountered natural hazards such as earthquakes, flooding, and landslides. The region is large, has a present population of about five million people, and is being urbanized rapidly.

The study is attempting, within three years, to identify earth science concepts and related empirical results that address regional land use problems and express them in a form that can readily be utilized. During the study a continuing appraisal of the results is being made through discussions with potential users.

The San Francisco Bay Region Study includes detailed consideration of topographic, geologic, geophysical, and hydrologic elements. Basic information on the soils and unconsolidated geologic formations of the region, a landslide inventory, and seismic data are important components of the geologic and geophysical program (see Table 6.7).

Local Planning

Regional data, although satisfying some needs at the local level, cannot satisfy all of them. Such local problems as detailed planning and construction require detailed geologic maps, soil analyses, drainage plans, and so forth. To produce these for the entire region requires a much greater effort than can be justified by regional planners. Such efforts are best undertaken by local authorities, and they should be the responsibility of local agencies and private consultants rather than state or federal agencies.

Traditionally, economic factors have decided the use of city land irrespective of ecological considerations. This practice has resulted in the loss of many social and natural values of land as well as the impacts on soils already discussed. McHarg (1969, 1970) has described a method whereby these values can be incorporated into urban planning. The method basically consists of mapping intrinsic environmental factors such as climate, hydrology, geology, soils, and wildlife habitats; these elements are important to all prospective land uses. The maps then are combined into a single composite that indicates (by color and tones used for the various factors) the intrinsic suitability of the land for various uses, such as residences, commerce, industry, conservation, and passive or active recreation. In addition, the composite indicates areas, on environmental grounds, where more than one use can be

Table 6.7. Geological and geophysical elements in the San Francisco Bay Region Environment and Resources Planning Study.

1. Active Faults
   a. Areal geologic and geomorphic investigations of suspected active faults and of sedimentary deposits and geologic structures in active fault zones
   b. Monitoring and analysis of microearthquakes (in conjunction with seismicity and ground-motion studies)
   c. Physical exploration of active fault zones
   d. Strain measurement and monitoring of known active fault zones (in conjunction with seismicity and ground-motion studies)
   e. Identification and mapping of submarine segments of active faults based on interpretation of marine geophysical surveys
2. Slope Stability and Engineering Behavior of Bedrock Geologic Formations
   a. Landslide inventory and characterization
   b. Geologic mapping — as a basis for other studies and interpretive reports
   c. Physical properties and engineering behavior
   d. Prediction of slope stability, erodibility, and other aspects of the engineering behavior and environmental problems of the bedrock geologic formations of the Bay region
3. Physical Properties and Engineering Behavior of Unconsolidated Geologic Formations
   a. Bedrock depth and configuration
   b. Thickness, character, and distribution of unconsolidated sedimentary units — as a basis for other studies and interpretive reports
   c. Physical properties and engineering behavior of unconsolidated deposits
   d. Prediction of engineering behavior and analysis of environmental problems of the unconsolidated geologic formations of the Bay region
4. Seismicity and Ground Motion
   a. Mechanics of earthquake generation — precise location of microearthquakes, strain measurements along active faults, and laboratory and model studies
   b. Seismic wave propagation in the crust — delineation of crustal structures and seismically sensitive sedimentary layers by reflection and refraction techniques
   c. Influence of local geologic and topographic conditions on strong ground shaking (relative amplification of seismic waves)
5. Mineral Commodity Utilization
   a. Inventory and evaluation of Bay region mineral commodities
   b. Determination of the social and economic impact of utilization — or nonutilization
   c. Development of strategy for deciding how, when, or if specific Bay region mineral commodities should be utilized
6. Undeveloped Land and Water Areas
   a. Cataloguing and mapping Bay region lands and waters that have significant scientific, educational, historical, and recreational values
   b. Analysis of the impact of geologic or hydrologic hazards, and mineral or water resources, upon present or potential nondevelopmental uses of Bay region lands and waters

supported; other factors may then determine which alternative use to employ there.

Once local urban development plans are formulated, one hopes on the basis of an enlightened land use policy and site inspection, it still is necessary to mitigate or guard against adverse impacts that may occur. Insofar as possible, practices should be avoided that lead to excessive soil erosion or slope failures, and control measures should be instituted to deal with sedimentation. It is beyond the scope and intent of this chapter to detail remedial measures for dealing with soil problems. The reader interested in pursuing this subject beyond the guidelines and precautions presented here should refer to the publications by Schwab and others (1966), Powell and others (1970), Leggett (1962), Lambe and Whitman (1969), and official publications of the U.S. Soil Conservation Service and Building Advisory Board of the National Research Council.

REFERENCES

Brown, E. H. 1970. Man shapes the earth. *Geogr. Jour.* 136(1):74–85.
Building Research Advisory Board. 1969. *Slope protection for residential developments.* Report prepared by the Division of Engineering, National Research Council, for the Federal Housing Administration.
Cannon, H. L., and J. M. Bowles. 1962. Contamination of vegetation by tetraethyl lead. *Science* 137(3532):765–766.
Corte, A. E. 1969. Geocryology and engineering. In *Reviews in engineering geology,* ed. D. J. Varnes and G. Kiersch, vol. 2, pp. 119–185. Boulder, Colo.: Geological Society of America.
Crawford, C. B., and W. J. Eden. 1967. Stability of natural slopes in sensitive clay. *Jour. Soil Mechanics and Foundation Division, Amer. Soc. Civ. Eng.* 93(SM4):419–436.
Dudley, J. H. 1970. Review of collapsing soils. *Jour. Soil Mechanics and Foundation Division, Am. Soc. Civ. Eng.* 96(SM3):925–947.
Ferrians, O. J., Jr., R. Kachadoorian, and G. W. Greene. 1969. *Permafrost and related engineering problems in Alaska.* U.S. Geological Survey Prof. Paper 678. Washington, D.C.: Govt. Printing Office.
Flawn, P. T. 1970. *Environmental geology: Conservation, land-use, and resource management.* New York: Harper and Row.
Gray, D. H. 1970. Effect of forest clear-cutting on the stability of natural slopes. *Bull. Assoc. Engrg. Geologists* 7(1&2):45–65.

Hackett, J. E. 1965. Ground-water contamination in an urban environment. *Ground Water* 3(3):27–30.

Holtz, W. G. 1968. Soil as an engineering material. *Jour. of Materials* 3(4):847–915.

Holtz, W. G., and H. J. Gibbs. 1956. Engineering properties of expansive clays. *Trans. Am. Soc. Civ. Eng.* 121:641–677.

Judson, Sheldon. 1968. Erosion of the land: Or what's happening to our continents? *Amer. Scientist* 56(4):356–374.

Kaiser, E. R. 1967. Refuse reduction processes. In *Proceedings, the Surgeon General's conference on solid waste management for metropolitan Washington, July 19–20, 1967,* ed. Leo Weaver, pp. 93–104. Cincinnati: U.S. Dept. of Health, Education, and Welfare, Public Health Service.

Kerr, P. F. 1963. Quick clay. *Sci. Amer.* Nov.:132–142.

Lagerwerff, J. V., and A. W. Specht. 1970. Contamination of roadside soil and vegetation with cadmium, nickel, lead, and zinc. *Environ. Sci. and Tech.* 4(7):583–586.

Lambe, T. W., and R. V. Whitman. 1969. *Soil mechanics.* New York: John Wiley and Sons.

Legget, R. F. 1962. *Geology and engineering,* 2nd ed. New York: McGraw-Hill.

Lofgren, B. E. 1969. Land subsidence due to the application of water. In *Reviews in engineering geology,* vol. 2, ed. D. J. Varnes and G. Kiersch, pp. 271–303. Boulder, Colo.: Geological Society of America.

McHarg, Ian. 1969. *Design with nature.* New York: Natural History Press.

——— 1970. Ecological values and regional planning. *Civil Engineering, Am. Soc. Civ. Engin.* 40(8):40–44.

Marsh, G. P. 1864. *Man and nature; or, Physical geography as modified by human action.* New York: Scribners. (1965 edition ed. by David Lowenthal. Cambridge, Mass.: Harvard Univ. Press.)

Marx, Wesley. 1971. *Man and his environment: Waste.* New York: Harper and Row.

Milligan, V., and L. G. Soderman, and A. Rutka. 1962. Experience with Canadian varved clays. *Jour. Soil Mechanics and Foundation Division, Am. Soc. Civ. Engin.* 88(SM4):31–67.

National Academy of Engineering and National Academy of Sciences. 1970. *Policies for solid waste management.* U.S. Dept. of Health, Education, and Welfare, Public Health Service Publ. no. 2018.

Poland, J. F., and G. H. Davis. 1969. Land subsidence due to withdrawal of fluids. In *Reviews in engineering geology,* vol. 2, ed. D. J. Varnes and G. Kiersch, pp. 187–269. Boulder, Colo.: Geological Society of America.

Powell, M. D., W. C. Winter, and W. P. Bodwich. 1970. *Community action guidebook for soil erosion and sediment control.* Washington, D.C.: National Association of Counties Research Foundation.

Purves, D., and E. J. MacKenzie. 1969. Trace-element contamination of parklands in urban areas. *Jour. Soil Sci.* 20(2):288–290.

Risser, H. E., and R. L. Major. 1967. *Urban expansion: An opportunity and a challenge to industrial mineral producers.* Illinois Geological Survey Environmental Geology Notes, no. 16. Urbana, Ill.: Illinois State Geological Survey.

Ross, W. G. 1967. Encroachment of the Jeffrey Mine on the town of Asbestos, Quebec. *Geogr. Rev.* 57(4):523–537.

Schoustra, J. and T. D. Lake. 1969. Los Angeles hillside developments put to test by recent rains. *Civil Engineering, Am. Soc. Civ. Engin.* 39(11): 39–42.

Schwab, G. O., R. K. Frevert, T. W. Edminster, and K. K. Barnes. 1966. *Soil and water conservation engineering,* 2nd ed. New York: John Wiley and Sons.

Scullin, C. M. 1966. History, development, and administration of excavation and grading codes. In *Engineering geology in southern California,* ed. R. Lung and R. Procter, pp. 226–236. Glendale, Calif.: Special Publ. of Los Angeles Section, Association of Engineering Geologists.

Seed, H. B. and I. M. Idriss. 1967. Analysis of soil liquefaction: Niigata earthquake. *Jour. Soil Mechanics and Foundation Division, Am. Soc. Civ. Engin.* 93(SM3):83–108.

Seed, H. B., and S. D. Wilson. 1967. The Turnagain Heights landslide, Anchorage, Alaska. *Jour. Soil Mechanics and Foundation Division, Am. Soc. Civ. Engin.* 93(SM4):325–353.

Soil Conservation Service. 1970. *Guidelines for the control of erosion and sediment in urban areas of the northeast.* Washington, D.C.: U.S. Dept. of Agriculture Publ.

U.S. Dept. of Interior. 1967. *Surface mining and our environment.* Washington, D.C.: U.S. Dept of Interior, Strip and Surface Mine Study Policy Committee.

Vadnais, R. R. 1965. *Quantitative terrain factors as related to soil parent materials and their engineering classification.* Soil Mechanics Series no. 10. Urbana, Ill.: Univ. of Illinois.

Varnes, D. J. 1958. Landslide types and processes. In *Landslides and engineering practice,* National Academy of Engineering and National Academy of Sciences Publ. 544, Highway Research Board, Special Report 29, pp. 20–47.

Wagner, A. A. 1957. The use of the unified soil classification system by the bureau of reclamation. *Proc. 4th Intern. Conf. Soil Mech. Found. Engrg.* (London) 1:125.

Wallace, R. E. 1969. Geologic factors in earthquake damage. In *CENTO conf. earthquake hazard minimization, Ankara, Turkey, 1968,* pp. 123–133. Ankara, Turkey: U.S. Economic Coordinator for CENTO Affairs.

CHAPTER 7

Risk from Nature in the City

Duane D. Baumann and Robert W. Kates

The modern city is the ultimate human artifact. Yet 3,800 years after the city of Mohenjo-Dara disintegrated in the rising of the Indus River, 1,900 years after Vesuvius engulfed Pompeii, and 215 years after earthquakes destroyed Lisbon, risk from nature persists in the city of man. The natural hazardousness of cities arises from the impact of natural events on an urban structure that at best is only partly designed to absorb, buffer, or reflect such events, and that at worst exacerbates them. The degree of hazard is a result of the frequency, duration, magnitude, and timing of natural events as well as of the extent of human adjustment to those events. The burden of hazard is twofold: (1) death and damage from events that exceed the human adjustments to hazards and (2) the continuing cost of adjustment in terms of wealth and energy.

Man is subject to numerous natural hazards, many of which are listed in Table 7.1. All of these common hazards can affect cities or their populations, depending upon regional location. Research into the nature and occurrence of natural hazards has in the last 15 years been closely linked to studies of human perception of these hazards and the adjustments people make to them. It has been recognized by both geographers and psychologists that the environment is viewed in varying ways by different individuals and societies. Even within a given society, the general public and the decision-makers — technicians, scientists, and administrators — may perceive environmental events in very

Table 7.1. Common natural hazards by principal causal agent. (After Burton and Kates 1964.)

Geophysical		Biological	
Climatic and Meteorological	Geological and Geomorphic	Floral	Faunal
Blizzards and snow	Avalanches	Fungal diseases	Bacterial and viral diseases
Droughts	Earthquakes	*For example:*	*For example:*
Floods	Erosion (including	Athlete's foot	Influenza
Fog	soil erosion and	Dutch elm	Malaria
Frost	shore and beach	Wheat stem rust	Typhus
Hailstorms	erosion)	Blister rust	Bubonic plague
Heat waves	Landslides	Infestations	Venereal
Hurricanes	Shifting sand	*For example:*	disease
Lightning strokes and fires	Tsunamis	Weeds	Rabies
Tornadoes	Volcanic eruptions	Phreatophytes	Hoof and mouth disease
		Water hyacinth	Tobacco mosaic
		Hay Fever	Infestations
		Poison Ivy	*For example:*
			Rabbits
			Termites
			Locusts
			Grasshoppers
			Venomous animal bites

different ways. In short, the manner in which a society perceives its environment will significantly influence the adaptations that are made.

In attempting to understand man's perception of environment, investigators have focused on natural hazards — "those elements in the physical environment harmful to man and caused by forces extraneous to him" (Burton and Kates 1964, p. 413). There are several advantages to studying hazards: (1) hazardous events have greater than normal magnitude and require many adjustments to mitigate or prevent damage and loss of life; (2) hazardous events are often catastrophic (in terms of damage) and, therefore, loom large in terms of human interest and priorities; and (3) they hence make a great impression on the human memory, and thus are particularly amenable to scientific investigation of human perception and values regarding nature.

This chapter assesses the natural hazardousness of urban areas and the trends in risk from natural causes. It is useful first to review differences that exist between the actual magnitude and frequency of hazardous events and the affected populations' perceptions of the magnitudes and frequencies. A discussion of several hazards then follows. Finally, some answers are provided to the question: Is natural hazard increasing in the city, and if so, what actions can be taken to reduce human risk?

THE NATURAL HAZARDOUSNESS OF A PLACE

The Example of London, Ontario

To appreciate the meaning of natural hazards to an urban population, it is useful to describe the experiences of a "typical" city. Studies by Hewitt and Burton (1971) indicate that London, Ontario, is such a place. But the discussion cannot focus on the city alone. To understand natural hazards in this city of some 200,000 people, it is necessary to consider the entire southwestern region of Ontario, because the spectrum of events giving rise to natural hazards results from environmental conditions throughout the area, the bulk of which stem from meteorological and related hydrological processes.

Ontario is significantly affected by severe convectional storms and tornadoes. In addition, London lies on the fringe of a heavy, lakeshore snowfall belt and, like all of southern Ontario, is highly susceptible to glaze storms. A major stream runs through London (the Thames, naturally), and it frequently floods owing to high spring runoff aggravated by ice jams. Hurricanes pose significant wind, rain, and flood hazards in late summer and autumn. Hailstorms, though frequent, cause little urban hazard, and drought, though rare, is basically a threat only to agriculture.

How can we characterize this complex of natural hazards? Within the region of southwestern Ontario, Hewitt and Burton expect (on the basis of past records and with differing degrees of assurance) the following severe events over a 50-year period: 1 drought, 2 windstorms, 5 snowstorms, 8 hurricanes, 10 glaze storms, 16 floods of the Thames, 25 hailstorms, and 39 tornadoes. What does that mean for the resident of London? For example, although a tornado will occur about every 1.3 years somewhere within the region, its recurrence is estimated at 400 years for urbanized areas and 2,000 years at any given point location within the region!

Let us personalize the London data. If we were young adults

spending the rest of our lives in London, we should expect sometime to see one truly great snowstorm, one hurricane, two major floods in the Thames, and at least three paralyzing glaze storms in which we would be without electricity for more than a week. We should not be greatly surprised by a tornado, nor by any of the other rare but possible disasters, such as a hurricane centered over the Thames basin or a glaze storm followed by a paralyzing snowfall.

How threatening, therefore, is nature to the London resident? In absolute terms it would not appear to be very threatening, if the experience of the past is a key to the future. At most, six natural disasters have been recorded in the past 100 years. Is, then, nature only a minor threat relative to hazards introduced by man? London was almost destroyed by fire in 1845; 180 died in the capsize of a ferryboat in 1881; and 19 died when the second floor of the City Hall collapsed in 1898. Further, a major fire occurs less than once per year and an explosion occurs once in 4 years. Where disasters are concerned, man and nature seem to be about equal threats.

A comparison of the occurrence of both man-made and natural disasters at London to similar events at other urban places bears out this assessment of the relative threats of nature and man. Hewitt and Burton examined the 1958 to 1967 occurrence of disaster (loss of 10 or more lives or $500,000 damage, or both) for 57 cities of about London's population (see Table 7.2). Disasters, it appears, occur about equally from natural and man-made causes, with an expectancy of slightly over three from each cause per century.This accords well with the experience of London over the past 100 years as well as with the record of disasters for all North America in a single year. Using 1967 as a reference year, we can calculate that disasters should occur once in 21 years. London, therefore, approximates the mean of hazardousness as measured by the disaster definition.

Table 7.2. Average frequencies of disasters, 1958–1967, for 57 cities. (After Hewitt and Burton, 1971).

	Natural	Man Made	Total
Total city-years	570	570	570
No. of disasters	17	18	35
Return period (years)	33.5	30.0	16.3

The Magnitude-Frequency Concept

It is apparent from the discussion of London, Ontario, that at most places only a few natural events will occur during a human lifetime that are deemed "disasters" by the affected populace. Most natural events — for example, rainstorms — occur very frequently but are of low magnitude. In other words, *most* storms are relatively small and do not seriously disrupt human beings or the terrain on which they live. Occasionally, however, a storm of great magnitude will occur, causing serious damage to the landscape and its inhabitants, loss of life, and disruption of the economy. Such a rare and spectacular work of nature is, in human perspective, a catastrophic event. We do not quickly forget such disasters, and our lexicon of environmental events is replete with examples of nature's destructive force — such as the Johnstown flood, the San Francisco earthquake, the Galveston hurricane, or the Donora smog.

Very often such events carry the names of cities, for the greatest destruction of life and property is in urban areas. Nature, however, does not draw fine distinctions between city and countryside; in both places events occur with varying degrees of intensity and frequency. The *magnitude* of an event refers to its size. Examples are the height of water attained during a flood, the rating of an earthquake on the Richter scale, or the depth of snow accumulated in a winter storm. *Frequency* refers to the number of times a given event occurs during some time period. Magnitude and frequency usually are inversely related; that is, events of great magnitude and force occur infrequently, and vice versa.

It is important that the magnitude and frequency of natural events be understood if scientists are to understand physical processes sufficiently to predict them. To intelligently prepare for natural hazards, communities must be aware of the frequencies at which events of different sizes are likely to recur. An effective image of these potentials has been created in the following analogy by Wolman and Miller (1960, p. 73):

A dwarf, a man, and a huge giant are having a wood-cutting contest. Because of metabolic peculiarities, individual chopping rates are roughly inverse to their size. The dwarf works steadily and is rarely seen to rest. However, his progress is slow, for even little trees take a long time, and there are many big ones which he cannot dent with his axe. The man is a strong fellow and a hard worker, but he takes a day off now and then. His vigorous and persistent labors are highly effective, but there are some trees that defy his best efforts. The giant is tremendously strong, but he spends most of his time sleeping. Whenever he is on the job, his actions are frequently capricious. Sometimes he throws away his axe and dashes wildly into the woods, where he breaks the trees or pulls them up by the roots. On the rare occasions when he encounters a tree too big for him, he ominously mentions his family of brothers — all bigger, and stronger, and sleepier.

Although the natural event of great magnitude (like the giant above) is seldom at work, it can cause great disaster in the city. An event of lesser magnitude (like the force of the man above) is generally less destructive, and also more easily prepared against; however, such events occur more frequently than those of great magnitude and, hence, they may *in total* cause more damage. Ordinary events (like the work done by the dwarf) are usually harmless, because they are of slight magnitude and because they occur so frequently that most communities have routinely adopted protective measures against them. Thus, over a term of decades the relative destructiveness of a natural hazard is clearly seen to be a function of its magnitude and frequency and the degree of community preparedness.

CLIMATIC AND HYDROLOGIC HAZARDS

It often is difficult to separate a climatic event from a hydrologic event because one is so closely connected to the other. Flooding, drought, hurricanes, and winter storms are excellent examples. In some cases, however, damage results directly from atmospheric components of the event — in the case of tornadoes, from pressure differentials and very high winds. The purpose of this section is to describe several climatic and hydrologic hazards that significantly affect urbanized places. The first part, on flooding, demonstrates the important relationship that exists between the frequency of a natural hazard event and adjustments that communities may make to combat the hazard. The second part, on tornadoes, illustrates that damage from natural hazards and adjustment to them is not merely a function of understanding the physical process, but is also a reflection of differing human perceptions and cultural attitudes. A discussion of drought in the city then focuses on problems faced by urban planners and other decision-makers. Finally, a section on winter storms briefly defines some problems encountered in communities where perception of and adjustment to a hazard is relatively high.

Flooding

Many urban places are situated on flood plains; these sites usually are level, fertile, on transportation routes, and, of course, near accessible water. Frequently — every few years or so — there is too much water, and flood plain cities are flooded (see Figure 7.1). More than 2,000 cities in North America are located on flood plains. A graph constructed from available flood frequency data on a fourth of these urban places shows a log-normal distribution (Figure 7.2). The figure shows that flooding in a city located on a flood plain occurs, on the average, once every two or three years.

Three insets in Figure 7.2 illustrate perception and adjustment in three cities: Desert Hot Springs, California, LaFollette, Tennessee, and Darlington, Wisconsin. These cities represent places of low, intermediate, and high flood probability, respectively. Response to the

Figure 7.1. A city in flood. The waters of the Red Lake River periodically flood Crookston, Minnesota (shown here on April 23, 1950; population 7,400). (Courtesy of U.S. Department of Agriculture.)

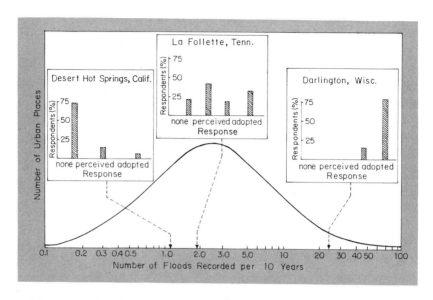

Figure 7.2. Flood frequencies for 496 urban places in the United States. Insets show response in three communities, each experiencing different flood frequencies per ten years. Response ranges from total ignorance (none), to two levels of perception (perceived), to adoption of countermeasures (adopted).

floods (illustrated by the bar graphs) is scaled from total ignorance (none), through two levels of perception (perceived), to adoption of measures to prevent and counteract flooding (adopted). The variation in people's perception of the associated hazard and adjustment to floods relates to the probable frequency of these events. For example, where floods occur often, as in Darlington, people make adjustments; where floods are infrequent, as in Desert Hot Springs, people make few, if any, adjustments in anticipation of flooding events. The majority of places, however, experience 1.4 to 4.0 floods per 10-year period; as exemplified by the LaFollette data, the inhabitants in such places are relatively uncertain whether to adjust to the hazard or not.

The log-normal distribution of places relative to extreme events has not been verified for other hazards, but many studies support the notion of increasing variation in perception and adjustment in areas of great uncertainty. Communities that experience disruptive natural events infrequently are generally those least prepared to cope with the event. If the residents and managers of a city recognize or perceive that a potentially hazardous event is the exception and not the rule, they are generally unwilling to invest in protective measures. In these places floods of a given magnitude will, therefore, cause greater damage than in communities that are prepared.

An interesting corollary that people often accept is exemplified in the expression "lightning doesn't strike twice in the same place." Once a major hazard – such as a 50-year or 100-year flood – has been experienced, there is an assumption that the place is "safe" for another 50 or 100 years. But flood probabilities are based on short-term stream records (see Chapter 5, pp. 101–102) and are not immutable. Also, nature is capricious and a 100-year flood one year may be followed by another 100-year flood the next year. Indeed, a community may find itself on the extremes of the probability curve during a short period of time. Finally, with respect to flood frequency, it must be remembered that urbanization may lead to positive feedback whereby flood hazards increase with city growth (see Chapter 5). Recognition of increased flood dangers may not keep pace with local urban development, and necessary protective measures may be ignored.

Generally speaking, urban and rural flood plain users perceive flood hazards differently (Burton and Kates 1964, p. 428). Urban users of flood plains are less sensitive to hazard potentials than are agricultural users, even where the frequency of hazard is approximately the same for both locations. This difference is largely attributable to the fact that agriculturists are directly affected by floods in the pursuit of their livelihoods and therefore have heightened awareness.

Tornadoes

Tornadoes are among the most feared and destructive natural events. These small funnel-shaped storms can generate winds up to 500 miles per hour and wreak awesome devastation in their path. Atmospheric pressure in the vortex of a tornado is so low that closed buildings may literally explode owing to the pressure differential. The path of tornadoes is erratic and cannot be predicted with precision; several blocks may be destroyed where tornadoes touch down in urban areas, whereas structures only a street away remain virtually undamaged (see Figure 7.3). As cities spread across the landscape, the probability of settled areas being struck by tornadoes increases.

Deaths caused by tornadoes have been continually declining in the United States, although the number of tornadoes has apparently been increasing (see Figure 7.4). The apparent increase in tornadoes is

Figure 7.3. Destruction by a tornado in Oak Lawn, Illinois, a southwestern suburb of Chicago. The arrow marks part of the 16-mile path of this April 21, 1967, storm, which destroyed 129 homes and killed 31 people. (Courtesy of the *Chicago Tribune*.)

largely accounted for by a growing and widespread tornado observation network. From 1916 through 1966 the annual average number of tornado-caused deaths was 193, but for 1953 through 1966 the average was only 122 deaths per year.

The exceptions to this decline, however, are dramatic — not only for a single year, but for a single storm. On April 11, 1965, 271 people were mortally injured by tornadoes that touched down in six midwestern states. In that year, over 300 persons were killed by tornadoes. However, even the peak years, when higher than average deaths result from tornadoes, show a pattern of decline. This is remarkable in light of increased urbanization and population growth.

The development of a national warning system has been influential in the steady decrease of tornado-caused deaths. Prior to 1952,

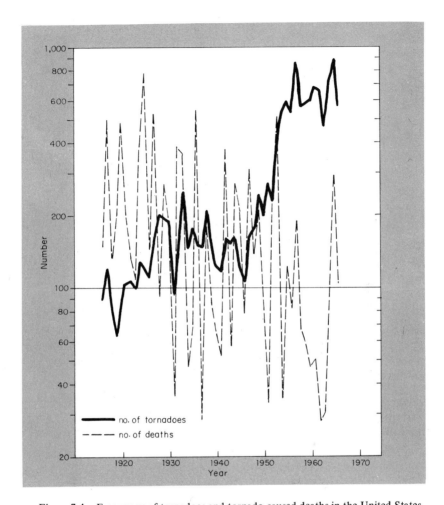

Figure 7.4. Frequency of tornadoes and tornado-caused deaths in the United States.

tornado watches and warnings were not issued by the U. S. Weather
Bureau, partly because of a belief by some that widespread panic would
spread throughout the public (Bates 1962). However, numerous lives
were saved at a U. S. Air Force base in a tornado-prone area after a
warning system was instituted in the late 1940's. In 1952 the Weather
Bureau undertook the responsibility of forecasting tornadoes. Consequently, as a more elaborate observation network was installed throughout the United States, the number of recorded tornado occurrences
rose sharply, while the number of tornado-caused deaths declined

(Figure 7.2). The efficiency of tornado watches and warnings may be illustrated in specific occurrences. For example, on June 8, 1966, when a tornado swept through a densely settled area of Topeka, Kansas, only 17 deaths were recorded; the combination of an efficient warning system and appropriate response to it by the citizenry kept deaths much lower than might have been expected.

From a spatial viewpoint the effects of the tornado hazard have not been uniform throughout the country, even if variations in population density and tornado frequency are considered. The greatest frequency of tornado deaths has occurred in the South. By 1953, the number of tornado deaths in the South was five times the average for the remainder of the nation (Linehan 1957, p. 17). One apparent explanation for the concentration of deaths is that the South has both a high population density and a high tornado frequency; this suggests that the highest *potential* casualties occur there. Potential casualties are those that theoretically would occur under given conditions of population density, the frequency of tornadoes, and the area of the average tornado. The potential casualties from tornadoes are highest in zones (1) from Dallas, Texas, through Topeka, Kansas; (2) from Chicago, Illinois, to Detroit, Michigan; and (3) in the densely populated Northeast (Sadowski, 1965). This contradicts the actual highest incidence of tornado-caused deaths, which, as we have seen, is located predominantly in the South.

Several possible explanations of this anomaly have been offered. One explanation focuses on the physical characteristics of the tornado. It may be that the storms in the South are more violent and that this accounts for the higher death rate. If the storms are more violent, one might expect a higher property damage rate along with the higher death rate. However, except for Georgia, the states with the highest property damage were not in the South; on the contrary, most of the Southern states are not even on the list of the ten states that incur the highest property damage from tornadoes (Flora 1954).

Some other hypotheses, instead of focusing upon variations in the physical characteristics of tornadoes, emphasize variations in the human environment. One frequently mentioned explanation stresses the type and quality of housing. In the South, for example, are homes more or less likely to have storm cellars than in other areas of the country? Or are homes in the South less well constructed? The relationship between quality of housing and tornado-caused deaths is not easily identified and measured, although it has been suggested that the average quality of housing in the South has been inferior and hence more susceptible to damage.

It has also been suggested that the efficacy of tornado warning systems may be of less value in the South than in other areas with equal or higher potential tornado casualties. In 1953, the first year in which the U. S. Weather Bureau made tornado forecasts available to American communities, the South recorded the greatest intensity of tornado-caused deaths. From 1953 on, the information on tornado forecasts has been available to all communities. Indeed, radio and television stations have regularly broadcast the warnings sent from the Severe Local Storm Center in Kansas City or by local observers. Not all communities employ civil defense sirens or have a tornado preparedness plan, however, and such measures are especially lacking in the South.

A person's perception of the hazard is an important factor related to the value of a warning system. People adjust to their environment, and the process of adjustment is influenced by individual personality, culture, and physical environment. Once ideas or perceptions are established, a person tends to maintain his personal set of ideas or cognitions about a particular phenomenon. Thus, a person's perception of environment accommodates both reality and his personal needs and dispositions.

By analogy to the previous discussion of flood frequency, one would expect the greatest adoption of adjustments to mitigate the effects of tornadoes in Oklahoma and Kansas, where the frequency of tornadoes per unit area is highest. Such adjustments logically include a higher proportion of storm cellars or basements, a public more sensitive to warnings, a public more informed of alternative strategies of action, and even a more complex and intricate organizational warning network. In general, these expectations are fulfilled in Oklahoma and Kansas. In contrast, along the eastern seaboard tornadoes occur so infrequently that many suggested measures for protection are never adopted. Communities do not test or utilize their civil defense sirens in preparation for an actual tornado; knowledge of adjustment alternatives is low, although fear of the tornado may be quite high.

In seeking an answer to why the South has a higher death rate, a study by Baumann and Sims (1972) considered areas with different degrees of tornado hazard. Personal interviews (420 in all) were completed in: Kansas and Oklahoma, a high hazard area; Connecticut and Massachusetts, a low hazard area; and Alabama and Illinois, representative of the middle range of tornado hazard where ambiguity is greatest. Each respondent was given a sentence-completion test to assess environmental perception.

Though findings are tentative, populations in areas with similar probability of tornado occurrence (Alabama and Illinois) have fundamental differences in perception of adjustments to the hazard. The Illinois resident, unlike the Alabama respondent, sees himself as personally responsible for directing his own life, whereas the Alabaman typically views himself as being more moved by external forces, especially God. The Alabama respondent's lower confidence apparently leads to the belief in "what ever will be, will be." The study also reveals that people in Illinois are more action-oriented, display more adaptive behavior when confronted with a tornado, and are more willing to accept available technology and recommended adjustments than are the Alabamans.

In summary, the data suggest that in environments with similar degrees of tornado hazard culture in part determines the effectiveness of a tornado forecast system. Attitudinal variations from city to city and from region to region must be considered in planning ways to minimize damages from tornadoes.

Drought
Most people think of drought as an agricultural phenomenon, an event from which the urban dweller is somehow immune. By and large this has been true in humid areas of the world, where natural supplies historically have been sufficient to meet demands for water. But in many areas of the world drought is a seasonal, or even nearly continual, facet of climate. Cities in such regions may have to draw water from great distances to assure their survival. This was true of ancient Mesopotamian cities, and it is true of Los Angeles today. The situation has become more serious as growing urban populations demand more and more water. Few modern cities, even in humid regions, are exempt from some threat of drought. Early Dutch settlers could hardly have guessed, for example, that someday New York City restaurants would stop serving water with meals and that the city's male residents would give up shaving in rather futile gestures to reduce the severity of periodic droughts.

Urban drought is not necessarily caused by insufficient precipitation, although that sometimes may be the case. Many droughts are caused by inadequate storage of available water to meet seasonal needs. Thus, drought in the city in part reflects inadequacies in water supply planning. Problems of municipal water supply have already been addressed in Chapter 5, particularly in terms of fluctuations in water demand, fluctuations in natural water supply, and the storage-yield relationship. In this chapter, urban water supplies and associated drought risks are viewed from the perspective of the water supply planner.

Alternative water management plans can be illustrated by four cities in Massachusetts (Fitchburg, Fall River, Worcester, and Pittsfield; see Figure 7.5). In the face of variable rainfall and in response to actual and anticipated demands for water, the planner seeks out and examines available, alternate sources of supply. In the genesis of water supply systems, these alternatives may be limited by the myopic vision of the planners, and, in existing systems, further constraints are implied by past decisions. Nevertheless, there is almost always a choice of size and timing of development and also of source (for example, groundwater or surface water; location, size, and quality of stream). Almost always, the question of development size and timing is one of balancing the costs of expansion against some notion of the costs of shortages to be expected in the absence of expansion.

Given these fundamental influences, then, the historical growth of a typical water system might take the following form (as illustrated by the demand and yield curves for Fitchburg in Figure 7.5A). Demand, as the product of innumerable individual decisions, varies continuously and generally upward, reflecting both a growing urban population and increases in per capita water use. In contrast, the development of reservoir systems occurs in large, discrete steps. This leads to a characteristic pattern of system growth whereby "overcapacity" is periodically introduced. Steady demand growth causes the eventual elimination of the overcapacity cushion, and this, in turn, leads sooner or later to further spurts in supply.

Now, it is reasonable to suppose that the impact of a given climatic event (for example, a period of abnormally low precipitation) will be different for systems with different relations between supply and demand. Thus, a system that has just completed a large addition to its capacity should probably be able to meet the demands of its customers better than one that has allowed demand to outrun supply. This notion is at the heart of our model of drought impact.

The basic supply capacity of a water system is a product of its

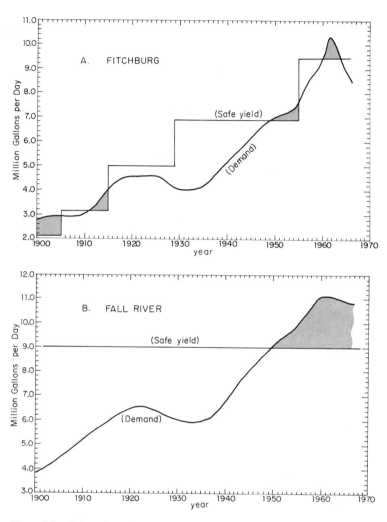

Figure 7.5. Comparison of average daily water demand with safe yield in four Massachusetts cities: (A) Fitchburg, (B) Fall River, (C) Worcester, and (D) Pittsfield. Shaded areas represent demand in excess of safe yield. Abrupt vertical changes in safe yield curves result from reservoir construction.

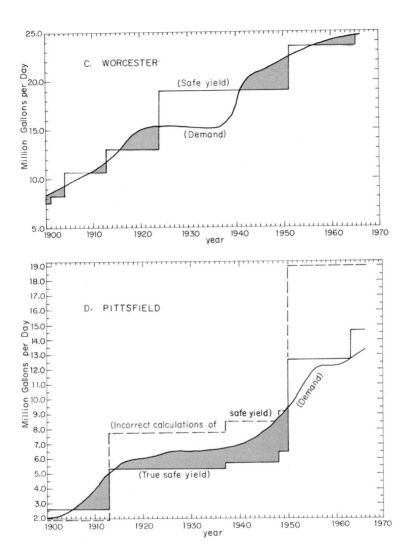

flow and storage characteristics. The term *safe yield* is generally used to refer to the supply capabilities of both groundwater and surface water sources. There is, however, nothing safe about safe yield, and for our purpose we might define its value as the flow per day of water that a system might reasonably be expected to provide 95 percent of the time. We may now measure the relative adequacy of an urban water system by the ratio of demand to safe yield. When demand/safe-yield ratio is high, the cushion of surplus capacity is low; when it is low, urban places are less vulnerable to conditions of low precipitation and low stream flow.

Distinctive strategies of water systems development have evolved for the four cities in Massachusetts (Figure 7.5). Fitchburg and Fall River show highly contrasting patterns of development. The development of water supply for Fitchburg shows a tendency to establish excess capacity on an incremental basis, thus minimizing the long-term risk of water shortage. Fitchburg even constructed a new reservoir when the demand/safe-yield ratio was less than 1.0. Fall River provides an example of the early establishment of a water supply that insured the city against the effects of water shortage for many years. Worcester and Pittsfield, Massachusetts (C and D on Figure 7.5), have displayed mixed patterns of growth. Pittsfield has had a number of reevaluations of safe yield that increased the apparent risk of shortage, but that did not result in immediate compensating additions to capacity. Worcester has added relatively often to its system, but the average size of these additions (as a percentage of the existing system size) has been relatively small.

The concept of drought hazard to a municipal water system is complex. The degree of hazard depends on perception of the hazard, physical opportunities, potential economics of scale, availability of emergency supplies, status of the urban treasury, the influence of decision-makers, and willingness to risk shortage.

Winter Storms
The winter storm is a natural hazard particularly disruptive to urban life. Cities, which are dependent on fast transportation and communication, can be crippled by a heavy snowfall or glaze ice accumulation. Spatial interaction within the city and with its tributary areas may be curtailed or stopped; emergencies may arise as supplies and distribution lines are cut (Rooney 1967, pp. 539–540). Heavy financial

losses may also accrue — both from lost or reduced economic activities and from the direct costs of combatting the hazard.

Cities respond to winter storms in different ways, and there is a high variability of investment in equipment and labor for snow removal. Places with much snowfall, such as Montreal, are geared to continuing snow removal throughout the winter; a two-inch snowfall is routinely cleared and life goes on "as usual." The same amount of snow may bring activities in San Francisco or Washington, D.C., to a halt. Similarly, adjustments to low temperature stress vary from region to region. In Tallahassee or Mobile, for example, most homes and buildings have inadequate heating plants and insulation to protect against near-freezing and lower temperatures. In contrast, Detroit and Chicago are prepared for low temperatures and residents regard cold periods as commonplace.

The pattern of urban adjustment to snow hazard is similar to that for floods. Cities with the highest probability of snowfall are generally best equipped to handle it. However, the worst disruptions often occur in the places that presumably are best prepared (Rooney 1967). One explanation is as follows: Snowfall usually is anticipated and cities annually allocate funds for its removal. Unfortunately, the question of magnitude and frequency is often overlooked and advance funding is based on so-called climatic norms. When snowfall exceeds these norms, no money is left to operate equipment. Detroit, Michigan, for example, found that it had exhausted its purchased salt supplies* and most of its labor appropriations by February 1970. Reliance on mean snowfall statistics had led to fixed and insufficient funding in a year of above-average snowfall. As a result, residential streets remained packed with snow and ice until natural thawing removed the hazard. Meanwhile, indirect costs to private and public sectors of the economy exceeded the amount that proper treatment would have cost.

GEOLOGIC AND GEOMORPHIC HAZARDS

Geologic and geomorphic hazards in the city have been discussed in Chapter 2 (earthquakes and subsidence), Chapter 5 (sedimen-

*Ironically, Detroit is situated directly over one of the largest salt mines in North America.

tation), and Chapter 6 (slope instability and erosion). Some less common hazards that depend upon regional location and specific site characteristics are volcanic eruptions, avalanches, and the breaching or collapse of natural lake impoundments. It is not the purpose of this section to discuss these hazards further on an individual basis; instead specific hazard events in cities are presented as case examples of hazard perception and adaptation.

Earthquakes are an excellent case in point. They occur suddenly and, for all practical purposes, without warning. Earthquakes also are responsible for some of the worst devastation wrought on cities and their populations. Although there has been considerable progress in the development of earthquake warning systems, there is little likelihood that a workable prediction method will be devised in the near future. Thus, although people generally know if they live in earthquake-prone zones, structural adaptations to mitigate earthquake effects, rather than evacuation, remain the normal precautionary response.

Over 150,000 earthquakes occur annually throughout the world. Most of these are small tremors imperceptible to humans, but about one earthquake a year (on the average) is of sufficient magnitude to cause serious destruction in cities. The number of people affected is related to how important man considers an individual earthquake to be. In 1958 one of the major earthquakes of the twentieth century occurred in Alaska. Because the epicenter and major repercussions were located in a practically unpopulated area, little notice was taken of the event — except by seismologists and other earth scientists. In contrast the 1964 Alaska earthquake, which struck with great force in the Anchorage area and other settled parts of the state (killing 115 people), was the focus of worldwide attention. Tsunamis (tidal waves) generated by the seismic shock caused major destruction or loss of life, or both, in Valdez, Kodiak, and Seward, Alaska, as well as in such distant points as Hilo, Hawaii, and Crescent City, California. Destruction of buildings, primarily due to collapse and movement of unstable soils and mantle, caused over $290 million damage in Anchorage alone (Rogers 1970).

Although Anchorage residents had long been aware that they lived in an earthquake zone, they took few precautions before 1964. Homes, schools, hospitals, and parts of the downtown business district were constructed on unstable earth materials — despite the fact that the U.S. Geological Survey had published information about the sliding

potential of these areas (Kates 1970, p. 17). Once a destructive earthquake has occurred, it might be expected that careful attention would
be given to the location and design of future buildings. This was indeed
the case — at first. Three categories of danger areas were scientifically
identified: high risk, nominal risk, and provisional nominal risk. What
followed tells us something about the rapid changes in individual
and societal attitudes that may occur once a disaster has passed:

> The area initially classified as high-risk was gradually reduced, strictly
> on scientific grounds. However, a major concession in the high risk area was the de-
> cision to provide funds to restore buildings but not to construct new ones. Other
> concessions have followed, leading to a major policy change in February, 1967,
> when FHA [the Federal Housing Administration] removed its restrictions on
> mortgage insurance in the two major risk areas, requiring only the promise that
> mortgage lenders make clear to prospective buyers the nature of the risk and their
> financial responsibility in case of earthquake recurrence. Local zoning of risk
> areas has not taken place. On the contrary, building permits have been issued for
> about $6 million worth of new construction in and adjacent to the L-K-Street-slide
> area. (Kates 1970, p. 26)

Thus the attitude of many individuals in Anchorage became: "We've
had our earthquake; there won't be another in our lifetime." Apparently the institutions created to protect the populace also were
swept along in the wave of new optimism or could not resist political
and economic pressures.

Ideally, recent experience with a hazard should improve perception and lead to better adaptation. This is illustrated by differing
responses to tsunami warnings issued in Crescent City, California, and
Hilo, Hawaii, at the time of the 1964 Alaska earthquake. Previous to
that date Hilo had experienced a tsunami generated by the May 23,
1960, Chilean earthquake, which killed 61 people and injured 282. This
disaster has been attributed to failure to heed warning sirens, the in-
explicable reluctance of some persons to leave the danger area, and the
belief of some persons that they were in a safe zone (Lachman and
others 1961). A carefully designed alert system was subsequently
established. It defined clear lines of responsibility and action for public
officials, disaster workers, and the public. Thus, when the 1964 tsunami
alert was sounded, Hilo residents evacuated danger areas in a safe and
orderly manner; no deaths resulted.

In Crescent City, the first alert — estimating the midnight arrival
of a tsunami — was received at 11:08 P.M. Door-to-door warning of
residents in dangerous areas did not begin until a second alert was re-

ceived at 11:50 P.M. and was still in progress when the first wave hit (Anderson 1970, p. 119). At least 11 lives were lost and 29 city blocks suffered damage. Less than a year later, Crescent City was issued another nighttime tsunami alert. Because of lessons learned in 1964 and because officials were sensitive to disaster cues, low-lying areas were quickly evacuated and much property was saved. Thus, as in the case of tornadoes, the effectiveness of a warning system depends on a combination of factors: efficiency and organization of the alert system, action of public officials, and public perception of and response to the hazard.

IS NATURAL HAZARD INCREASING IN THE CITY?

What are the trends of risk from nature in urban areas of North America? In absolute terms, damage and the cost of adjustment have increased as a function of the increase and concentration in wealth and population accompanying urbanization (Dacy and Kureuther 1969). At the same time, corresponding increases in deaths have not occurred; indeed deaths have decreased both in absolute and in per capita terms. For many hazards, the number of damage-causing events (some not recorded) may have diminished with the population's increased capacity for adjustment. But the potential for catastrophic events (in terms of impact on man and his cities) has clearly increased. Extrapolating the impact of an earthquake of the same magnitude and low per capita death and damage ratio as the Alaska earthquake of 1964 to California would forecast a super disaster of 2,000 dead and $6 billion damage. Calculations for an intense hurricane stalled over New Orleans provide a similar estimate of death and damage.

The potential for serious but noncatastrophic damage is even more clearly on the increase. This was demonstrated for floods by Roland Holmes (1961), who suggested that urbanization of previously unoccupied flood plains causes increased risk. Other hazardous effects of urban growth — brush fires, floods, earthslides, and land slips — have been identified for Los Angeles (Van Arsdol and others 1967). All are characteristic of the fast-growing areas of southern California.

Finally there are urban environmental hazards that are quasi-natural in origin. Principal among these are man-made pollutants,

conveyed or concentrated by natural processes of air and water, discussed in Chapters 3, 4, and 5. In most urban parts of the country,
their presence is clearly increasing, although there are some notable
exceptions.

It is difficult to obtain time series data of any sort. It is especially difficult to obtain adequate time series of damage data (clearly
our recording and perception of damage improves in time) and costs of
adjustment (we are still trying to define these costs for most hazards).
Yet it appears worthwhile to draw up a tentative balance sheet at
present — to estimate both the current death and damage rates from
different natural hazards and the public and private costs of adjustment
to them. These data then can be contrasted with quasi-natural and
man-made hazards. We know that deaths have decreased and damage increased from natural hazards. Although we do not know, we do suspect
that per capita damage rates (discounted for growth in wealth and
total social costs) have moved upwards in toto — especially if one considers the long-term increase in catastrophic potential, the new sources
of hazards, and the rising costs per unit of adjustment for certain
hazards.

SOME RECOMMENDED ACTIONS

In light of the continued increase in population and urbanization, what strategies can man implement to mitigate the expected losses
from natural hazards? One course is to develop a greater thrust by
the federal government. This is not novel. Already, examples can be
found in federal policy regarding water quality standards and the
National Flood Insurance Act of 1968. If the federal government would
initiate guidelines and regulations concerning the type of human occu-
pance and human response necessary in hazard zones, then a further
decrease in deaths and property damage might be expected. The initial
effect of governmental regulations should be to reduce the great variation that now exists in human adjustment to specific natural hazards.
As in the formulation and development of water quality standards, the
federal government could call upon each state to formulate specific
regulations that a given federal agency, such as the Office of Emergency
Preparedness, could then evaluate and either approve or return for

modification. In the event of a disaster, federal assistance could be with-held from those states, local governments, and individuals who did not comply. In fact, one proposal for a suggested national disaster insurance program requires participants to purchase insurance within one year if they wish to be eligible for federal disaster assistance.

Let us now be more specific by providing examples related to floods, tornadoes, and drought. As mentioned previously, the National Flood Insurance Act was passed in 1968. In addition to provisions for flood loss compensation, the act includes plans to control future occu-pance of flood plains so that there will be a reduction in flood damage potential. Similarly, local governments and states could be required to enact specific zoning ordinances near the flood plains, to formulate emergency plans, and to require individuals to adopt specific flood-proofing measures. The effect would be a decrease in the damage poten-tial, which since 1936 has continued to increase.

A few strategies can reduce the magnitude of tornado-caused damage. If tornado shelters were required for new home construction in hazardous areas, a further reduction in loss of life could be expected. Communities could be required to develop preparedness and emergency plans, which are either absent or woefully inadequate in most com-munities today. For example, installation of sirens *throughout* the area of cities or alarms installed in television or radio sets could reduce loss of life — especially for tornadoes that occur at night. Moreover, if residents would merely open their windows, damage on the periphery of a tornado path might be significantly lessened. And it could be required that all new housing be constructed according to minimum standards of safety, decency, and sanitation, as prescribed by the Secretary of Housing and Urban Development, and in conformity with applicable building codes and zoning regulations. Finally, public school curricula could easily include a program on the human implications of the tornado storm. Again, disaster assistance could be withheld from those communities that did not develop and implement approved tornado preparedness plans.

Concerning municipal water supply, the focus should be not solely on the effects of drought, but also on efficiency in the provision of the municipal water supply. Assistance could be granted only to those communities that maintained a specified water-use/safe-yield ratio and a demonstrated efficiency in the provision and distribution of water. Concerning distribution, for example, only specified low levels of unmetered (and hence unpaid-for or wasted) water would be tolerated, a frequently monitored metering system would be maintained, and price mechanisms would be changed to reduce peak demands. With respect to the source of supply, communities could be directed to seek and select the least-cost alternative in the provision of a specified safe yield, and if they did not comply, they could be deprived of federal assistance to the amount of the chosen, more costly, alternative.

These suggested remedies are partial and somewhat speculative, but unless federal and state governments act, losses from natural hazards in our ever growing urban areas will continue to set new records.

REFERENCES

Anderson, W. A. 1970. Tsunami warning in Crescent City, California, and Hilo, Hawaii. In *The great Alaska earthquake of 1964: Human ecology,* pp. 116-124. Washington, D.C.: National Academy of Sciences.

Bates, F. C. 1962. Severe local storm forecasts and warnings and the general public. *Bull. Amer. Meteor. Soc.* 43:288-291.

Baumann, Duane, and Cliff Russell. 1970. *Social and economic implications of the urban snow hazard.* Washington, D.C.: U.S. Office of Water Resources Research Report no. 37.

Baumann, Duane, and John Sims. 1972. The tornado threat: Coping styles in the North and South. *Science* (in press).

Burton, Ian, and Robert Kates. 1964. The perception of natural hazards in resource management. *Natural Resources Jour.* 3(3):412-441.

Dacy, D. C., and Howard Kureuther. 1969. *The economics of natural disaster.* New York: Free Press.

Flora, S. D. 1954. *Tornadoes of the United States.* Norman, Okla.: Univ. of Oklahoma Press.

Hewitt, Kenneth, and Ian Burton. 1971. *The hazardousnous of a place: A regional ecology of damaging events.* Toronto: Univ. of Toronto, Dept. of Geography Research Publ. no. 6.

Holmes, Roland, 1961. Composition of flood losses. In *Papers on flood problems,* ed. G. F. White, pp. 7-21. Chicago: Univ. of Chicago, Dept. of Geography Research Paper no. 70.

Kates, Robert. 1970. Human adjustment to earthquake hazard. In *The great Alaska earthquake of 1964: Human ecology,* pp. 7-31. Washington, D.C.: National Academy of Sciences.

Lachman, Roy, Maurice Tatsuoka, and William Bonk. 1961. Human behavior during the tsunami of May, 1960. *Science* 133(3462):1405-1409.

Linehan, R. J. 1957. *Tornado deaths in the United States.* Washington, D.C.: U.S. Weather Bureau, Tech. Paper no. 30.

Rogers, George. 1970. Economic effects of the earthquake. In *The great Alaska earthquake of 1964: Human ecology,* pp. 58–76. Washington, D.C.: National Academy of Sciences.

Rooney, John F., Jr. 1967. The urban snow hazard in the United States: An appraisal of disruption. *Geogr. Rev.* 57(4):538–559.

Russell, Clifford, Robert Kates, and David Arey. 1970. *Drought and water supply: Implications of the Massachusetts experience of municipal planning.* Baltimore: Johns Hopkins Press.

Sadowski, Alexander. 1965. *Potential casualties from tornadoes.* Washington, D.C.: U.S. Weather Bureau (National Weather Service).

Van Arsdol, M. D., F. Alexander, and G. Sabagh. 1967. *Human ecology and the metropolitan environment: Environmental hazards in Los Angeles.* Final Report, U.S. Public Health Service Contract PM 86–62–163.

Wolman, M. G. and J. P. Miller. 1960. Magnitude and frequency of forces in geomorphic processes. *Jour. of Geology* 68(1):54–74.

CHAPTER 8

Noise and the Urban Environment

Gordon M. Stevenson, Jr.

From the days of the earliest cities, noise has been an invisible but integral part of the urban environment. In ancient Rome the poet Horace complained of the noise made by heavy wagons on cobblestone roads, and Caesar barred chariots from certain parts of the city at various times of the day and night. In later centuries Marcel Proust built cork panels into his study to keep out the noise of the Paris streets, and Francis Scott Key threatened lawsuits to halt the nightly barge traffic past his home in Washington, D.C.

Ever since the Industrial Revolution began, but especially in the last 50 years, the accelerating growth of technology and population has been accompanied by a steady escalation in urban noise levels. Recognition of the scope and significance of this phenomenon has thus far been much slower than the growth of the noise itself.

The purposes of this chapter are to discuss the physical nature of noise; to examine its varied sources and distribution in the urban context; to explore the effects and costs of such noise; and to note some of the social, political, and legal problems facing those who are concerned with noise.

THE NATURE OF NOISE

Noise has been defined by the American National Standards Institute as: (1) any undesired sound and (2) an erratic, intermittent, or statistically random oscillation. There are three facets to the phenomenon of sound: the *source*, an object or material that is vibrating; the *transmission* of the vibration (usually through air but also through solids and liquids); and the *effect*, that is, the perception of the vibration, which includes both the "hearing" of it and other physiological and emotional reactions to it.

One of the best descriptions of the sound-production process is that given by Theodore Berland:

As the sound source vibrates — be it violin string, tuning fork, loudspeaker, auto muffler, or whatever — it pushes against the air, then returns to its original position. Then it pushes again, and returns, and so forth, until it is spent or is turned off. This vibration produces alternating dense and sparse bands of air. The result is cordon after cordon of dense air spreading outward from the sound source, much as ripples do on water after you throw in a pebble . . . It is important to understand that it isn't the air that moves in waves; it's the *sound* that moves in waves through the air. (1970, pp. 4-5)

Noise — any unwanted sound — can be measured at the sound source, at whatever point it is heard, or at any point in between those two. Noise has two major dimensions: pitch (that is, frequency) and amplitude (that is, intensity). *Pitch* is determined by how rapidly the sound source vibrates. It is measured by the number of sound waves passing a given point in one second. For example, if a tuning fork vibrated 500 times per second, then the pitch or frequency would be 500 cycles per second (cps), or, more commonly, 500 Hertz (Hz; in honor of the German scientist H. R. Hertz). The average young adult can hear sounds with frequencies from approximately 20 to 20,000 Hz. For reference, the lowest and highest notes on a piano keyboard have pitches of 20 Hz and 4,000 Hz, respectively.

In contrast to pitch (or frequency), *amplitude* (or intensity) reflects the depth or height of sound waves above and below a median line. It generally is measured in terms of *decibels* (dB), on a decimal scale that was named in honor of Alexander Graham Bell. The decibel scale spans the amazingly wide range of sound pressures that the human ear can detect. Thus, 0 dB represents the threshold of detectable sound for normal young ears (0.0002 microbars of pressure), and 1 dB represents the smallest change in sound pressure, or intensity, detect-

Table 8.1. Typical overall sound levels. Measurement in parentheses indicate distance from the sound source. (After Committee on Environmental Quality 1968.)

Noise Source	Decibels	Noise Source
	140	(Threshold of pain)
Hydraulic press (3')	130	
Large pneumatic riveter (4')		
Pneumatic chipper (5')		Boiler shop (maximum level)
	120	
Overhead jet aircraft–4 engine (500')		
Unmuffled motorcycle		Jet engine test control room
	110	Construction noise (compressors
Chipping hammer (3')		and hammers) (10')
Annealing furnace (4')		Woodworking shop
		Loud power mower
Rock and roll band	100	
Subway train (20')		
Heavy trucks (20')		Inside subway car
Train whistles (500')		Food blender
	90	
10-HP outboard (50')		Inside sedan in city traffic
Small trucks accelerating (30')		
		Heavy traffic (25' to 50')
	80	Office with tabulating machines
Light trucks in city (20')		
Autos (20')		
	70	
Dishwashers		Average traffic (100')
		Accounting office
Conversational speech (3')		
	60	
	50	Private business office
		Light traffic (100')
		Average residence
	40	
	30	
		Broadcasting studio (music)
Whispering	20	
Breathing	10	
(0.0002 microbars)	0	

Table 8.2. Decibels related to sound intensity

Decibels	Units of Intensity
150	1,000,000,000,000,000
100	10,000,000,000
50	100,000
40	10,000
30	1,000
20	100
10	10
1	1

able by the same ears. Table 8.1 provides a comparison of decibel levels for various common noise sources in the modern urban environment.

One important characteristic of the decibel scale is that it is a logarithmic rather than a linear scale. Thus, for example, while 10 dB represents an intensity level approximately 10 times greater than 1 dB, 20 dB produces an intensity level of about 10 times (rather than 2 times) greater than 10 dB. Table 8.2 illustrates this logarithmic relationship of decibel to intensity. One consequence of the logarithmic relationship between decibels and intensity is that a small increase in the decibel level of a noise may represent a significant increase in subjective annoyance. Both annoyance and other effects of noise in fact depend on many variables, including the duration, pattern, and pitch of the noise, the distance of the noise source from the individual, the time of day or night that it occurs, and the individual characteristics of the person affected. Nevertheless, the intensity or decibel level of the noise remains one of the key variables, and often the most critical one, in terms of its human impact.

Starting from the basic decibel scale, a great variety of other scales have been developed for accurately evaluating the quality of human response to noise. Sound level meters, for example, measure decibel levels on either the flat, C-scale network, dB(C), which Table 8.1 is based upon, or the weighted, A-scale network, dB(A). The latter scale was developed after it was discovered that the human ear generally is less sensitive to lower than to higher frequencies of sound. On the A-scale about 40 decibels are filtered out of the measurement at lower frequencies, and thus a noise source with considerable energy in those frequencies will have a lower dB(A) reading than dB(C) reading.

Another important variation, developed to reflect human response to aircraft noise more accurately, is the *perceived noise decibel* (PNdB), which is discussed below in connection with aviation noise.

THE SOURCES AND DISTRIBUTION OF NOISE

One useful dichotomy of noise sources is between those produced indoors and those produced outdoors. This chapter focuses on the latter because they tend to be more noticeable and annoying to the city dweller (both outside and inside his dwelling), but it is important to realize that indoor noises are also a significant and troublesome facet of the urban environment.

As an overview, there are three major sets of sources for noises generated indoors, and five for noises generated outdoors. Indoor noises originate in: (1) the apartment and house, (2) the office and factory, and (3) the discotheque and other places of amusement. Specific sources in the apartment and house are both human and mechanical; they include loud voices and heavy footsteps, radio, television, and stereo equipment, plumbing and air conditioners, and noisy appliances such as vacuum cleaners, disposals, washing machines, and food blenders. For reasons of economy, the great majority of both apartments and houses have been designed and built with comparatively little attention to acoustical considerations. As a result, noises often are carried with relatively little muffling or structural softening into the neighbors' dwellings.

Industry and the discotheque are special cases. In both situations the individual is drawn directly to the noisy site for particular personal reasons, so that there is usually no invasion of privacy problem comparable to that which can occur in the residential context. Also, in both cases the intensity of the noise is often quite high, frequently falling in the 80–110 dB range, which can cause both temporary and permanent hearing loss. These and other extended effects are set forth in the section on effects.

Outdoor sources of urban noise fall into five broad categories, of which *transportation* of all forms is the most serious. The others include *construction* work of all types, *industrial operations*, the *individual human being* (including such activities as shouting and loud playing of transistor radios), and various *miscellaneous* noises, such as the clanging of metal garbage cans and lids on the street at all hours and the air-conditioning machines attached to the windows of apartment and office buildings.

Before analyzing these sources, it should be pointed out that European and some other countries run far ahead of the United States in measuring and controlling urban noise. Thus, much of the material referred to here stems from European investigations. One reason for the disparity in research is because European countries tend to be more densely populated, the effects of noise were more obvious and were recognized more quickly in Europe than in North America. Although the situation is now changing, in the United States, for instance, there is still less awareness of noise as a problem, less research into its effects, and less committment to enforcing the few existing regulations. There is no organization in the United States at any level of government whose overall study of noise can compare with that of the Greater London Council. As R. A. Baron has noted:

> This *local* government lab has researched the acoustic profile of tall buildings, the noise contour of urban motorways, techniques for shielding residential sites from roadways, techniques for soundproofing windows and providing sound-trapped ventilation, scales for evaluating the relationship between different types of windows and aircraft noise intrusion . . . Also investigated was the effect of traffic vibration on historic buildings . . .
>
> Where can the American public go for similar information? The only way we can learn about the impact of traffic noise and vibration and construction blasting is when it cracks a water main and floods the neighborhood. (1970, pp. 198–199)

Community Noise Surveys

Despite the recent American lag in noise research, some of the earliest community noise surveys were done in the United States. They were precipitated in the 1920's largely by increases in the volume of motorized transportation in urban areas and by advances in the technology of measuring noise. These surveys were designed to determine (1) the sources and noise levels that were most responsible for complaints, (2) the ambient (or background) noise levels in certain areas, and (3) practical bases for proposed zoning regulations and control ordinances. E. E. Free, Science Editor of *Forum* magazine, made the first significant audiometer surveys of New York City street noises in 1925 and extended his measurements to skyscraper offices in 1928. The later survey demonstrated that noise from Manhattan's canyon-like streets tended to reverberate up to the twelfth floor with only slight diminution. Noise gradually decreased from that point upward to about the twentieth or twenty-fifth floor.

Spurred by mounting complaints, in 1929–30 the city of New York itself undertook the first comprehensive citywide noise survey. (For a concise review of that landmark effort, plus the next 25 years of outdoor noise surveys, see Hardy 1955.) In addition to its measurements, the New York City study classified the key sources of noise, in terms of complaints, as follows:

1. Private motor traffic	36 percent
2. Public transportation (including trains, elevated railways)	16
3. Radios	12
4. Collection and deliveries (including garbage pickup)	9
5. Whistles and bells	8
6. Construction activity	7.5
7. Vocal (individuals; groups)	7
8. Miscellaneous	4.5

For comparison, a New York City newspaper poll in 1956 resulted in the following ratings of irritating urban noises (Still 1970, p. 79):

1. Refuse trucks and clanging garbage cans
2. Automobile horn-blowing
3. Truck and bus acceleration
4. Loud radio and television sets
5. Aircraft noise
6. Unmuffled motor exhaust
7. Street repairs
8. Sound trucks
9. Riveting and other construction work

Important community noise surveys have been conducted in Chicago, in Düsseldorf and Dortmund, Germany, in London, and in Tokyo. Chicago's two-year survey from 1947 to 1949 involved different types of intracity areas, seasonal conditions, and hours of the day, and it was apparently the first such survey to measure octave-band sound-pressure levels. In the 1950's a German acoustics laboratory mapped noise in the Düsseldorf area from the standpoint of social hygiene, and a decade later a comprehensive noise map was drawn for Dortmund, with measurements made at 1,449 points in industrial zones and along important streets. A comprehensive survey of more than

36 square miles of Central London in the early 1960's automatically made tape recordings once each hour throughout the day and night at 540 different points. This study showed that at 84 percent of the points road traffic noise predominated, at 7 percent industrial noise was the most significant, and at 4 percent construction operations were predominant.

The Tokyo study, conducted in 1965 and 1966, analyzed noise in residential, suburban, commercial, light industrial, and heavy industrial zones. Seventeen typical areas, each of about two dozen acres, were chosen in each type of zone, and at 20 different points in each of the areas noises were measured on the dB(A) scale. Measurements were made at various definite intervals throughout the day and night. Figure 8.1 shows typical noise levels in a commercial zone along a tramway and within a suburban zone.

Surface Traffic Noise

Turning to specific sources of noise, one finds general agreement that streets are the greatest source of exterior noise in the city. As one governmental report stated: "Traffic noise radiating from the freeways and expressways and from midtown shopping and apartment districts of our large cities probably disturbs more people than any other source of outdoor noise. Although aircraft noise is much more intense, the exposure time is substantially less than that of a round-the-clock, continuous highway noise" (Anderson 1970, p. 16). The traffic noise level in the downtown area of a modern city generally exceeds 70 dB, except during the very early morning hours. A recent survey of traffic noise made outside the sixteenth- and seventeenth-floor windows of three New York City hotels revealed noise levels up to 100 dB in the 4,800 to 10,000 Hz bands (Still 1970, p. 64).

The nature of traffic noise depends mainly upon the type, quantity, and speed of the vehicles involved, plus the quality of the road surface and the tires on the vehicles. Trailer trucks produce the most intense and varied noises. Figure 8.2 shows the various sources of truck noise. Trucks are capable of generating noise of 90 dB at freeway speeds, owing in great measure to tire noise. Off the freeway trucks commonly generate levels of 70 to 90 dB owing to inadequate or faulty muffling equipment, to general engine noise during acceleration, and to brake squeal. In fact, it is possible for a large truck with an extremely defective muffler to produce as much noise as 90 to 100 passenger

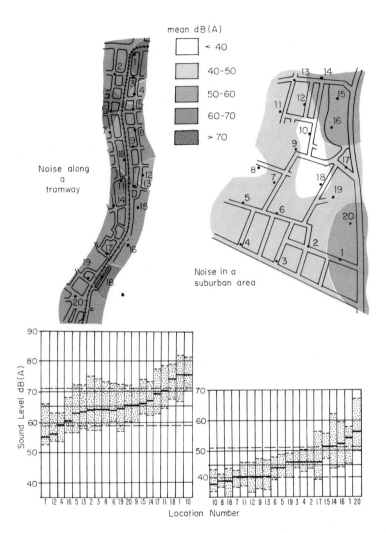

Figure 8.1. Noise levels along a tramway in a commercial district and in a suburban area in Tokyo. Points on the chart represent average dB(A) levels at corresponding points on the map. Vertical lines show range of dB(A) over 24-hour period. (After Mochizuki and Imaizumi 1967.)

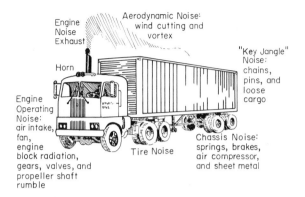

Figure 8.2. Sources of truck noise. (After Goodfriend 1968.)

cars traveling simultaneously. Thirty-nine percent of all truck mileage in the United States is on urban streets (H. Close, in Dickerson 1970, p. 48). Figure 8.3 shows the volume of truck traffic on a crosstown mid-Manhattan street and suggests why such traffic is the most *pervasive* source of noise in most cities.

Following closely behind trucks in terms of noise annoyance are buses (particularly when starting and stopping), motorcycles, sports cars, and other passenger cars. The most disturbing components of these vehicles are their exhaust and horn noises. In addition, significant noises are also produced by the engine itself, by the gears during acceleration, by the tires (especially at higher speeds), by the brakes, and by the slamming of doors. Motorcycle and motorbike noise, which is more prevalent in Europe than in the United States, is usually caused by direct exposure of engine cylinders without adequate mufflers, caused in turn by customer preference for the louder machines. In the United States the number of motorcycles is increasing rapidly. For example, the number of motorcycles licensed in Chicago increased from 5,500 in 1965 to 9,400 in 1966 to 12,500 in 1968 (Berland 1970, p. 162). Highway traffic in general also is increasing rapidly. Figures 8.4 and 8.5 show the present magnitude of freeway traffic in the greater Los Angeles area and its expected growth within the next two decades.

Despite the considerable research that has been done into the generation of noise by motor vehicles, city planners and highway planners did almost nothing prior to the 1970's to control the growth of highway and street noise: "There have been very few occasions in which knowledge of projectable highway noise has been used as a factor in planning highway locations, giving due regard for the environ-

Figure 8.3. Truck traffic on a crosstown street in midtown Manhattan, New York City. (Department of Water Resources photograph by Vincent J. Lopez.)

Figure 8.4. 1970 freeway traffic volume in the Los Angeles area. (After Branch 1970.)

mental values of the communities through which the highways must pass" (McGrath 1968, pp. 352–353). A prime example of locating urban residences near a serious highway noise impact is the massive set of apartment units built in New York City at the eastern end of the George Washington Bridge and directly above the heavily traveled Cross Bronx Expressway. The hazards of both noise and exhaust fumes were never adequately recognized at the planning stage. Increasing population density, housing needs, and scarcity of urban land will continue to produce similar situations. Thus it is important both to design such structures carefully, with appropriate insulation, and to give prospective tenants fair warning of the probable noise levels to which they will be exposed.

Figure 8.5. Estimated 1990 freeway traffic volume in Los Angeles area. (After Branch 1970.)

The United States government did not begin seriously to consider the factor of potential noise radiation in the location and construction of federally supported highways until 1967. One factor contributing to the recognition of noise as a significant factor in highway planning was the controversy throughout the 1960's over the proposed stretch of interstate highway to run along the New Orleans riverfront past the French Quarter's historic Jackson Square. Local opposition to the proposed location of the highway sparked studies (funded by the Department of Housing and Urban Development) of the potential noise and other environmental effects of using that location, which already had a high ambient noise level due to surface traffic. The noise study led to tape recordings of local traffic noise at seven locations in the area and at four daily times. Projections of probable noise levels (if the elevated road were built as first proposed) indicated that uncomfortably high levels of speech would be needed to communicate in the historic area. The study persuaded planners to give serious additional consideration to alternate designs for the roadway, including depressed alignments.

Though the above episode is encouraging, efforts at all levels of government to control surface transportation noise during the 1960's were "insignificant in terms of the scope, magnitude and severity of the existing problem" (Committee on Environmental Quality 1968, p. 18). Significant alleviation will only come through (1) improvements in vehicle equipment and regulations to enforce their use and maintenance (plus pressure and desire to enforce those regulations); (2) restrictions on truck and other traffic *in* certain locations, and *to* certain hours of the day; (3) improvements in the location and design of dwelling units; and (4) giving greater consideration to noise radiation in highway design. Improved highway design involves overall highway location, the construction of various protective barriers, and, in some cases, the lowering of the highway surface below ground level. Figure 8.6 indicates how various types of highway design can attenuate traffic noise nearby; the elevated designs are less effective than the illustrated alternatives at distances of several hundred feet.

Aviation Traffic Noise

Aircraft noise emerged as a serious community problem in the late 1940's and early 1950's with the increasing use of jet aircraft by the *military* and the increasing volume of *commercial* air traffic. The direct intrusion of the noise itself, as well as the indirect effect of decreasing residential property values near airports, stimulated public concern. Both factors continue to be important

The problem of aviation noise worsened and increased in complexity with the advent of commercial jet service (during 1958–1960). As the volume of that service has expanded, jet noise has become a serious problem in many areas and an acute one in some, such as Los Angeles and New York. Figure 8.7 provides a comparison of various aviation noises with surface traffic noises in terms of perceived noise decibels (PNdB) and indicates that *jet* noise is significantly louder to the human ear than the noise of *propeller* aircraft (and both are louder than surface traffic sources).

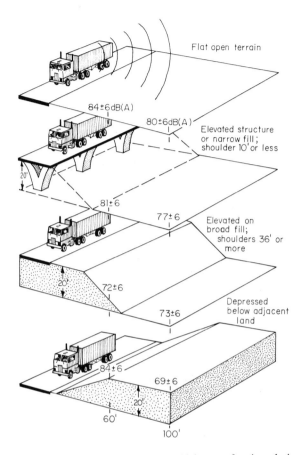

Figure 8.6. Noise attenuation near highways of various design. Data for diesel truck noise, 5–6 feet above ground level. (After Beaton and Bourget 1968.)

The concept of PNdB is the one most commonly used in discussing aircraft noise today. It was developed in the 1950's as an aid in accurately assessing the degree of annoyance caused by aviation noise. The PNdB scale is more high-frequency weighted than the dB(A) scale, because the higher-frequency noise components of jet noise were found to be more irritating to the human ear than are lower-frequency noises. Any jet-noise PNdB level would be about thirteen units higher than the corresponding dB(A) measurement.

Aside from their increased power thrust at takeoff, the main

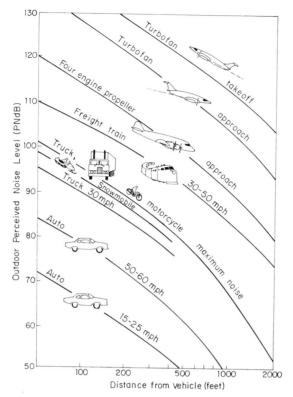

Figure 8.7. Typical transportation noise levels. (After Dickerson 1970.)

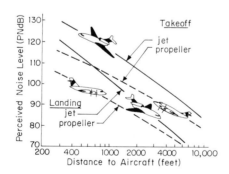

Figure 8.8. Comparison of perceived noise made by jet and by propeller aircraft on take-off and landing. (From Federal Aviation Administration, 1963.)

reason for jets being more irritating than earlier aircraft is their increased noisiness when approaching the airport. They do not "glide in" quite as simply as propeller craft do. They are really "flown down," faster and at a shallower angle. As a result, when jets are at the same horizontal distance from the end of the runway as propeller aircraft are, they usually are closer to the ground. Then, upon landing, jets emit a high-pitched compressor whine that is very loud. Figure 8.8 contrasts the differences in perceived noise on landings and takeoffs of both types of planes. Near the largest airports it is common for families to be exposed to a landing (or to a takeoff, depending on the wind pattern) every 90 seconds for several hours during peak traffic periods.

Spreading Impact of Aviation Noise

Aviation noise is an increasingly serious problem both because aviation volume is rapidly developing and because population density around airports has been steadily increasing. In 1967 Louisiana Representative Hale Boggs provided Congress with the following dramatic example of urbanization in an airport area:

When the site for this airport was chosen in 1943, it was in an area that was really almost rural — it was some 15 to 20 miles from the center of New Orleans and the City of Kenner, and the surrounding area at that time was not developed by residential or business construction to any extent.

Needless to say, the noise of aircraft of that day had little adverse effect on the sparsely populated surrounding community. But then coincidentally with the introduction of jet aircraft in 1960, a tremendous expansion of population growth took place in Kenner and the surrounding area of East Jefferson Parish. Today New Orleans International Airport is surrounded on three sides by thickly populated, well-developed residential and business community . . .

With the larger jet aircraft being built and employed to handle the ever-growing passenger traffic, there are no hours in the day when the citizens of nearby communities such as Kenner in my district may find relief from the noise. (*Congressional Record*, November 15, 1967)

Figure 8.9 provides graphic evidence of the pattern and intensity of residential growth in the Howard Beach area of New York, just west of J. F. Kennedy International Airport. For numerous reasons similar patterns of growth have occurred, and are still occurring, around most of the world's major airports. Improved land-use controls are only of marginal utility with regard to the many areas that are already densely developed, but they should be invoked where sparse settlement surrounds present airports and developing future airports.

1955

1962

1969

Figure 8.9. Residential growth pattern in the Howard Beach area, just west of J. F. Kennedy International Airport, New York, 1955–1969. (Courtesy of R. Dixon Speas Associates and Lockwood, Kessler, and Bartlett, Inc.)

There are, however, many difficulties with implementing land-use controls near airports. Aviation noise is a metropolitan as well as an urban phenomenon, geographically cutting across many political jurisdictions, each of which jealously guards its right to zone its own land. At the same time, every individual reacts to jet noise differently, so that it has been thought to be extremely difficult to set precise noise limits for zoning purposes. In the 1960's the Federal Aviation Administration (FAA), with the aid of the Department of Housing and Urban Development and various consultants, began to make serious and sophisticated efforts to map out present and projected noise levels in various urban areas, and to relate past complaints to potential noise levels in the future. The underlying pattern for these maps is seen in Figure 8.10, showing the various areas affected by aircraft noise near Chicago's O'Hare Airport. These projections are based upon the concept of the *noise exposure forecast* (NEF), which involves a detailed correlation of projected traffic growth, types of aircraft involved (because different jets have different noise configurations), and frequency and pattern of operations throughout each 24-hour day. Thus, in the smaller zone in Figure 8.10 the calculated NEF in 1970 was estimated to be 40, whereas the larger zone experienced an estimated NEF of 30. Past complaints suggest that residents in 30 NEF areas may complain, perhaps vigorously, and concerted group protest action might be expected from those living in areas of 40 NEF (McGrath 1968, p. 350). In the Chicago case, the FAA estimated in the 1960's that traffic expansion from 1965 to 1975 would increase the 30 NEF area around O'Hare Airport from 72 to 123 square miles, increasing the affected population from 236,000 to 432,000, the affected schools from 86 to 142, and the affected hospitals from 4 to 6.

The most comprehensive technical report to date on any one area focused on Boston's Logan International Airport (Franken and Standley 1970). The noise exposure contours for 1967 and 1975 (estimated) flight operations in the Boston area are illustrated in Figures 8.11 and 8.12. Another analysis, of J.F.K. Airport in New York, determined that there the noise exposure area of 40 NEF would encompass approximately 36 square miles and over 373,000 residents by 1975. At the same time the projected 30 NEF area will cover 120 square miles with a population exceeding 1.7 million (McGrath 1968, p. 350). In 1968 the latter area already included 112 schools, 37 public parks, and a dozen hospitals.

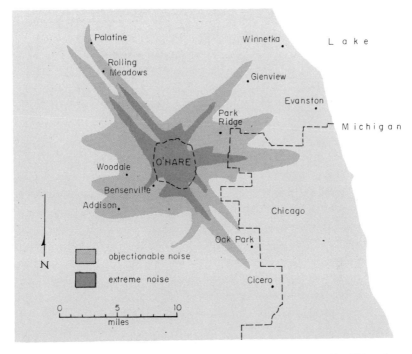

Figure 8.10. 1970 noise exposure forecast contours for areas surrounding Chicago's O'Hare International Airport. (After Mecklin 1969.)

Some Remedial Measures

Resolution of the jet noise problem will have to come about through a *combination* of (1) land-use controls; (2) research into the reduction of engine noise at the source; (3) refitting of jets with modified engines; (4) insulation of dwelling units already near flight paths; and (5) the use of greenbelts and new, heavily insulated buildings near airports as a buffer to preexisting residential units.

Also, other modes of air travel will be introduced on a significant scale in the near future, such as vertical- and short-takeoff-and-landing (V/STOL) aircraft, including helicopters, and measures must be taken to counteract the noise they will produce. Supersonic aircraft, which continuously produce a sonic boom along their paths when flying faster than the speed of sound, when they eventually operate commercially will present unique noise exposure unless they are legally prevented from flying over land areas at supersonic speeds. V/STOL vehicles

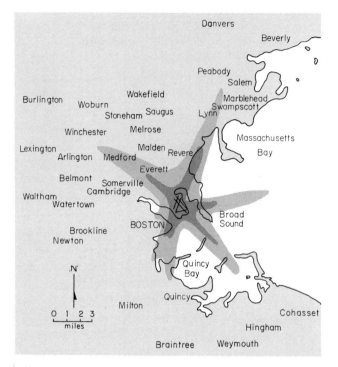

Figure 8.11. 1967 noise exposure forecast contours for areas surrounding Boston's Logan International Airport. Inner contour line denotes 40 NEF, outer contour line 30 NEF. (After Franken and Standley 1970.)

appear to present a much more immediate noise problem. They will be able to take off and land on extremely short runways, and many planners are convinced that they will ultimately operate regularly between the centers of different cities. For example, they could easily land along the Hudson and East rivers in midtown Manhattan, as well as on top of the covered railroad tracks at Union Station in downtown Washington, D.C. The 1968 *National Airport Plan* of the Federal Aviation Administration recommended 25 STOL-ports for the West Coast and the New York–Washington, D.C., corridor, including nine in New York City. Because of high noise levels from STOL-craft and helicopters, all central city landing sites must be selected carefully, and zoning and building code regulations must be used effectively to decrease noise exposure. For example, downtown landing pads might be flanked by industrial structures. Controversies such as the continuing

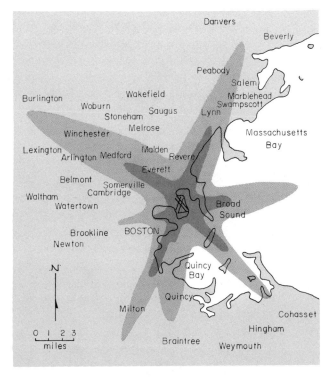

Figure 8.12. Estimated 1975 noise exposure forecast contours for areas surrounding Boston's Logan International Airport. Effects of supersonic transport are not included. Inner contour line denotes 40 NEF, outer contour 30 NEF. (After Franken and Standley 1970.)

one over the use of the Pan American Building in New York City for a helicopter pad should stimulate additional forethought in the selection of sites. A similarly useful episode is the controversy over a proposed Washington-to-Baltimore helicopter service, which has involved an extended legal battle between several citizens' groups, the Civil Aeronautics Board, and those seeking to institute the service. As part of the battle, the citizens' groups developed a detailed map (see Figure 8.13) to show the many areas in Washington where noise from helicopter overflights would tend to be incompatible with present land use.

Other Key Noise Sources

Of all the other sources of noise in the urban environment besides surface and aviation traffic, construction, demolition, and street

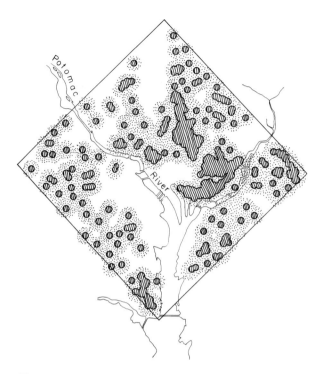

Figure 8.13. Washington, D.C., land uses incompatible with noise from helicopter overflights (based on standards recommended by the Department of Transportation). Shaded areas represent noise sensitivity zones around hospitals, schools, and colleges within Washington's original boundaries. Not shown are additional zones around several hundred private and parochial schools and churches. (From a brief filed on August 19, 1968, by Concerned Citizens et al. with the Civil Aeronautics Board in Docket no. 17665.)

repair generate the most intense and intrusive noise. In addition to an average of 80,000 street repairs and 10,000 demolitions per year, New York City, for example, always has a high number of construction projects in progress. These involve equipment operated by loud diesel engines and substantial numbers of noisy air compressors, as well as pile-driving, riveting, and blasting operations to remove bedrock. The noise of an individual air compressor generally exceeds 100 dB at the source. Figure 8.14 shows the common sight of a number of those machines in simultaneous operation at one location. To reduce disruption from construction and street repair noise, cities must encourage

Figure 8.14.   Battery of air compressors at work on excavation project in New York City. (Department of Water Resources photograph by Vincent J. Lopez.)

research, development, and especially the use of quieter equipment. A surprising amount of this type of machinery is already on the market, although at somewhat higher prices than the noisier equipment. Most cities also have the power to control the hours in which such equipment is operated.

Another set of intrusive city noises stems from railroad, subway, and elevated train systems. Noise from this source is annoying both to people living along the rights-of-way and to many passengers on the trains. The use of air-conditioned coaches greatly alleviates noise impact for the rider. Much of the noise from trains results from the clickety-clack of metal wheels on metal rails and their squeal when rounding corners. Two methods for reducing those sounds are: (1) continuous welded rails, some of which have been installed in the New York City transit system and (2) the use of rubber wheels, as in the Montreal and Paris systems. Using the *sone* measure of loudness (which accentuates the value of the more annoying, higher frequencies), Figure 8.15 shows that an 80 percent reduction in loudness may be achieved by substituting rubber wheels for steel wheels.

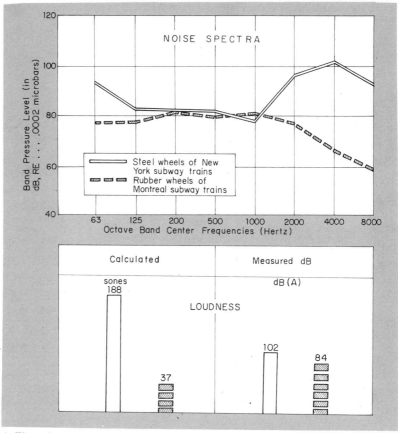

Figure 8.15. Comparison of subway noise generated by New York trains with steel wheels and Montreal trains with rubber wheels. (After Anderson 1970.)

Other important sources of outdoor noise are industrial operations, garbage and trash collections, and air-conditioning equipment. Industrial noises are caused in large part by: "air intake and discharge ducts or openings from fans and compressors or valves, engine intakes and engine and turbine exhausts, pumps, and pump and engine radiation and steam discharge noise . . . [and] out-of-doors yard operations. These include warehousing of steel and lumber, scrap yards, and truck and rail-freight-handling yards " (Anderson 1970, p. 45). Reduction of the impact of such noise can, and will eventually, be achieved through the development and installation of quieter fans and muffling equipment, the effective enclosure of noisy outdoor operations, the appropriate insulation of preexisting dwelling units, and the effective zoning of such operations away from residential sections. Although Chicago has had a zoning ordinance since the 1950's limiting manufacturing noise to specified decibel levels, this country generally has lagged behind the European countries in terms of incorporating noise-abatement criteria into its zoning regulations.

Noisy garbage and trash collections are particularly irritating to people when they occur at night or in the very early morning. Purchasing power and local licensing authority are the keys to alleviating this disturbance. Substantially quieter garbage cans and garbage trucks are on the market. New York City recently purchased some trucks of this kind, and Paris has required the use of quiet trash cans since 1959. Citizen initiative can help persuade local governments to invest in such trucks (or specify their use by independent contractors) and to bar nighttime and early morning trash and garbage collections.

The noise from air conditioners comes from modern cooling towers atop apartment buildings and from the smaller individual units in apartment and office windows. Where small units are placed in row after row on several floors of a building, the noise can approximate the roar of a waterfall. That noise may please some people, but it is very annoying to others, particularly at night. This kind of noise will be controlled through the development of quieter equipment, some of which is presently available, and the enforcement of regulations specifically designed to curb such noise. Several cities — including Beverly Hills, California, and Coral Gables, Florida — have passed local ordinances attempting to control the noise level of air-conditioning units.

Other sources of irritating outdoor noise in the city include: transistor radios and other electronic equipment, sound trucks, power mowers and chain saws, police, fire and ambulance sirens, ice cream trucks, noisy pets, children at play, rock bands, and teen-agers and adults at parties. All such noises can and should be regulated to some extent by local ordinance and police power. Although often it is difficult to set limits, efforts should be made. Without sufficient sustained community interest, however, optimum noise control will not occur.

THE EFFECTS OF NOISE

Temporary and Permanent Hearing Loss

Exposure to excessive noise can cause both temporary and permanent loss of hearing, depending upon (1) the nature and intensity of the noise, (2) the proximity of the individual to the source, (3) the duration and frequency of exposure, and (4) the physical condition of the individual. *Threshold shift* is the technical term for such hearing loss; it refers to a diminution in the ability to detect weak auditory signals, rather than to a complete and total loss of hearing. If the decrease in sensitivity eventually vanishes, it is termed *temporary* threshold shift (TTS); if not, it is *permanent* threshold shift (PTS).

The exact mechanism by which the shift occurs is not clear, but the phenomenon itself is familiar to anyone who has had a loud firecracker go off very close to him. Any steady noise over 80 dB(A) can produce some change in auditory threshold, and noise in excess of 105 dB(A) will produce permanent threshold shift in the normal ear if exposed daily over a substantial period of time. To date there is no known way to restore noise-induced PTS. Currently there is considerable research on this subject, and it is not yet clear whether exposure to levels of noise between 80 and 105 dB(A) for shorter periods will produce any substantial PTS in the normal ear.

It *is* clear that substantial numbers of people are regularly exposed for various durations to noise levels exceeding 80 dB. One Carnegie-Mellon University study of American occupations found that 24,000 boilermakers were regularly exposed to 110 dB, 63,000 weavers to 102 dB, 162,000 taxicab drivers to 85 dB, 182,000 bus drivers to 90 dB, 199,000 excavation machine operators to 110 dB, 270,000 stationary engineers to 116 dB, more than 1 million foremen to 80 dB, 1.5 million truck drivers to 95 dB, and more than 2 million mechanics to 80 dB (Berland 1970, p. 156). Obviously, all such persons are running some risk of both types of hearing loss. Substantial numbers of teenagers also run such risks both in electric rock bands and in discotheques and other places where amplified music regularly averages 90 to 100 dB or higher (Still 1970, p. 49).

Occupation-Related Costs

Occupation-related costs include (1) compensation claims by employees, (2) losses due to noise-induced inefficiency, and (3) costs of insulating and muffling equipment and insulating work areas. Two court cases (in New York and Wisconsin), in 1948 and 1951, opened the door to workmen's compensation for noise-induced *gradual* hearing loss (even though the employees still were able to work an eight-hour day and had lost neither time nor wages on account of their disabilities).

Although the awards in those cases were small (approximately $1,600 each), the potential total value of such claims is likely to be well over $500 million. Several years ago one expert estimated the total to be $450 million on the conservative assumptions that the average award per claim would be $1,000 and that only 10 percent of those eligible would in fact file (Glorig 1961). As of 1968 the average award per claim was closer to $2,000, yet the number of claims was still very small, a fact that reflects both a general lack of awareness of gradual hearing loss and an unwillingness to press such claims against one's employer (Committee on Environmental Quality 1968, p. 34).

The other two types of costs from occupational noise are more obvious than the potential compensation claims. Before World War II it was estimated that office noise was costing American business over $2 million per day through inefficient operation, and by the 1960's that figure was estimated to have doubled (Bell 1966, p. 12). Along with reduced output, both general communication difficulties and increased accident rates (due in part to high noise levels) should be included with these costs. The development and purchase of additional equipment to control occupational noise is another obvious cost.

Interference with Speech, Sleep, Leisure, and Education
General annoyance and interruption of various daily activities represent another set of effects on humans that can be distinguished from both hearing loss and the physiological and psychological effects noted later. Much of the research on the annoyance effects of noise has been associated with studies of jet aircraft noise, because of its growing magnitude in the past decade. Noise may interfere with normal living activities, including TV and radio reception and enjoyment, rest and sleep, reading and concentrating, telephone and other personal communication, and with various types of recreation and entertainment, such as outdoor barbecuing and outdoor concerts.

The interference of noise with classroom activity in schools near airports has tended to serve as a catalyst in some areas to ignite community interest in the extended effects of noise. Several acute areas are near Los Angeles International Airport. According to the Superintendent of Schools of the city of Inglewood, which borders on that busy airport:

Oral communication becomes impossible each time a jet aircraft passes near our schools. This means that approximately 165 teachers and 4,000 students must stop all class discussion until the aircraft has progressed beyond the schools. The result of such disruption goes beyond the actual time involved in the passage of the aircraft, and each class must again have its attention focused on what was being done before the interruption . . . Our teachers tell us that as the number of jet planes increases they find classroom instruction increasingly difficult, and it is their feeling that considerable loss in the educational program results. (Quoted in Baron 1970, p. 112, from testimony before Congress)

In November 1968, one elementary school in nearby Westchester was closed, and 55 pupils had to be relocated, because of the interference of jet noise with teaching. A second Westchester school was closed down for the same reason two years later. As one final example, three schools within a mile and a half of a major airport were found to average 40 to 60 daily interruptions in classroom listening due to aviation noise (Still 1970, p. 200).

Effects on Property Values

The interference of noise with daily living depresses residential property values near the source of the noise. Such properties also tend to take a longer time to sell than do similar units in less noisy areas. Transportation noise causes the most serious depression of property values. This effect, however, relates only to the residential value of the land — its *underlying* value for potential commercial or industrial purposes may increase in such a situation. The homeowner, though, if he sells, usually cannot obtain the higher value because the area is zoned for residential use only. It has been shown in Canada that residentially zoned land near railroad tracks may be depressed below whatever its normal value would be, unless it is 500 to 1,000 feet from the right-of-way. In Sacramento County, California, foreclosed homes bordering on a freeway took 10 months longer to sell than did similar foreclosed houses in the same tract located farther from the highway (Baron 1970, p. 90).

Aircraft noise causes the greatest diminution of residential property values, although this effect is very hard to measure. In 1961 real estate assessments were reduced as much as 20 percent immediately around Los Angeles International Airport; this caused a $120,000 tax loss to the county from an estimated $1.5 million reduction in valuation. Similar reductions occurred the following year near what is now Kennedy Airport in New York. One of the most dramatic examples of this depression occurred in a very unusual 1970 court decision. A California judge awarded over 500 plaintiffs a total of more than

$740,000 in damages for property losses due to the noise impact of jets
operating out of the city-owned Los Angeles International Airport
(*Aaron v. City of Los Angeles*, Los Angeles County Superior Court case
no. 387799, February 5, 1970). The total figure represented preliminary
individual awards ranging from $400 to $6,000, determined on the
basis of loss in the value of the land itself as well as the improvements
on the land.

Other Physiological and Psychological Effects

Finally, urban noise contributes to the general atmosphere of
stress and tension that city dwellers live and labor within. The human
body (including the fetus) reacts to noise even when the individual
is asleep, or when he believes that he has become used to the noise.
Scientists have demonstrated that noise stimuli can cause the sleeper's
blood vessels to constrict, and change his heart rate and muscular
tone, without waking him. A number of researchers have even implied
that there is a meaningful connection between noise, hearing loss,
and coronary heart disease. Their arguments suggest that there are links
between constant exposure to noise levels in the modern city and
increases in tension, hypertension, and heart disease.

Medical experts also believe that excessive noise can be an un-
suspected triggering agent for allergies, ulcers, and even mental illness.
An English study, reported in *The Lancet*, a medical journal, in December 1969 discovered that the percent of individuals closely exposed
to the noise of London's Heathrow Airport that required treatment for
mental illness was higher than the percent of people living farther from
the noise. Though there is as yet slight agreement about relations
between noise and physiological and psychological human health, the
arguments are sufficiently plausible to cause research to expand.

SOCIAL, POLITICAL, AND LEGAL FACETS

A great many people still believe that noise is simply one price
that must be paid for technological progress in urban environments.
Prior to the 1960's in the United States there had been virtually no
federal action and very little meaningful action at state and local levels
to control noise. New York City established the first formal office of

noise abatement at the local level in this country in 1969. Although most states had long since legislated against faulty mufflers, and many cities had purported to regulate automobile horn-blowing, such laws were invariably phrased in vague, technically imprecise terms such as "no unnecessary noise" or "no excessive noise." The imprecision was due in large part to the primitiveness of early noise-abatement technology. In addition, such laws were hard to enforce both because of their vagueness and because there usually was little community support for their enforcement.

Today there are more technically precise laws, but lack of enforcement and lack of support for enforcement remain serious problems. For example, five years after enactment of legislation by New York State in 1965 placing specific decibel limits on highway traffic noise, the problem was as severe as ever. Given our democratic political structure (within a federal scheme), much of the noise in our urban environments will continue unabated until such time as a *significant* number of citizens strongly support its control.

Another problem, directly related to the lack of laws and poor enforcement, is that the regulatory steps that *are* eventually taken are usually partial steps, in part because persons who are to be most directly affected are neither aware that the steps are being taken nor care much at that point in time. The 1968 revised New York City building code is a case in point. There has never been any national code for dwelling sound control in the United States (despite the existence since 1938 of such codes in Europe). The 1968 New York City code was in fact the *first local code* in this country to incorporate significant noise control provisions, and yet those that were adopted are still criticized as being weak. The rating for walls, for example, is reputedly below the lowest reported standard in Europe. The floor-ceiling impact noise ratings are so low that perhaps 75 percent of the tenants will be dissatisfied. Noise intrusion is permitted from lobbies and hallways, and there is no provision for rating appliance noises or for regulating noisy toilets.

At the federal level, despite the fact that the majority of Congressmen primarily represent nonurban areas, some very significant steps were taken in 1968. First, Congress passed Public Law 91-411, which gave the FAA an official mandate for the first time to attempt to regulate aircraft noise. In the same year, an amendment added a new requirement to the Walsh-Healey Public Contracts Act. It specified that employers holding contracts with the federal government worth over $10,000 (and involving over 20 employees) would have to ensure that the noise in their plants did not exceed 90 dB, if they wanted to retain their contracts and obtain new ones. Although that control is salutary, it is also 5 or 10 dB above the level regarded by most experts as a safe one in terms of avoiding hearing loss (threshold shift).

The legal and political problems of people living near airports are particularly difficult. First, there is a disinclination to complain about noise in the first place, a feeling that it would be useless. Once complaints are lodged, it is hard for many to rebut the arguments that aviation noise is "the price of progress" for aviation growth, that it is "in the national interest," and that someone else is always really "responsible" for the noise (pilots, airline management, manufacturers, airport operators, or the federal government). Beyond those are arguments that safety factors preclude altering landing patterns, that economic factors preclude accelerated research to attain quieter engines, and that the federal constitution and federal legislation have preempted other legal steps, that could otherwise be taken by *states* to control noise caused by interstate commerce. Finally, in the courts the concept of "the legalized nuisance" precludes injunctions against airport noise, and the law of evidence often makes it difficult to prove property devaluation conclusively. However, as the 1968 legislation and the 1970 *Aaron* case suggest, property owners should be able to make some headway in both the courts and the legislatures in the future.

What is needed above all is a consciousness both that noise *is* an increasingly serious problem and that appropriate concerted action *can* produce meaningful results at the federal, state, and local levels, as well as in the courts.

REFERENCES

Anderson, N. 1970. *Toward a quieter city.* New York: Report of the (New York City) Mayor's Task Force on Noise Control.
Baron, R. 1970. *The tyranny of noise.* New York: St. Martin's Press.
Beaton, J., and L. Bourget. 1968. Can noise radiation from highways be reduced by design? In *Highway Research Record,* no. 232, pp. 1–18. Washington, D.C.: National Academy of Sciences, Highway Research Board.

Bell, A. 1966. *Noise: An occupational hazard and public nuisance.* Geneva: World Health Organization.

Berland, T. 1970. *The fight for quiet.* Englewood Cliffs, N.J.: Prentice-Hall.

Branch, M. 1970. *Outdoor noise and the metropolitan environment: A case study of Los Angeles with special reference to aircraft.* Los Angeles: Dept. of City Planning.

Chalupnik, J., ed. 1970. *Transportation noises: A symposium on acceptability criteria.* Seattle: Univ. of Washington Press.

Committee on Environmental Quality (of the U.S. Federal Council for Science and Technology). 1968. *Noise: Sound without value.* Washington, D.C.: Govt. Printing Office.

Dickerson, D., ed. 1970. *Transportation noise pollution: Control and abatement.* National Aeronautics and Space Administration, Langley Research Center, and Old Dominion University.

Federal Aviation Administration. 1963. *A citizen's guide to aircraft noise.* Washington: Govt. Printing Office.

Franken, P., and D. Standley. 1970. *Aircraft noise and airport neighbors: A study of Logan International Airport (Boston).* Tech. report prepared by Bolt, Beranek & Newman for the U.S. Dept. of Transportation and the Dept. of Housing and Urban Development.

Glorig, A. 1961. The problem of noise in industry. *Amer. Jour. of Public Health* 51:1338–1346.

Goodfriend, L. 1968. Control of highway noise. In *Proc. of the Rutgers Noise Poll. Conf., May 22, 1968,* pp. 11–23. New Brunswick, N.J.: Rutgers College of Agriculture and Environmental Science.

Hardy, H. 1955. Twenty-five years' research in outdoor noise. *Noise Control* 1:20–24.

Harris, C., ed. 1957. *Handbook of noise control.* New York: McGraw-Hill.

Hildebrand, J. 1970. *Noise pollution and the law.* Buffalo: W. S. Hein.

McGrath, D., Jr. 1968. City planning and noise. In *Noise as a public health hazard,* ed. W. Ward and J. Fricke, pp. 347–359. Washington, D.C.: American Speech and Hearing Association.

Mecklin, J. 1969. It's time to turn down all that noise. *Fortune* Oct.: 130–133ff.

Mochizuki, T., and A. Imaizumi. 1967. City noises in Tokyo. *Jour. Acoust. Soc. Japan* 23:146–67.

Stevenson, G. 1972. *The politics of airport noise.* Belmont, Calif.: Duxbury Press.

Still, H. 1970. *In quest of quiet.* Harrisburg, Pa.: Stackpole Books.

Ward, W., and J. Fricke, ed. 1968. *Noise as a public health hazard* (proceedings of a conference held in Washington, D.C., June 13–14, 1968). Washington, D.C.: American Speech and Hearing Association, ASHA Report 4.

types of vegetation can be observed; these range from weed patches on vacant lots and construction sites, to distinctive ribbons of herbs and grasses along roadways and footpaths (Bates 1935), to volunteer shrubbery in unused corners of industrial areas, to aquatic vegetation in city streams and lakes.

The Interstitial Forest

An interstitial forest characterizes the older, single-family, residential areas of most cities, as well as the commercial districts of many towns. This forest contains numerous large shade trees that were either planted long ago or naturally established prior to settlement and allowed to remain. The interstitial forest may form a nearly continuous canopy over streets and buildings in these areas, in marked contrast to other parts of the city. In larger cities the central business districts, areas of old multiple-family dwellings (row-houses, and so forth), and industrial zones are so built up that there is little room for trees (or, given space, tree growth is difficult). The newer suburbs usually are unshaded, too, because mass development techniques – dominantly used since World War II – have stripped the land of preexisting trees, and planted trees have not yet matured. In sparsely wooded regions, such as the Great Plains, urban forests appear as oases.

In natural forest regions, such as the northeastern United States, forests cover many interstices between settlements as well as within them. Traditionally a leftover in the landscape, the woods are gaining increasing value and use as sites for expensive low-density dwellings and for urbanite recreation. This growing tendency toward quasi-preservation – together with the abandonment of agricultural lands that land speculators have allowed to revert to forest – appears to have maintained the total amount of forested space in megalopolitan regions over the past 10–15 years. And megalopolis is surprisingly heavily wooded. The Washington-to-Boston megalopolis is, for example, about half forested. Thus, the interstitial forest is an important vegetational feature both within the city and between cities in urbanizing regions.

Parks and Green Space

Parks and green areas, which occur in patches relatively uninterrupted by human structures, constitute the second major type of urban vegetation. This separate class is based as much on psychological and cultural functions as on plant physiognomy. Parks and green areas are places where the urbanite may envelop himself in nature without great distraction by the usual city activities. Most city parks are publicly owned and are maintained in large part for the public. But there are many demands upon parks, and they must serve multiple leisure-time uses. Vegetational variety enhances multiple uses, and in fact may help to define them. This explains why so many green areas are a mélange of trees, lawns, gardens, and pathways.

There is much variation in the size and other characteristics of urban green spaces. Several examples from New York City may be cited. Central Park (see Figure 9.1), designed by Frederick Olmstead and Calvert Vaux in the 1850's, is a descendant of idealized English landscapes of the century before. This famous 843-acre park has served, in turn, as an inspiration or model for numerous other parks. Jamaica Bay Wildlife Refuge is a different kind of green space — primarily a marshland devoted to wildlife. It is located less than 10 miles from Times Square and was visited by more than 75,000 people in 1970. In contrast, a mini-park of only 2,500 square feet, Paley Park, serves as a mid-Manhattan refuge for two to three thousand people each day; 17 locust trees and vines of kudzu and ivy give this urban green space

Figure 9.1. Central Park and neighboring Manhattan. This famous 843-acre park has been an outstanding urban green space for more than a century. (Courtesy of H. Armstrong Roberts.)

Figure 9.2.   Paley Park, a mini-park in mid-Manhattan. This park, with only 42 feet of frontage on 53rd Street, was established in 1967. (Courtesy of the Greenpark Foundation.)

its character (Figure 9.2). Greenbelts (circular parks surrounding cities or parts of them), which may serve as a buffer between conflicting land uses, are another type of green space; the greenbelts around London and some of its satellite communities are well known. The kinds and uses of urban parks and green space have been subject to much recent discussion (for example, Shomon 1971; Wallace 1970; Guggenheimer 1969). Given the increasing leisure time and mobility of the urbanite, many parks and green areas geographically beyond the urban area now *function* somewhat as urban parks; thus, for instance, Cape Cod and Shenandoah National Park temporarily become extensions of the city each summer, especially on weekends.

Gardens

Man evolved as a creature of the forest and its edges, and so craves the natural companionship of trees in the artificial city. So, too, does the garden signify the necessity of man to live close to nature, the provider of food. Thus the garden, like the woods, historically has satisfied other than aesthetic needs. Man's need for gardens is probably, in part at least, ingrained in our humanness.

City gardening is not a recent invention. Ornamental gardens were grown by ancient Egyptians in patios and on roofs and balconies. The Greeks considered the famed hanging gardens of Babylon, which flourished about 600 B.C., to be one of the seven wonders of the world. These monumental gardens may have been built on protruding hillside terraces supported by large arches and columns and on roofs; they may have included elaborate fountains and cascades. The history of urban gardening reveals many diverse and interesting practices (Wright 1934), with a tendency toward increasingly formal and geometrical designs until about two centuries ago.

Today a variety of gardens is cultivated in the city (see, for example, Brett and Grant 1967; Lees 1970). Indoor gardens – in greenhouses, covered courtyards, and home window boxes – may contain casual groups of lush tropical plants. Most front gardens in American suburbs are little more than decorative edgings next to houses and along property lines. In back yards strip gardens, which may include hedges or fences, help provide privacy, and small kitchen gardens also are popular. Residential gardens in Europe and Latin America generally are more private, being contained behind walls. In an attempt to overcome the starkness of downtown areas, where ground for gardens is minimal, modern cities are beginning to reemploy the ancient idea of the rooftop garden (Figure 9.3).

In addition to satisfying man's innate and intangible psychological needs, the urban garden may serve several other functions. These provisions may be summarized as (1) enclosures of space for privacy in crowded environments; (2) green thumb recreation for the urbanite; (3) fresh vegetables and fruits for human consumption; (4) food and

Figure 9.3. Kaiser Center Roof Garden, Oakland, California. This 3-1/2 acre garden, which overlies a garage and shops, contains a large variety of exotic shrubs and trees. All plants are watered by an automatic sprinkler system. Six thousand cubic yards of soil were used in its construction. (Courtesy of the Kaiser Corporation.)

habitat for urban wildlife; and (5) aesthetic pleasure through the multiple effects of garden plant form, color, texture, and odor.

Lawns

The lawn has become a prime symbol of suburban living in America. It is a vegetation type that also is widely cultivated in other parts of the city and in other countries. In North America the "ideal" lawn is held to consist of close-cropped grass (without any broad-leaved herbs) of uniform texture and a rich green color. Such intensive mono-culture of turf grass requires almost constant maintenance, including mowing and the application of water, fertilizer, and herbicides.

The history of this important urban artifact, the lawn, is interesting and sheds light on its nature today. Unlike gardening, which originated in hot regions, lawn-making arose in cool, moist climes (predominantly England). Grass yards may first have been maintained by domestic animals (such as sheep, goats, and cattle) grazing around the homes of their keepers. By the early seventeenth century Francis Bacon wrote in an essay on the ideal garden that "nothing is more pleasant to the eye than green grass finely shorn." During the eighteenth century the English lawn and the open park landscape that it dominated turned the tide against the geometrical exactness of the French garden. This landscape concept, successfully promoted for English manors by William Kent and Lancelot "Capability" Brown, was exported to America, where it became the ideal of not only the new gentry but the egalitarian bourgeois as well.

Today through our suburban lawns we may try to assert our role as "lord of the estate." In reality, however, the present role of the suburbanite in relation to his lawn is pathetic. With his power mower he artificially assumes the cropping function of domestic animals that have long since disappeared. The primary pay off from this activity is maintaining social "appearances" in the neighborhood and property value. Other uses of the lawn appear to be secondary, despite common statements to the contrary. (These conclusions are shown in an un-published study of lawns and attitudes in Ann Arbor, Michigan, by Robert Reynolds.) Both the importance and the difficulty of maintaining a "good" lawn are suggested in Figure 9.4.

The strength of the lawn as a cultural tradition is reflected in the fact that home lawns in the United States cover about five million acres and stimulate an expenditure of about $3,000,000,000 each year (Wadleigh 1968).

Much energy and water and many minerals are misspent on growing green lawns, especially in hot, dry regions. For instance, tremendous quantities of water are used to irrigate lawns in cities such as Denver and Los Angeles, which hence may appear from the air as green patches in an otherwise brown environment. The sale of topsoil and grass turf for instant lawns in suburbia has become big business. Frequently the first thing a developer will do in a new area is scrape off

"Everything goes with the house except the lawn. They're taking that with them."

Figure 9.4. Drawing by Shirvanian. (©1971 *The New Yorker Magazine,* Inc.)

the topsoil to sell for lawn establishment in neighboring, just-constructed residential areas (which earlier were stripped of their natural soil wealth for sale elsewhere).

There are several alternatives to present lawn practices. Commercial interests are promoting ground cover that requires even greater expenditure per unit area than do present lawns, such as artificial turf (for example, Astroturf and Tartanturf) and pavement. Unfortunately, the financial profits extracted from such schemes will not take account of considerable environmental costs to society — for example, the problems of urban runoff and flooding, reduced groundwater recharge, and especially urban heating all will be exacerbated (see Chapters 3 and 5). Alternatives that are more sound ecologically, and also require much less work than the traditional lawn, include creeping plants other than grass (for example, periwinkle, English ivy, pachysandra) and mixtures of grasses and other low wild plants (now commonly thought of as "weeds"). The "weedy" lawn should proudly

be referred to as an "American heritage lawn," because plants that
have migrated from many foreign lands are included.

DYNAMICS OF URBAN VEGETATION

The existing plant life in a city may be viewed, in broad terms,
as resulting from several filtering processes by man. Some of these
human actions are purposeful and direct, whereas others are inadvertent
and indirect (and hence more difficult to understand and control).
During urbanization the original plant cover is differentially destroyed,
the remnants forming fairly predictable vegetational patterns. Man
brings new plants into the city and tends them; he also creates conditions favoring the growth of other, aggressive, "weedy" invaders.
Thus, urbanization subtracts and adds various kinds of plants. Man's
attempts to manage the distribution and abundance of plants in the
urban flora are worked against by numerous complex repercussions of
urban activities — most important, the plants' water and mineral relations commonly are disrupted and their edaphic and atmospheric
environments are contaminated.

Clearing of Preexisting Vegetation
Urbanization of a region is almost always preceded by widespread destruction of native vegetation, usually with an intervening
period of agricultural practice. This modification of the plant cover by
man in advance of the city is not unrelated to urbanization. Historically,
as cities in a wooded region have proliferated and grown, they have
intruded on the forests of their hinterlands to obtain lumber for building and wood for fuel, as well as to furnish agricultural land on which
food for the city could be grown. In Europe the Middle Ages was
the major period of forest clearing (Darby 1956); in North America
extensive deforestation spread from the east coast westward to the
grassy plains during the nineteenth century (Curtis 1956).
Today land use — and vegetation — are roughly zoned as concen-
tric rings near cities, more or less according to J. H. von Thünen's
classical model. The needs of the urban ecosystem together with land
rent, which generally increases near the city and its center, promote (or
allow) the following approximate sequence of land use zones, going

toward the city: (1) forests, or lands with other wild vegetation; (2)
general farms; (3) intensive, specialty farms; (4) former farmland, being
held for speculation; (5) high-class residential suburbs; and (6) middle-
class urban residences. An interesting perspective on the environment-
vegetation dynamics within nodes along a similar sequence of wild
to urban conditions has been provided by Dansereau (1971).

The spatial relationship between the degree of urbanization and
forest cover in and around a typical American city, Philadelphia, is
indicated in Figure 9.5. The percentage of area in marshes, like that in
forests, increases away from the city. The pressure to develop these
open (undeveloped) lands is suggested by the high average value of undeveloped land within 10 to 15 miles of downtown Philadelphia. The
changing percentages of forest lands and marshes near Philadelphia
are primarily functions of urban growth. In general much of the forest
was cleared for agricultural use well in advance of urbanization. Forests
cover less than 4 percent of the area within 10 miles of the city center.
In contrast, they represent more than 38 percent of all land beyond 30
miles from the city center. Marshes are filled and destroyed more as

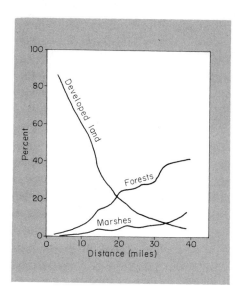

Figure 9.5. The distribution of developed
land, forests, and marshes, by distance from the
center of Philadelphia, 1960. (Based on data
from Toulan 1970.)

a result of urbanization than as a result of preceding agricultural practices. The period 1930–1960 saw unparalleled growth and changes in the nature of the metropolitan region. The size of the urbanized area expanded much faster than did the population. Philadelphia's developed area increased from 110,000 to 430,000 acres as the outer radius of the circle of urbanization increased from less than 8 miles to 16 miles during the thirty years (Toulan 1970, p. 55).

Introducing and Tending Plants in the City

Man superimposes additional plant species on the remnants of preexisting vegetation left during urbanization. These plants that are added to the city include both existing species from afar and new horticultural varieties (or cultivars) developed by man. Most of these introduced and new plants, like some of the old, require intensive tending for survival. In contrast, some alien organisms — especially those inadvertently brought into the city — may thrive in city conditions without man's conscious aid (many weeds in a vacant lot are good examples).

There are books of information about thousands of horticultural varieties for the garden and lawn. But our brief discussion here will focus on trees, which are conspicuous elements of the city's vegetation and also relatively easy to measure and understand. In most cities, street trees are systematically planted and maintained by the municipal government (see Figure 9.6). Ornamental and shade trees on private property are more a reflection of individual tastes (of both past and present property owners). There are surprisingly few geographical surveys within a city of either component.

Table 9.1 lists the primary street trees growing in two cities at two periods (chosen because of the availability of data). In about 1910 the city of East Orange, New Jersey (population 34,000 then), had 47 species represented in its 10,953 street trees. About 32 percent of the species, constituting about 20 percent of the trees, were not native to the area. Three fourths of all the trees were maples (four species), and only eight species were represented by more than 1 percent of the community's street trees. Comparison of these data with modern figures for another American city (Ann Arbor, Michigan — see Table 9.1) are suggestive (certainly not demonstrative) of historical changes in street tree planting, which also tend to be supported by other information: (1) a city's street tree flora is becoming more diverse (Ann Arbor's

Figure 9.6. Locust trees and flowers in planters along Main Street, Ann Arbor, Michigan. Until a few years ago, when traffic lanes were narrowed, the central business district shown here was nearly barren of greenery. (Courtesy of Johnson, Johnson & Roy.)

flora consists of more than 73 species plus many horticultural varieties); (2) introduced species and horticultural varieties are gaining increased prominence, both floristically and vegetationally (in Ann Arbor these groups make up about half of the street tree flora and about 30 percent of the trees); and (3) many more kinds of trees are being represented by significant numbers (16 of Ann Arbor's species constitute 1 percent or more each of the total street trees).

The trend toward increased planting of different and exotic types of trees along streets both increases the variety of vegetational ex-

Table 9.1. Common street trees in two American cities, as percentages of total trees and by land of origin. Only trees exceeding 1 percent of the total are listed. (East Orange data are from Solotaroff 1912, p. 248.)

East Orange, New Jersey, as of c. 1910			Ann Arbor, Michigan, as of 1971		
Species	Percent of Total Trees	Origin	Species	Percent of Total Trees	Origin
Red maple (Acer rubrum)	26.0	Native	Sugar maple (Acer saccharum)	24.2	Native
Sugar maple (Acer saccharum)	20.4	Native	American elm (Ulmus americana)	13.7	Native
Silver maple (Acer saccharinum)	20.3	Native	Green ash (Fraxinus pennsylvanica)	9.2	Native
Norway maple (Acer platanoides)	11.1	Europe, Caucasia	Norway maple (excl. vars.) (Acer platanoides)	8.9	Europe, Caucasia
American elm (Ulmus americana)	9.1	Native	Silver maple (Acer saccharinum)	7.6	Native
Carolina poplar (Populus Xcanadensis)	6.7	Hybrid (betw. American and European spp.)	Hopa crab (Malus Xsp.)	4.4	Hybrid
Horse chestnut (Aesculus hippocastanum)	1.6	Europe	Black maple (Acer nigrum)	3.5	Native
American linden (Tilia americana)	1.2	Native	American linden (Tilia americana)	2.4	Native

Species	Value	Origin
American sycamore (*Platanus occidentalis*)	2.0	Native
White oak (*Quercus alba*)	2.0	Native
Skyline locust (*Robinia* Xsp.)	1.6	Hybrid
Pines (*Pinus* spp.)	1.4	Various
London plane tree *Platanus Xacerifolia*	1.3	Hybrid (betw. American and Eurasian spp.)
Siberian elm (*Ulmus pumila*)	1.1	Asia
Littleleaf linden (*Tilia cordata*)	1.0	Europe
Box-elder (*Acer negundo*)	1.0	Native

Total number of trees = 32,451
Total species = 73+

Total number of trees = 10,953
Total species = 47

periences for urbanites and ecologically hedges a city's tree investment
against massive losses due to one or several specific diseases (such as
Dutch elm disease). Diversification also is promoted by commercial tree
nurseries, each of which, to peddle its own special cultivars, urges
cities to "buy something new and different this year"; one city forester
has compared this with Detroit's perennial new car approach to life.

Although urban areas have been diversifying their street tree
plantings during recent years, the total number of street trees in many
cities has remained about constant (that is, the number planted each
year approximates the number removed). For example, New York City
plants about 5,000 street trees annually (at a cost of three quarters of
a million dollars) while removing over 5,000 trees (at a cost of about
half a million dollars); thus the number of street trees remains about
800,000. Similarly, in 1968 Lansing, Michigan (which has about 35,000
street trees), planted 1,498 trees and removed 1,573 trees; of the latter
406 were newly planted trees and 642 were dead or diseased elms.

The American elm has long been an outstanding feature of the
eastern U.S. landscape. The tree's arching branches rise to 100 feet
above the streets of many towns. But unfortunately Dutch elm disease
has killed most of these magnificent shade trees during the past few
decades. This disease, introduced from abroad by man, has transformed
urban forests to such an extent that it merits discussion here. Further,
it is an example (albeit extreme) of numerous introduced diseases —
including the gypsy moth (introduced in 1869) and the chestnut blight
(introduced in 1904).

Dutch elm disease is caused by a fungus (*Ceratocystis ulmi*) and is
mainly carried from tree to tree by elm bark beetles (*Scolytus multi-
striatus*). Both the fungus and the bark beetle were inadvertently
imported into North America from Europe, the fungus probably on a
shipment of logs for veneer manufacturing in about 1930. Since then
the disease has spread until it now extends from Quebec and Georgia
west to Oklahoma and South Dakota. An isolated attack has been
recorded on the street elms of Boise, Idaho. All American and European
species of elm are attacked (although some highly resistant clones
are now being developed) and infection almost always results in death.

Cities practice various control measures to delay the infection
and death of elms. Insecticides (formerly DDT, now primarily methoxy-
clor) are extensively sprayed on trees to kill the beetle, and infected
trees may be removed and destroyed. Nonetheless, trees still can be

infected through natural root grafts between closely spaced trees. Communities are having different degrees of success in controlling Dutch elm disease, but the fact remains that at present all "controls" are only partially effective. Still, such delaying tactics can allow a high proportion of elms to remain and give trees of other kinds that are planted nearby time to mature.

Table 9.2 indicates recent annual rates of elm loss in a number of midwestern United States cities, together with the type, extent, and duration of spraying program. The differential success of the control measure is evident. In the 1950's before great numbers of trees were lost, most of these communities had an average of one elm tree for every two to seven residents. Now some cities have only a few hundred elms left. Obviously different cities have adjusted differently to the disease threat, depending on such factors as public attitude toward the trees, the location of the elms, environmental effects of the sprays, perceived effectiveness of various control measures, and the cost of materials, equipment, and labor. The cost factor is great; in Michigan alone $9 million was spent in 1964 on control and removal of diseased elms.

The Dutch elm disease tide has not been turned. Pathologists think that conditions are ripe for its spread to California, where the bark beetle now occurs in 20 counties. Many California cities contain numerous mature elms. Sacramento, for example, has 15,000 elms, of which 436 grow within a two-block radius of the state Capitol.

Less is known generally about the trees of the urban forest that grow on private property than about municipally maintained street trees. However, a sample survey of trees on private land in Ann Arbor indicates some interesting distributional relations between tree species frequencies and period of urban settlement (see Figure 9.7). Some species — notably mulberries, elms, and ailanthus (or tree of heaven) — decrease outward from the central, older parts of the city. Conversely, the conifers and the oaks are much more common on private land that was urbanized less than a hundred years ago. Fruit trees (including crab, cherry, and apple) are most significant on land developed since the Second World War. In general, the size of trees declines outward from the city's center; this reflects the date of planting and the age of trees. However, the inner city contains the greatest variation in size, because many older trees, especially elms, have been removed there and replaced by younger trees of other species. The curve in Figure 9.7

Table 9.2. Losses of American elms to Dutch elm disease in some midwestern cities. (Data as of 1970, from a survey conducted by the city of Midland, Michigan.)

City	Population (1960)	Peak no. of American Elms	Loss of Elms per Year (1970)	Program of Control by Spraying in 1970	Year Spraying Stopped
Ypsilanti, Mich.	21,000	10,000	1.0% (2,000 left)	total[a]	—
Pittsburgh, Pa.	604,000	25,000	1.2	none	1968
Birmingham, Mich.	26,000	8,000	1.5	total[a]	—
Evanston, Ill.	79,000	19,000	c. 2.0	total[a]	—
Flint, Mich.	197,000	62,000	2.0	total[b]	—
Midland, Mich.	28,000	15,000	c. 3.0	partial[a]	—
Elmhurst, Ill.	40,000	15,000	3.0	total[a]	—
Detroit, Mich.	1,670,000	310,000	3.2	partial[a]	—
Dayton, Ohio	262,000	20,000	4.5	none	—
Saginaw, Mich.	98,000	20,000	4.5	total[a]	—
Pontiac, Mich.	82,000	2,600	5.8	none	1969
Rochester, N.Y.	319,000	50,000	6.0	none	1960
Ann Arbor, Mich.	67,000	10,000	7.0	partial[a]	—
Toledo, Ohio	318,000	72,000	10.0	none	1964
Coldwater, Mich.	9,000	11,000	10 to 20	none	1963
Milwaukee, Wisc.	741,000	127,000	? (62,000 left)	none	1966
Battle Creek, Mich.	44,000	4,700	? (400 left)	none	1963

[a]Methoxyclor sprayed in 1970.
[b]Benlate sprayed in 1970.

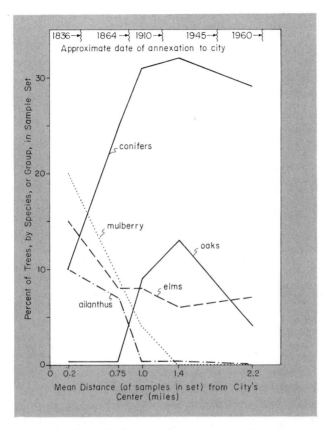

Figure 9.7. Urban distributions of some trees on private property
in Ann Arbor, Michigan. Curves based upon two-block samples at
each of 23 systematic grid intersections. Data from several sample
locations were combined as follows: 0.2 mile from center, 2
samples with 154 trees; 0.75 mile, 4 samples with 292 trees; 1.0
mile, 8 samples with 762 trees; 1.4 miles, 4 samples with 215 trees;
and 2.2 miles, 5 samples with 255 trees. (After unpublished study
by Mary Robinson 1967.)

depicting distribution of elms certainly was steeper several decades ago.
The distributions primarily reflect changing tastes in trees through
Ann Arbor's history, although several other factors probably are important as well: (1) mulberries and ailanthus are "weed" trees that can
establish themselves naturally, with a longer period for such establishment in older parts of the city; further, they are tolerant of extreme
urban conditions and may survive where some other species cannot;

(2) many conifers cannot tolerate extreme urban conditions and may, in part, be environmentally excluded from the inner city; and (3) most oaks in the middle-aged areas of Ann Arbor (where they grow in high proportion) may be remnants of preurban forests (or spreading forms of earlier open, rural places); this is indicated by their large size.

Finally, this section should mention some inadvertent floristic and vegetational changes occurring in the city, although these are poorly understood. Weeds may migrate into the city without man's aid. Once there, the urban habitat may be favorable to them in part because many of these plants evolved on human-disturbed sites in Europe and Asia (that is, they are adapted to areas of human occupance). This explanation helps account for the numerous alien weeds that are successfull in North American cities. Further, plant evolution undoubtedly is continuing in cities, according to the principles outlined by Edgar Anderson (for example, 1956), which show how environmental disturbance stimulates hybridization. These exciting ideas deserve detailed examination in urban areas.

Detrimental Urban Processes

Urban plants, especially trees, are subject to a number of environmental stresses that are absent or less severe in the countryside. These urban processes combine to limit the kinds of plant life that can survive in the city, and their action must be appreciated if management of vegetation in the city is to be successful. The discussion here concentrates on the detrimental effects of urban processes on trees, although many other plants are affected similarly.

The city, compared with a forest setting, is hostile to tree growth. The tree commonly must withstand reduced supplies of water and oxygen in the paved-over soil. The normal cycle of nutrient minerals is interrupted as man removes grass, leaves, and limbs from the ground rather than allow their incorporation into the soil. In contrast, other substances — some of them deleterious in kind or quantity — may be applied to soil: pesticides and road salt, for example. Also, a number of air pollutants produced by urban activities greatly influence plant life, even though the contaminants are present only in low concentrations. Man may injure plants by direct mechanical means, such as during construction and by excessive pruning. This section discusses these various detrimental processes in turn. Several additional effects of the city should be noted in passing. Many city trees are in the open and hence more susceptible to damage by wind or ice than are forest trees. Finally, although the death of many urban plants is directly attributed to biotic disease, the aforementioned stresses make the plants much more vulnerable to disease than they otherwise would be.

Drought and Poor Aeration

The roots of plants require an adequate supply of water and oxygen. The quantities of these requisites are reduced in the city by paving, ground compaction, and soil filling. Most precipitation falling in the city is quickly carried off in drains; hence, little moisture can infiltrate into the ground for plant usage. Street trees, whose roots may have only several square feet of unpaved ground from which to absorb water and air, are especially affected. In just one season an oak tree may give off 120 tons of water through its leaves, and that water must be replenished from the soil.

The problems of this man-induced drought in the city are compounded during periods of subnormal rainfall. A progression of plant symptoms develops, with death a common terminal condition. Wilting is followed by yellowing or browning of leaves; the stems of trees may split or grow cankers, and the upper portions of the plant may be progressively damaged until recovery is impossible. With regard to soil aeration (the process by which gases produced or consumed under the soil surface are exchanged for gases in the aerial atmosphere), several feet of fill-dirt deposited on the ground over tree roots will damage or kill the tree by cutting off oxygen from active rootlets. Similarly, traffic (even foot traffic) can compact surface layers of the ground sufficiently to injure plants whose roots are growing beneath. Normally soil aeration is improved naturally by soil animals, such as earthworms, which by their movement increase the pore space through which both air and water move. But in the city soil, paving, compaction, and pesticides reduce both the diversity and the number of these organisms.

Mineral Deficiencies

All higher plants require an adequate supply of 16 chemical elements for normal growth and health.* Oxygen and carbon are derived

---

*The nine macronutrients, required in substantial quantities, are carbon, oxygen, hydrogen, nitrogen, phosphorus, potassium, sulfur, magnesium, and calcium; the seven micronutrients, of which only slight amounts are needed, are iron, boron, copper, zinc, molybdenum, manganese, and chlorine.

from carbon dioxide in the air and hydrogen is obtained from soil water. The plant usually obtains the other 13 elements in solution through the soil. Many urban soils are deficient in one or more of these essential plant nutrients. Further, the uptake of nutrients by city plants is influenced by other urban impacts; urban drought, for instance, may restrict nutrient uptake to the point that nutrient deficiency occurs. In city plants the symptoms of deficiency generally are confusing because they are not nearly so well understood as such symptoms in agricultural crops; furthermore, symptoms of nutrient deficiency in urban plants usually are confounded by other urban environmental effects.

Mineral deficiencies in urban vegetation, most notably of nitrogen, phosphorus, and potassium (which are required in large quantities), are usually a result of man's interrupting of cyclic flow of nutrients — which move from soil to plant leaves and animal consumers and back to the soil for recycling as leaves fall and organisms die. In the city man disturbs this cycle by collecting lawn clippings, raked leaves, plucked weeds, and remains of garden plants and either burning them or disposing of them through municipal refuse collections. The urbanite may in part replenish major nutrients by applying mineral fertilizer, especially to lawns and gardens (where deficiency symptoms are most commonly recognized); but he usually neglects trees, and urban trees are serious victims of nutrient cycle disruption.

Contamination by Road Salt, Heavy Metals, and Pesticides

Soil and vegetation in cities are contaminated by various substances that may injure plants. Roadside vegetation is particularly affected. Increasing amounts of rock salt (sodium chloride) and calcium chloride are being applied to North American roads for deicing; over seven million tons were used in the winter of 1966–67, a fourfold increase since 1954. Heavy metals emitted by motor vehicles also may have an impact. Finally, pesticides are applied to vegetation with pronounced effects that were not intended.

The injurious effects of salt on urban trees were recognized as early as 1912 by Solotaroff — who illustrated tree damage from nearby dumping of salt used in freezing ice cream! Today, as much as 20 tons of salt per year may purposely be applied to a single mile of roadway to melt ice and snow. The vegetational consequences have become

Figure 9.8. Roadside vegetation damaged by salt.
Kentucky bluegrass killed and American elms severely
damaged in Arlington, Virginia. (Courtesy of Horace
V. Wester, National Park Service.)

widespread and striking (Figure 9.8). One investigation of these effects
typifies conclusions reached by many researchers:

> Salt-damage injury to vegetation is serious. As observed in the Washington,
> D.C. area, trees, shrubbery and turf may be killed in a single season; however, the
> more typical reaction for shade trees is the production of chronic symptoms
> such as stunted growth and foliage scorch . . . The damage undoubtedly greatly
> shortens the life of affected trees, and in the process makes the trees very unattrac-
> tive for ornamental purposes. (Wester and Cohen 1968, p. 354)

The degree of plant injury depends upon numerous factors, including the inherent susceptibility of different plant species, the amount
of salt applied to the road, the proximity of the plant to road, the

timing of the application with respect to snow-plowing (which piles salt and snow along the roadside), soil characteristics (including depth and duration of frost in the soil), and the amount of saltwater runoff prior to ground thaw. Low springtime precipitation helps maintain toxic levels of salt in the soil; irrigation of affected soils will leach out some of the salt and help prevent plant damage.

The relative resistance of different species to road salt is not well known, but in general oaks and Norway maple are more tolerant than hemlock, sugar maple, and elm. Likewise, the specific physiological mechanism responsible for plant damage is debated; however, sodium ions, toxic to plants in high concentration, may substitute for potassium or antagonize the uptake of other essential nutrients and thereby induce nutrient deficiencies.

Heavy metals are another type of contaminant of roadside soils and vegetation (see Chapter 6), though their effects on plants are poorly understood. The residues of gasoline, motor oil, and car tires, which include cadmium, nickel, lead, and zinc, are deposited directly on plants and also accumulate in surface soil. The toxic effect on plants of high concentrations of zinc is recognized, and lead may injure shallow-rooting plants such as grasses. The biological effects of metals deserve much more investigation.

The use of chemical pesticides may have inadvertent and deleterious effects, as well as intended effects, on urban vegetation. Huge amounts of pesticides are applied in urban places (including suburbia) — about 40 percent of the annual dollar sales of pesticides in the United States (Wadleigh 1968). Herbicides, applied to kill unwanted plants, frequently do unintended damage by drifting to neighboring areas. For example, herbicides sprayed to control roadside vegetation (a common practice) have caused tree damage 300 feet back from the road in the Connecticut Arboretum. Undesired leaf loss, distorted growth, and dieback may occur from such accidents. Other pesticides, such as those sprayed in gardens to control insect pests, may indirectly injure plants in several ways, including by drastically reducing the number and variety of organisms that live within the soil and are responsible for soil health.

Air Pollution

It is now widely recognized that numerous air pollutants, although present in only very low concentrations, severely affect plant

life. And a mixture of air pollutants fouls the air of virtually every
city — exhaust from motor vehicles, smoke and gases from combustion
for power generation, waste products from industrial processes, and
others (see Chapters 3 and 4). Air pollutants may act to reduce food
production in plants (by destroying chlorophyll and disrupting photosynthesis), causing injury of various sorts. At the extreme, vegetation
has been nearly exterminated near certain industries. Toxicants in
the air may also suppress growth, cause dwarfing, produce browning or
spotting of leaves, or cause other effects short of death, as well as death.

Table 9.3 lists the major contaminants of urban air that injure or
destroy vegetation, together with their important sources, plant symptoms produced, and thresholds of injurious exposure. The greatest
threat by far is from gaseous pollutants; particulate matter generally is
regarded to be of minor importance, although deposition of dust
particles on leaves may inhibit photosynthesis.

Many usual symptoms of injury from air pollution are similar to
injuries caused by other agents (such as mineral deficiency or drought).
Likewise, damage by different pollutants may be confusingly similar.
The *injury threshold* is the minimum amount of contaminant that will
cause visible injury. Even though the plants in a city must endure continuous exposure to contaminated atmosphere, the thresholds for
chronic injury (that is, low concentrations continuously or intermit-
tently present over long periods, such as weeks or years) are less well
known than acute levels (that is, the higher concentrations that will
damage after only short periods of exposure). The damage thresholds
for many plants are considerably below the pollutant concentrations
usually occurring in many American cities.

Injury to plants in the city by air pollution is an excellent (albeit
disturbing) example of positive environmental feedback loops in operation. The botanical effects of a given concentration of a specific pollutant usually are accentuated by two types of environmental interactions:
(1) the presence of other pollutants and (2) other changes in the plant's
urban environment. For example, ozone and sulfur dioxide together
produce a synergistic action such that plant injury occurs at concentrations below the threshold levels of either of the separate gases. In other
words, an ordinarily harmless concentration of sulfur dioxide combined
with an ordinarily harmless concentration of ozone can produce ozone-
type injury. Similarly, the presence of other environmental stresses
in the city may serve to lower the injury threshold of an air pollutant.

Table 9.3. Impact of various air pollutants on vegetation, including sources, symptoms, and injury thresholds. (After Mukammal and others 1968 and Hindawi 1970.)

Pollutant	Sources	Plant Symptoms of Injury	Injury Threshold	
			Parts per Million (ppm)	Periods of Exposure
Sulfur dioxide (SO$_2$)	Combustion of coal, fuel oil, and petroleum; oil refineries	Bleached areas on leaves; yellowing of leaves; growth suppression; leaf-fall; reduction in yield	0.3 0.05	8 hours season
Nitrogen dioxide (NO$_2$)	High-temperature combustion of gasoline, oil, gas, and coal in internal combustion engines and power plants; manufacture of acids	Dead spots between veins and on margins of leaves	2.5 0.5	4 hours season
Hydrogen fluoride (HF)	Phosphate rock processing; aluminum refining; iron smelting; brick and ceramic works; fiber glass manufacturing	Dead tip and margin of leaves; yellowing of leaves; leaf-fall; dwarfing; lower yield	0.0001	5 weeks
Chlorine (Cl$_2$)	Leaks in chlorine storage tanks; hydrochloric acid mist	Bleaching between veins and dead tip and margin of leaves; defoliation	0.10	2 hours
Ethylene (CH$_2$)	Automobile and truck exhaust; incomplete combustion of coal, gas, and oil; chemical manufacture	Yellowing of leaves; leaf-fall; failure of flower to open; flower dropping; stimulation of lateral growth	0.05	6 hours
Ozone (O$_3$)	Photochemical reaction of hydrocarbons and nitrogen oxides from fuel combustion (esp. in automobiles); refuse burning; and evaporation from petroleum products and organic solvents	Flecks and bleached spots on leaves; early leaf-fall; growth suppression	0.03	4 hours
Peroxyacetyl nitrate (PAN)	Same sources as ozone	Discoloration (silvering or bronzing) on undersurface of young leaves	0.01	6 hours

There is limited evidence that the following common urban conditions tend to increase a plant's susceptibility to air pollution damage: decreased light intensity (peroxyacetl nitrate, PAN, is an exception), increased temperatures, and deficient nutrition. The urban reduction of humidity and soil moisture tends, however, to counter these effects; plants near wilting, for instance, are quite resistant to air pollution damage because of their reduced rate of gas exchange with the atmosphere.

Different kinds of plants are differentially susceptible to air pollution damage. Further, a given species may be nearly immune to injury by one pollutant and highly susceptible to another.Generally, susceptible trees include oaks, beech, hemlock, fir, white pine, Scots pine, and spruce. Among smaller plants, lichens are notoriously liable to injury; numerous studies have shown them to be scarce in metropolitan areas and often totally absent from the central city.

Mechanical Impacts by Man

Human activities can cause direct mechanical damage to urban vegetation. Injury to tree roots during construction work, which decreases tree stability and allows entry of diseases, is a commonplace example. Careless pruning also may open a tree to attack by disease. Equally serious is the aesthetic damage inflicted on some trees by pruning, especially to clear paths for overhead wires. Collision by vehicles is another significant cause of tree injury in the city. And vandals wantonly destroy or damage many trees, especially young ones.

SOME PLANNING CONSIDERATIONS

Knowledgeable planning can, and should, enhance the vegetational environment of urban man. It also is apparent that such planning must consider the complex dynamics of urban processes. To continue our focus on trees, Table 9.4 lists some kinds of trees with special environmental characteristics (more information can be found in U.S. Department of Agriculture 1949; Edwards 1962). Useful and detailed suggestions for fostering tree planting and maintenance in the city are presented in a report by the American Society of Planning Officials (1968) and in the Proceedings of the International (formerly National)

Table 9.4. Trees with special characteristics for urban planting. (After American Society of Planning Officials 1968.)

Characteristics	Kinds of Trees
Resistant to extreme city conditions	Tree of heaven, box-elder, white mulberry (all grow where nothing else will, but are not generally desirable)
Resistant to most city conditions	Norway maple, horse chestnut, green ash, hawthorn, ginkgo, London plane, honey locust, red oak, linden, European hornbeam
Fast growth	Red maple, white ash, ginkgo, green ash, honey locust, European larch, cucumber tree, pin oak, black locust, mountain ash, American linden, Chinese elm, pitch pine, red pine, white pine, Scots pine
Privacy and protection	Evergreens or mixtures of evergreens and deciduous trees, euonymus, firethorn, lilacs, mock orange
Resistant to air pollution	Birch, catalpa, elms, ginkgo, hawthorns, London plane, magnolia, tree of heaven, English oak, tulip tree
Resistant to most biotic disease and insects	Russian olive, ginkgo, honey locust, Kentucky coffee tree, golden rain, sweet gum, cucumber, sweet bay, magnolia, sour gum, sourwood, and cork
Resistant to ice damage	Beech, catalpa, ginkgo, golden rain, hawthorn, hop hornbeam, horse chestnut, locust, oaks, yellow birch
Flowers and color	Dogwood, English hawthorn, honey locust, golden rain, tulip, cucumber, sweet bay, magnolia, beach plum, Japanese cherry, black locust, fringe-tree, flowering fruit trees
Sweet scents	Silver wattle (*Acacia*), amur maple, silk tree, English hawthorn, laurel or sweet bay, sorrel or sourwood, magnolias, citruses, pines and balsams
Edible fruits that attract birds	Cotoneasters, flowering crabapple, sapphire berry, spreading juniper, hawthorn, sumacs, hollies
Weak-wooded (break in storms)	Chinese elm, silver maple, mountain ash
Prone to drip on cars	Birches, elms, lindens
Prone to clog drains and sewers	Willow, poplar, silver maple, catalpa, elms, some locusts, lindens, black walnut, horse chestnut

The left margin indicates an arrow ranging from "Favorable" (upper portion) to "Detrimental" (lower portion).

Shade Tree Conference. Steps toward solving many problems of urban tree maintenance are presented by Pirone (1959). However, initiation of planning and maintenance rests on broad recognition of their need.

The strong case for urban greenery has more grounds than simply aesthetics and promotion for economic profits. Plants have virtues for alleviating social and physical environmental problems in the city. There is great need to incorporate both physical and social environmental values, along with enlightened aesthetic, educational, and economic values, into urban planning. But social and physical scientists unfortunately have shunned studying and communicating these values, for complicated historical reasons mentioned in Chapter 1.

The dominant ecological models for vegetation analysis and interpretation are plainly inadequate for explaining the nature of most urban vegetation — either the overall pattern or individual patches. The concepts of plant succession and energy cycling, for example, contribute little to understanding the city's dynamic vegetational mosaics. New perspectives — of kinds traditionally avoided by students of plant cover — are needed. Reality dictates that emphasis on "natural" processes must shift to human activities, attention on presumably close-knit plant "communities" should shift to the environmental adjustments of individual plants, and predilection for studying native species in wild habitats should give way to more investigation of alien, ornamental, and weedy species in the city. This is not to suggest that there are no existing ecological or geographical concepts for describing and explaining urban vegetation. Rather the problem has been neglected and existing approaches cannot readily be applied unmodified in the city. Hence, this chapter is a set of early, hesitating steps into the field.

REFERENCES

American Society of Planning Officials. 1968. *Trees in the city.* Chicago: Planning Advisory Service Report no. 236.

Anderson, Edgar. 1956. Man as a maker of new plants and new plant communities. In *Man's role in changing the face of the earth,* ed. William L. Thomas, Jr., pp. 763–777. Chicago: Univ. of Chicago Press.

Barber, John C. 1971. Urban forestry as the U.S. Forest Service sees it. *Arborist's News* (Urbana, Ill.) 36(7):73–77.

Bates, G. H. 1935. The vegetation of footpaths, sidewalks, cart-tracks and gateways. *Jour. Ecol.* 23(2):470–487.

Brett, W. S., and K. Grant. 1967. *Small city gardens.* London and New York: Abelard-Schuman.

Curtis, John. 1965. The modification of mid-latitude grasslands and forests by man. In *Man's role in changing the face of the earth,* ed. William L. Thomas, Jr., pp. 721–736. Chicago: Univ. of Chicago Press.

Dansereau, Pierre. 1971. Dimensions of environmental quality. *Sarracenia* (Montreal), no. 14.

Darby, H. C. 1965. The clearing of the woodland in Europe. In *Man's role in changing the face of the earth,* ed. William L. Thomas, Jr., pp. 183–216. Chicago: Univ. of Chicago Press.

Edwards, P. F. 1962. *Trees and the English landscape.* London: G. Bell.

Guggenheimer, E. C. 1969. *Planning for parks and recreation needs in urban areas.* New York: Twayne.

Hindawi, I. J. 1970. *Air pollution injury to vegetation.* U.S. Department of Health, Education, and Welfare National Air Pollution Control Administration Publ. no. AP-71. Washington, D.C.: Govt. Printing Office.

Lees, C. B. 1970. *Gardens, plants and man.* Englewood Cliffs, N.J.: Prentice-Hall.

Li, H. L. 1969. Urban botany: Need for a new science. *BioScience* 19(10): 882–883.

Ministry of Housing and Local Government, Great Britain. 1958. *Trees in town and city.* London: H. M. Stationery Office.

Morel, Henri, and Jean Gottmann. 1961. The woodlands, their uses and wildlife. In *Megalopolis: The urbanized northeastern seaboard of the United States,* ed. Jean Gottmann, pp. 341–383. New York: Twentieth Century Fund.

Mukammal, E. I., C. S. Brandt, R. Neuwirth, D. H. Pack and W. C. Swinbank. 1968. *Air pollutants, meteorology, and plant injury.* Geneva: World Meteorological Organization, Tech. Note no. 96.

Pirone, P. P. 1959. *Tree maintenance,* 2nd ed. New York: Oxford Univ. Press.

Shomon, J. J. 1971. *Open land for urban America.* Baltimore and London: Johns Hopkins Press.

Smith, David M. 1969. Adapting forestry to megalopolitan southern New England. *Jour. of Forestry* 67:372–377.

Solotaroff, William. 1912. *Shade trees in towns and cities.* New York: John Wiley and Sons.

Toulan, Nohad. 1970. The distribution and value of open land in the Philadelphia area. In *Metropolitan open space and natural process,* ed. David Wallace, pp. 53–80. Philadelphia: Univ. of Pennsylvania Press.

U. S. Dept. of Agriculture. 1949. *Trees, the yearbook of agriculture.* Washington, D.C.: Govt. Printing Office.

Wadleigh, C. H. 1968. The application of agricultural technology. In *Soil, water and suburbia,* ed. National Conference on Soil, Water and Suburbia, pp. 41–53. Washington: Govt. Printing Office.

Wester, H. V. and E. E. Cohen. 1968. Salt damage to vegetation in the Washington, D.C., area during the 1966–67 winter. *Plant Disease Reptr.* 52(5):350–354.

Wright, Richardson. 1934. *The story of gardening.* New York: Dodd, Mead.

CHAPTER 10

The City as Habitat for Wildlife and Man

Forest Stearns

This chapter might also be titled "A Biologist Views the City." Biologists are accustomed to thinking in terms of organism-environment interactions. They deal with populations that live, grow, diminish, and sometimes disappear. Species prosper in environments to which they have become adapted through evolutionary processes. Habitat is a place in which to live; it can be described, examined, and modeled mathematically. The habitat of man can be studied in much the same way as that of any mammal; the heavily trampled bluegrass sod in a park gives clues to the behavior and preferences of the human population just as the browse line on white cedar in a northern Michigan swamp speaks for the white-tailed deer.

In his book, *A Different Kind of Country,* Raymond Dasmann (1968, p. 239) asserts that the urban planner needs some of the same understanding that all range and wildlife managers require — an appreciation of the overwhelming importance of habitat: "If you protect the habitat, the range, the environment, the future of the population is relatively secure. If you allow the habitat to be destroyed, the population will cease to exist." This is true whether it be elephants, whitetailed deer, whitefaced cattle or man. This chapter considers habitat in the city, first with reference to birds and mammals and finally as it affects man.

HABITAT: A DEFINITION

Habitat means different things to different people. For our
purpose let it encompass water, food, cover, breeding space and group
territories, and the amenities essential to a reasonable quality of life. In
nature, several of these requirements are provided by vegetation, either
directly or indirectly. A variety of plants furnish energy for herbivores
and thus are the energy base for the carnivores and detritivores of
other trophic levels.

A variety of plants is essential, not only to provide food for
many different animals, but also to prevent catastrophe from eliminat-
ing an animal population when a particular food crop fails. Similarly,
plants furnish cover — physical protection from precipitation, wind,
heat, and cold, as well as visual protection from predators and privacy
for the individual. Vegetation is vital even within the city. Man-made
structures may provide cover from the elements and from prying
eyes, and garbage cans or birdfeeders may be sources of food, but vegetation remains the key to habitat.

Water too is an essential component of habitat; water may be
limited, but in North America it is rarely scarce enough to eliminate
wildlife if other requirements are met. In places and periods of abundant
water the diversity of both vegetation and wildlife commonly increases.

URBAN WILDLIFE HABITATS

Diversity of urban vegetation permits diversity in the fauna. In
most cities one can find a broad range of vegetation types. Plant communities may include a patch of annual weeds on a dry cinder fill,
a cattail marsh in a roadside ditch, a narrow stretch of prairie along a
railroad, or an old deciduous forest preserved in an "undeveloped" city
park. Many successional communities are to be found — weedy lawns,
abandoned fields rich in forbs, and brush patches — as well as types
cultured by man: ornamental shrub plantings, vegetable patches, formal
flower gardens, and park savannas.

In metropolitan areas where the original landscape was hilly or

rolling, and where rivers, lakes, or marshes were present, ample opportunity for habitat diversity usually remains. Such areas, aided by a
modicum of intelligent planning and a degree of benign neglect, can
provide young *Homo sapiens* as well as other, wild species with appropriate conditions for development.

A variety of natural and cultural factors may influence habitat
development. The original nature of the physical landscape and the
degree of its destruction are important. The human population frequently imposes stringent limits on other plant and animal populations;
some cultures and some individuals invite wildlife or at least will
tolerate inconvenience from animals and birds, others will not. Controls
of urban wildlife populations may pose problems not met in the wild.
Predation may occur, but often the prey selected are not the weaker
members of the population. Vehicle predation, for instance, results
more from chance than chase.

Man's cultural activities commonly serve to limit habitat diversity at the micro scale. The intensive cultivation of both large and
small areas of short grass lawns is the general rule, as is the open
savanna-like park. Occasionally diversity is abruptly reduced when
officials, compelled by citizens' complaints, go on a weed-cutting binge.
Our obsession with neatness results in mowing brushy railroad rights-
of-way and even prairie patches in full flower (Stearns 1967).

Useful urban habitats include parks, cemeteries, dumps, greenbelts, railroad and utility rights-of-way (see Figure 10.1), institutional
grounds, riverbanks, industrial wasteland, open storm sewers, church-
yards, lakefronts, private lawns and gardens, and alleys.

As other chapters have shown, the urban habitat also suffers
from a catalogue of man-made hazards, affecting both man and beast.
City air is heavy with carbon monoxide, sulfur dioxide, ozone, PAN,
and particulates. Similarly, streams, ditches, lakes and even transient
pools are contaminated with organic oils, solvents, heavy metals,
and insecticides. Such water pollutants pose serious problems for waterfowl and fish. Vehicles — major predators — are everywhere; their
abundance emphasizes the need for animal travel corridors. Television
towers and guy wires kill many birds overflying cities during migrations.
The domestic cat, as well as the feral cat and dog, provide a frequent,
albeit more natural, type of predation. They in turn are preyed upon
and partially controlled by man (Beck 1971).

Figure 10.1. Hidden riches. Habitat and travelway for birds and small mammals in and along a utility line right-of-way. (Photograph by J. Klopatek.)

WILDLIFE IN THE CITY

What lives in these green and gray places within earshot of the rushing traffic? John Kiernan (1959) in his *Natural History of New York City* describes a surprising variety of wildlife to be found within the boundaries of that great city. Daily, news stories attest to a similiar variety in other urban places. The gulls in Boston harbor, the foxes of New York's Central Park, the raccoons of Madison, and the nesting teal of St. Paul are familiar examples. Some species, like the pigeon and the gray squirrel, are so well adapted to man and so familiar that the press ignores them. However, such creatures are of profound interest to man and are fed and watched by many, old and young alike.

Adaptation to Life with Man

The four-legged and winged life of the city may be grouped into three broad categories: (1) those species adapted to life with man and at least partly dependent upon him for food, cover, and nesting sites; (2) those that tolerate man and sometimes take advantage of him (the species of agricultural lands and suburbs); and (3) those that shun man, the species of wild forests, grasslands, and deserts, for whom small units of habitat usually are inadequate. Waterfowl are a special group whose presence is dependent upon suitable bodies of water. During migration, waterfowl may be seen in, over, and about most cities.

Birds adapted to a life dependent on man include the pigeon, starling, English sparrow, nighthawk, chimney swift, and herring gull; the mammals include Norway rats, house mice, cats, and dogs. However, by far the greatest number of urban vertebrates are not wholly dependent upon man, but take advantage of his activities and tolerate him. This group includes a long list of birds, especially those of the forest edge and open ground, such as the blue jay, robin, woodpecker, catbird, cardinal, crow, grackle, flicker, meadowlark, and oriole, and such mammals as the gray squirrel, cottontail rabbit, raccoon, chipmunk, skunk, bat, red fox, and opossum. The birds of the wild lands are seen in the city only during migration and then briefly. The larger wild-land mammals generally avoid city contacts with man, though coyotes have been observed on the outskirts of Milwaukee and Denver and have become residents of other cities. White-tailed deer are killed almost daily on streets and highways in urban areas; and the autumnal invasion of black bear into Duluth, Minnesota, and Marquette, Michigan, are well documented.

Much useful habitat for small animals and birds exists along streams and lakes, in parks (both forested and open), in backyards, and in the many "neglected" areas of the city. For example, the Menominee River Valley forms the industrial heart of Milwaukee and boasts a great concentration of heavy industry, materials storage, railroad yards and truck terminals. Despite these disparate human activities, wildlife finds food, water, and cover along the railroads, in the forgotten corners of storage yards, and in the narrow green corridors along fences and between buildings (see Figure 10.2). Here, with the Norway rat, live the rabbit, fox, and other mammals, as well as starlings, sparrows, and pigeons. The railroad yards of St. Paul and the docks at Superior,

Figure 10.2. Diverse wildlife habitat provided by water and vegetation in an industrialized area, the Menominee Valley in Milwaukee. (Photograph by J. Klopatek.)

Wisconsin, support sizable populations of ring-necked pheasants; these birds subsist on grain dropped during loading and transit. Sometimes habitat is created as a side benefit of modern technology. Water discharged by a power plant in Milwaukee warms the receiving stream enough to allow ducks to overwinter in an otherwise frozen and inhospitable environment. Canada geese, in places as distant as Rochester, Minnesota, and Carney's Point, New Jersey, have taken advantage of the same phenomenon. Large open bodies of water are even more useful. Almost 20,000 ducks, grebes, gulls, and other birds use the Milwaukee lakefront each winter.

During the 1930's and 1940's peregrine falcons substituted tall buildings for cliffs, and nested high on the man-made ledges in New York, Montreal, and other East Coast cities. The falcons hunted starlings and pigeons, thus serving as a beneficial predator. Widespread use of the pesticide DDT (which comes to be concentrated in the avian carnivore) brought an end to this relationship; East Coast peregrine falcon populations declined and have now disappeared (Hickey 1969).

The nighthawk is a familiar city bird, and its adaptation to flat gravel roofs for nesting has been studied in Detroit. Trees are used

for roosting. The bird has maintained territorial patterns, adjusting
these to urban conditions. The size of the home range appears to be
related to the abundance of flat roofs. In areas where flat roofs are
common, more birds can settle and home ranges are smaller (Armstrong
1965). In coastal cities, gulls also have used flat roofs as nesting sites.

Like the chimney swift, the European stork now nests almost
exclusively on human structures. The storks return year after year
to nest on the same rooftop or chimney. Barn and screech owls, too, are
often recorded as city dwellers. The large barred owl has been observed
hunting over the incinerator dump on the Milwaukee lakefront, and
the sparrow hawk is a frequent urban nester. Neglected window ledges,
steeples, attics, and the arches of bridges are commonly used by several
species of birds, especially the ubiquitous pigeon.

Areas used for refuse disposal commonly provide rich substrates
on which weedy plants thrive and produce both large quantities of
seed and a rank cover of stems and leaves. Cemeteries, zoos, institutional grounds, stream valleys, and steep bluffs like railroad embankments provide good habitat, largely because these areas frequently
remain untrimmed, unmowed, and unused by man.

The popular literature includes an abundance of observations of
animals and birds in the city and suburban fringe. Newspapers feature
unusual sightings and doings of animals and birds at every opportunity.
Despite these indications of public interest, there is a dearth of solid
research on both urban wildlife and wildlife habitat. This is matched in
considerable measure by the dearth of work on the biology and nonstructural habitat of urban man. For example, Sinton (1970) has
pointed out the need to study the detritus food chain of the city relative to wildlife populations. Likewise, little is known about the behavior
of animals and birds in the city. Those species considered to be pests —
the rat, the house mouse, and the English sparrow, for instance — have
been studied; but about others there is much mystery.

Problems for Man

City wildlife populations at times reach problem levels, although
rarely (except for highly adapted animals such as the rat, pigeon, and
starling) do they present problems of the magnitude posed by the kites,
crows, rooks, and jackdaws that stole food from children in medieval
London (Fitter 1945). In winter, hungry mice and rabbits strip the bark
from woody plants in city parks and home plantings. In suburban

areas, raccoons may strew garbage indiscriminately night after night. Confined herds of large herbivores, whether held purposefully (as they are in Buesch Park, St. Louis) or unintentionally (as was the Arsenal deer herd in St. Paul), may eliminate both woody and herbaceous vegetation and destroy their habitat as effectively as the wild deer of the Kaibab plateau in Arizona.

Occasionally an urban animal will develop a special taste for some plant prized by man and will achieve instant notoriety. This was the case of the gray squirrels of the U. S. Embassy in London, whose appetite for crocus bulbs almost resulted in their extermination by man.

Life in the city has had an impact on the food preferences of many animals, as illustrated most dramatically by the rhesus monkey in India. In contrast to their forest relatives, the city monkeys prefer cooked vegetables and roasted and spiced foods. These monkeys live by pilfering and show other distinctly urban patterns. Through its association with man and the urban environment the urban monkey has developed some behavioral characteristics resembling those of urban *Homo sapiens*: he is aggressive with other monkeys and sometimes with humans. However, the dominant male is more inclined to share food with his urban fellows than is the forest male. In general the urban animal is more responsive to new situations and shows more complex responses than the rural animal (Singh 1969). Similar adaptations to city life are evident in many animals and birds — the evening grosbeak becomes addicted to sunflower seeds and the chipmunk to peanut butter.

Urban birds and mammals must also be examined as vectors of human disease. Until there is more knowledge about this point, a few cases of human disease may wipe out progress in the development of wildlife and human habitat.

IMPROVING WILDLIFE HABITATS: THE NEED FOR DIVERSITY

What can be done to improve habitat for wildlife in the city? The general answer has already been indicated. Areas of diverse vegetation must be retained or developed. These areas must have suitable interconnections and be of sufficient size to support viable populations and to provide a buffer against people and traffic. Water is important;

Figure 10.3. Habitat lost. Channelization has destroyed valley bottom vegetation and habitat, Milwaukee County, Wisconsin. (Photograph by J. Klopatek.)

natural bodies of water must be protected and new ones created where needed. The channelization of streams to hasten storm drainage has been a major factor in reducing habitat (see Figure 10.3).

In any habitat program, vegetation is the prime requisite; for both man and animals it provides shade, reduces wind speed and noise, and ameliorates climatic extremes. Vegetation is a direct source of food, and it supports the insects and other invertebrates that in turn are food for many birds and animals. Vegetation also provides essential physical sites for nesting, dens, and escape.

The importance of diversity needs frequent emphasis. Variety is, above all, a buffer against calamity. Diverse soils with many different conditions of moisture and light provide suitable seed beds and support for a variety of plants. Each plant species may individually produce only a small yield, but when all are combined the crop includes a good mix of seeds, fruits, and buds. Variety in plant growth also produces a multiplicity of habitat situations and thus increases the niches available for wildlife. For example, open meadows and lawns attract some birds, patches of shrubs others, and wooded areas many more. Space with food in proximity must be available for nesting territories. Species diversity in both plants and animals is a major factor in community stability, a rule which appears to apply to urban as well as to wildland situations.

In making provision for ample and diverse vegetation and for water, there are many specific measures that can be taken to improve urban wildlife habitat.

Perhaps the greatest opportunity lies with individual home owners; their activity can be greatly enhanced by the cooperation of industrial firms and municipal government. Presently, open grass lawns predominate in residential areas. More trees and shrub patches are needed. The species chosen may influence human as well as wildlife habitat. For example, thorny shrubs may effectively direct human traffic while also providing food and nesting areas for wildlife. Hidden fencing may be combined with shrub plantings to form mini-refuges for wildlife, while simultaneously protecting man from predators of his own species. Erosion of a steep bank at the University of Wisconsin was virtually eliminated by a dense planting of vining and thorny shrubs; the planting also forms an excellent habitat for small mammals and birds.

One of the most important steps for improvement of wildlife habitat in the city is a program of "planned neglect." Hollow trees should be cut only when they offer a real and frequent hazard to man. They are needed as food sources and den trees. The impulse to mow every small segment of park, lawn, and vacant lot must be resisted. Cure of the mowing syndrome will allow the growth of patches of weeds useful as food, although occasional disturbance is essential if weed patches are to persist. Outdated city ordinances against weeds should be revised to eliminate controls on the strictly agricultural weeds and those plants whose contribution to human allergies is more imagined than real.

New habitats may occur as by-products of other activities. We anticipate that plantings now made chiefly for aesthetic considerations will soon be augmented by widespread use of plants in erosion control, noise reduction, wind and air pollution control, and perhaps wildlife habitat development. Park management methods clearly influence breeding bird populations; the removal of brush and the tendency to overprune shrubs and small trees decrease the number of bird species and increase the height at which nests of shrub-dwelling species are found (Burr and Jones 1968). Small changes in park management would make considerable improvements in habitat.

Birds and animals take to heart the expression, "It's a nice place to visit, but I wouldn't want to live there." Man should do the same. If the essential habitat needs of a species are only partially satisfied, members of that species may exist, but under stress, in competition with other species (or with other populations of their own) that are better adapted to that environment.

HABITAT REQUIREMENTS FOR MAN

In the case of *Homo sapiens* we need both appreciation for and understanding of habitat requirements beyond the essentials of food, air, water, and shelter. To complicate our considerations, we find that man uses compensating mechanisms to improve his immediate habitat — from awnings and air conditioning to furnaces and fireplaces. When, as often happens, such improvement is inadequate, urban man escapes to the countryside. That large part of the human population who cannot afford habitat alteration and who cannot escape at intervals into other surroundings is trapped in a stressful environment just as surely as is the Michigan white-tailed deer in a browsed-out winter deer yard.

With the growth of vast urban complexes and the destruction of large community green areas and local neighborhood pockets of diversity (often on the questionable premise of a bigger tax base), the automobile has become the only means of escape. Thus destruction of local habitat triggers a feedback mechanism that precipitates habitat destruction in an ever increasing area. The ultimate cost of providing substitute habitats and means of reaching them will greatly exceed the return in taxes from the land that was converted.

Basic Biological Needs

Most students of cities have chosen to ignore the basic biological nature of man. Architects deal in exterior form, aesthetics, and sometimes function; landscape planners in "design principles"; politicians in short-term solutions to immediate problems; economists in monetary profits and losses (for example, the influence of interest rates on the housing market); regional planners in trends and projections (thus often perpetuating past mistakes); and engineers in single-factor solutions to hasten the flow of water, sewage, or automobiles from one place to another. Few try to grasp the complexity of the interactions, and no one yet speaks clearly for human habitat and the unvoiced needs of man. Indeed, the biologist too has neglected the city and is likewise at fault.

It was only very recently that man left his ancestral savanna setting — where he gleaned food from the trees and shrubs, drank from the rivers, and jumped abruptly aside at the sound of danger — to congregate in villages and cities. In an evolutionary sense, he finds himself suddenly part of a vast aggregation of men, dependent upon others for the essentials of life and with little control of his surroundings or his fate. Man's physiology, reproductive processes, and behavioral responses indicate all too clearly his mammalian origins. His cities, especially those designed for private vehicular travel, show a vast disregard for these same origins (Figure 10.4). Thus it is no surprise that urban man is subject to a greater incidence of stress-induced disabilities than is his rural counterpart.

Territoriality

Beyond the essential physical needs to eat, breathe, sleep, and excrete, there are several less obvious, but deepseated, biological needs that man shares with other animals. These needs — for personal space, for territorial elbow room, for contact with other animals and with plants, for social interaction within small clans and family groups, and for diversity in surroundings — all derive from our prehuman origins. Man's needs likewise are conditioned by the cultural background of each population. Let us explore the nature of urban human habitat, from the densely built and aging inner city to the sprawling suburbs dotted with look-alike ranch houses.

In recent years, perhaps the outstanding example of disregard for human needs has been the attempt to house low-income families in

Figure 10.4. What does urban man need besides parking? Rear view of an apartment complex in Milwaukee. (Photograph by F. Stearns.)

high-rise apartment complexes fringed in places with a useless border of clipped green lawn. The social deterioration resulting from this attempt is now well known and has been demonstrated in American cities from New York to San Francisco. The inhabitants of these cages lack contact with soil and nature, and without territory or safe travel-ways they are at the mercy of human predators whose traits have developed in the behavioral sink of the dying city. Children at play on the ground are isolated from mothers aloft, all sense of community is lost, and regulations prove worse than useless. To quote Edward T. Hall (1968, p. 169), "The high-rise has proved to be the new source of anomie in ghetto life."

The suburbanite also faces problems of space and lack of environmental control. With low ranch houses sprawling side by side, the suburban dweller suffers noise and disruption from packs of small children moving across his land, and his nose is offended by the greasy smoke from his neighbor's barbecue. Although lacking privacy, he dares not erect hedge, fence, or wall to define his territory; such action would not conform to neighborhood mores. In the older portions of American cities and everywhere in Europe, hedges, fences, and walls prove valuable in defining territory and reducing stress. In the modern suburb, transient cultural values, fixed in restrictive "setback" ordinances, for example, detract from habitat quality.

Vegetation alone is not adequate to provide "cover" for urban man. However, it provides shade, cushions and cleans the wind, and blocks sound; by setting limits on vision, vegetation may increase privacy and thus reduce the stress of intraspecies contact.

Pathways

With man as with other animals, travelways provide opportunity to attain the environmental diversity so essential for development of the young and for sanity of the mature individual. Hall (1968, pp. 164–165) notes that theories have developed that consider both "sensory deprivation and information overload. Man can suffer from both, and an excess of either can destroy him. An adequate environment balances sensory inputs and provides a mix that is congenial as well as consistent with man's culturally conditioned needs."

Locations of animal travelways are based on habit and instinctual considerations of safety. Urban man also needs paths that can be easily and safely trod. Such passageways should be partially protected from the elements and should provide diversity in sensory impact as well as reasonable security. Not the least of the values of human travelways is that of health — they are designed for walking — and thus the mainly pedestrian city is a worthy goal for biological as well as aesthetic reasons.

Travelways involve questions of scale. The space needed varies with the species of animal, with its ecological niche, and with the age cohort involved. The mature ruffed grouse may range over 40 acres, the suburban cottontail an acre, and the black bear 10 square miles. A three-year-old child is satisfied in his own backyard. As he grows older and more venturesome, his range increases and at the age of 10 he may search for stimulation over six or eight blocks. The adolescent human, reaching the breeding age, may cover many miles in a single day.

The ancient pattern of juvenile dispersal is less evident in man than in birds or mammals, whose young of the year leave the home territory to establish areas of their own. However, not many years ago it was usual for a young man of 16 or 18 to leave home to make his own way. Despite crowding in the city and social pressures to remain at home, the urge for dispersal persists, and male competition is frequently evident within the family.

Some Recommendations

For a balanced urban habitat we must provide brood cover for small children, safe territory for youthful exploration, flocking, trysting, and roosting habitat for young adults, and, finally, stable and well defined territories for older cohorts. The vacant lot in his block is of far more value to a five-year-old than is the park located three or four blocks away. Likewise, the elderly need readily accessible, comfortable, and quiet parks. With man as with wildlife, scale and distribution of green areas are important.

Diversity in man-made structures is likewise essential to quality human habitat. Such diversity may result from age, from material, and from form. Structural variety combined with dynamic vegetation will provide a beneficial mix of sensations.

With man as with wildlife, water is at the core of life. The visual impact of water, even without the prospect of physical contact, is enough to excite the human senses. Urbanites indirectly reveal their preference by the price they are willing to pay to live near water. Despite the value of water bodies, their maintenance is difficult in urban areas. The engineer tends to look upon lakes, streams, and swamps as areas to be conquered by filling, channeling, and draining. Water and wetland areas should be retained for quality habitat, not used for waste disposal.

The effects of neighborhood destruction and dissolution resulting from urban renewal or expressway construction must be mentioned. In these cases the familial and tribal ties originating with the progenitors of man have again been disregarded, with resulting loss to the city and its stability.

Iltis (1968, p. 117) in an outstanding essay has summarized the habitat needs of man as a magnificent compromise: "The optimum human environment is one in which the human animal can have a maximum contact with the natural (evolutionary) environment in which he evolved and for which all our basic processes are genetically programmed, yet in which at the same time the many advantages of civilization are not sacrificed." We have not had time to adapt either our hormone systems or our brains to the anthill psychology necessary for survival in modern urban habitats. We lack reassurance provided by contact with the soil, we are jammed in with strangers from other families, clans, tribes, and cultures, with no territory to claim. Thus it is hardly surprising that urban men show pathological patterns similar to those that Calhoun (1962) developed experimentally in rats or that Konrad Lorenz (1966) noted in other animals.

Homo sapiens may well survive past the year 2,000 without drastic changes in his attitudes or actions, but if so, the quality of the life he leads will not be the same. Habitat quality is the first victim of unbridled population growth and Detroit may soon be indistinguishable from Calcutta. The mayor of any large city knows that today his city operates in continuous and deep crises, crises that neither he, Madison Avenue, the federal government, nor the networks can talk away. Often, even those needs basic to mere animal survival — food, suitable air, shelter, and personal protection — are lacking.

Why is it important to improve habitat? I submit that one cannot separate the problems of mere survival from those of quality; they are inextricably related. Improvement of the habitat of wildlife and of man the mammal is one way to improve greatly the life of urban man.

REFERENCES

Armstrong, J. T. 1965. Breeding home range in the nighthawk and other birds: its evolutionary and ecological significance. *Ecology* 46:619–629.

Beck, A. M. 1971. The life and times of Shag, a feral dog in Baltimore. *Natural History* Oct.:58–65.

Burr, R. M., and R. E. Jones. 1968. The influence of parkland habitat management on birds in Delaware. In *Trans. 33rd North American Wildlife and Natural Resources Conf.,* pp. 299–306. Washington, D.C.: Wildlife Management Institute.

Calhoun, J. B. 1962. Population density and social pathology. *Sci. Amer.* Feb.:139–148.

Dasmann, R. F. 1964. *Wildlife biology.* New York: John Wiley and Sons.

——— 1968. *A different kind of country.* New York: Macmillan.

Fitter, R. S. R. 1945. *London's natural history.* London: Collins.

Hall, E. T. 1968. Human needs and inhuman cities. In *The fitness of man's environment,* Smithsonian Annual no. 2, pp. 163–172. Washington, D.C.: Smithsonian Institution.

Hickey, J. J. 1969. *Peregrine falcon populations; Their biology and decline.* Madison: Univ. of Wisconsin Press.

Iltis, H. H. 1968. The optimum human environment and its relation to modern agricultural preoccupations. *The Biologist* 50(June):114–125.

Kieran, J. 1959. *The natural history of New York City.* Boston: Houghton-Mifflin.

Leopold, Aldo. 1949. *Sand County almanac.* New York: Oxford Univ. Press.

Lorenz, Konrad. 1966. *On aggression.* New York: Harcourt, Brace & World.

McHarg, Ian. 1969. *Design with nature.* Garden City, N.Y.: Natural History Press.

Rublowsky, John. 1967. *Nature in the city.* New York: Basic Books.

Shepard, Paul, and D. McKinley, ed. 1969. *The subversive science; Essays toward an ecology of man.* Boston: Houghton-Mifflin.

Singh, S. D. 1969. Urban monkeys. *Sci. Amer.* July:108–117.

Sinton, J. W. 1970. Wildlife in the city: A problem in values. AAS Symposium 1970. *Urban Ecology Today.* (Mimeo) 15 pp.

Stearns, F. W. 1967. Wildlife habitat in urban and suburban environments. In *Trans. 32nd North American Wildlife and Natural Resources Conf.*, pp. 61–69. Washington, D.C.: Wildlife Management Institute.

U.S. Dept. of Interior, Bureau of Sports Fisheries and Wildlife. 1968. *Man and nature in the city: A symposium.* Washington, D.C.: Govt. Printing Office.

ABOUT CONTRIBUTORS

WILFRID BACH (b. 1936) is an air pollution climatologist in the Department of Geography at the University of Hawaii, Honolulu, Hawaii 96822. He earned degrees from the University of Marburg and the University of Sheffield (Ph.D., 1965). He has held faculty appointments at McGill University and the University of Cincinnati. Interdisciplinary aspects of atmospheric pollution and the urban environment are the focus of Bach's teaching. His major research projects deal with the practical applications of air pollution diffusion theories, scattering theory, and suspended particulate pollution theory to air quality control and city planning. As Chairman of the University of Hawaii's Air Pollution Task Force, he is involved in setting air quality standards for Hawaii and establishing instrumentation procedures there. He is the author of *Atmospheric Pollution* (McGraw-Hill, 1972).

DUANE D. BAUMANN (b. 1940) is on the faculty of the Department of Geography at Southern Illinois University, Carbondale, Illinois 62901. He holds degrees in geography from Illinois State University and Clark University (Ph.D., 1967). Baumann's research has focused on human adjustment to natural hazards, information processing, and cognitive models of decision making in resource management, especially water resources. In 1969 he served as Chairman of the Massachusetts Board of Higher Education's Committee on Environmental Control. He is a member of the U.S. Commission on Man and Environment of the International Geographical Union.

REID A. BRYSON (b. 1920) is Director of the Institute for Environmental Studies at the University of Wisconsin, Madison, Wisconsin 53706. He is Professor of Meteorology and Geography at Wisconsin and was formerly Chariman of the

Meteorology Department (which he helped establish in 1948). Denison University honored him with a D.Sc. degree in 1971. Bryson has served on numerous national scientific committees, including the National Academy of Sciences–National Academy of Engineering Environmental Studies Board. His research publications span a wide range of interests – meteorology, geography, oceanography, hydrology, and archaeology. He presently is studying climatic history and climatic change as related to air pollution.

THOMAS R. DETWYLER (b. 1938) is a bio- and physical geographer in the Department of Geography, the University of Michigan, Ann Arbor, Michigan 48104. He earned an undergraduate degree in botany at the University of Michigan and a Ph.D. degree in geography at Johns Hopkins University (1966). His teaching interests are concentrated in plant geography and man's impact on environment; he teaches an interdisciplinary course on the latter subject with Donald Gray. Relations between vegetation and various dynamic processes, especially geomorphic processes, and perception of environmental quality have been subjects of Detwyler's recent research. He is the author of *Man's Impact on Environment* (McGraw-Hill, 1971).

DONALD F. ESCHMAN (b. 1923) is Professor of Geology, and former Chairman, in the Department of Geology and Minerology, the University of Michigan, Ann Arbor, Michigan 48104. Eschman is an alumnus of Denison University and Harvard University (Ph.D., 1953). He has been on the Michigan faculty since 1953 and is presently Director of the Environmental Studies Program in the College of Literature, Science, and Arts. His research interests include the Cenozoic history of the Rocky Mountains and the geology of Michigan, with special interest in the glacial geology and deglaciation of the state.

DONALD H. GRAY (b. 1936) is on the Civil Engineering faculty at the University of Michigan, Ann Arbor, Michigan 48104. Gray earned three degrees at the University of California, Berkeley (Ph.D., 1966). His professional interests include teaching and research in soil mechanics, soil erosion and stability problems, clay technology, and problems of solid waste. He is currently directing a research project concerning the effects of forest clear-cutting on the stability of slopes. With Thomas Detwyler he teaches the course "Man's Impact on Environment" at Michigan.

ROBERT W. KATES (b. 1929) is a professor in the Graduate School of Geography at Clark University. The University of Chicago awarded him a Ph.D. in geography in 1962. Kates has published on numerous aspects of environmental perception, particularly perception of and adjustment to hazards associated with water. He was a member of the President's Committee on the Alaska Earthquake and a major contributor to the committee's volume, *Human Ecology*. He currently is completing a study of agricultural drought in Tanzania as part of an international cooperative study of environmental hazard.

MELVIN G. MARCUS (b. 1929) has been on the geography faculty at the University of Michigan since 1964; he was Chairman of the Department of Geography for four years. He has served as Chairman of the National Commission on College Geography and as Chairman of that group's Panel on Physical Geography. His research in glacier climatology in Alaska, British Columbia, and the Yukon spans a period of more than twenty years. Marcus holds degrees from the universities of Miami, Colorado, and Chicago (Ph.D., 1963). He served on the faculty at Rutgers University from 1960 to 1964.

JOHN E. ROSS (b. 1926) is Associate Director of the University of Wisconsin's Institute for Environmental Studies in Madison. He earned degrees at Oregon State University and the University of Wisconsin (Ph.D., 1954). Except for service in the U. S. Army, Ross has been associated with the University of Wisconsin since 1948. Currently he is developing research and instructional programs in environmental studies. His specific research is on the function of technical information in environmental management and its use in resolving environment conflicts, as in locating atomic power plants.

JOHN C. SCHAAKE, JR. (b. 1936), is on the Civil Engineering faculty at the Massachusetts Institute of Technology, Cambridge, Massachusetts 02139. He holds both baccalaureate and doctoral degrees from Johns Hopkins University (in sanitary engineering and water resources, Ph.D., 1965). Schaake was a faculty member at the University of Florida from 1966 to 1968. His current interest is in improvement of water resources planning in the United States and abroad, with emphasis on the water problems of cities and the procedures that urban areas can use to manage water resources. His research has emphasized the uncertain nature of hydrologic events in water resources planning. Schaake is Secretary of the American Society of Civil Engineers' Urban Water Resources Research Council.

FOREST STEARNS (b. 1918) earned a B.A. degree at Harvard College and advanced degrees from the University of Wisconsin (Ph.D., 1947). Before joining the faculty at the University of Wisconsin at Milwaukee in 1968, Stearns was project leader in environmental research at the U. S. Forest Services' Southern Forest Experiment Station (1957–1961) and project leader in wildlife habitat research at the North Central Forest Experiment Station (1961–1968). He has been an editor of *Ecology* since 1962. Urban ecology and the rural-urban interface, landscape productivity, plant phenology, and wildlife habitat are the foci of Stearns's present research.

GORDON M. STEVENSON, JR. (b. 1938), is an associate attorney with Bingham, Dana, and Gould, Boston, Massachusetts 02110. He earned a B.A. degree at Williams College and graduate degrees at the University of California, Los Angeles (M.A. in political science, 1963), Columbia University (Ph.D. in public law and government, 1970), and Harvard University (J.D. 1970). Stevenson currently is practicing general law and pursuing special interests in noise abatement. He is the author of *The Politics of Airport Noise* (Duxbury Press, 1972).

PETER VAN DUSEN (b. 1929) is Associate Professor of Geography at Eastern Oregon College, LaGrande, Oregon 97850, where he is active in an environmental teaching program. He holds degrees from the University of Florida, University of Oregon, and University of Michigan (Ph.D., 1971). In addition to Van Dusen's professional work in cartography and art, he has research interests in man's interactions with natural resources, especially water. He is chairman of the LaGrande · city planning commission.

INDEX

Page numbers for tables and figures are in italics

Accidents, 97
Agricultural land, urbanization of, 136–137
Air circulation in city, 60
Airplanes. *See* Aviation
Air pollution, *52*, 66–68, 83–88; and topography, 48; particulate, 57–58; in New York City, 69–71; diurnal variation, *85*; by automobiles, 92–93; influence on vegetation, 252–255. *See also* Atmospheric Dust
Alabama, 182
Alaska, 151–152, 188–189
Anchorage, Alaska, earthquake, 150–151, 160–161, 188–189
Anderson, N., 220
Ann Arbor, Michigan, *141*, 236; influence of topography on growth, 37; trees in, 240–243, 245–248
Appalachian Mountains, 32–34
Aquifer, 126
Arlington, Va., *251*
Atmospheric dust, in England, 145
Atmospheric environment, as component of urban ecosystem, 20
Automobiles. *See* Transportation
Aviation, traffic noise, 208–217, *218*, 223–225

Baltimore, 97, 106, 124
Baron, R. A., 200
Bauer, William F., 115
Berland, Theodore, 196
Beverly Hills, Calif., 221
Biological environment, as component of urban ecosystem, 20
Biological requirements of urban man, 14–15, 17–18
Birds, 264–267
Bluefield, W. Va., 32–33
Boston, 111, 120, 264; growth by land filling, 41–43; lead, 66; freeways, *73*; drainage and sewerage, 111–114; aircraft noise, 214, *216–217*
Brandywine Creek, Pa., 103, 107
Brazil, urban slums, *36*
Bruges, Belgium, coastal changes near, 47–48
Burton, Ian, 171–172

Cadmium contamination, 146–147, 252
California, 121, 190, 224, 245; earthquake

hazard, 45; pollution by automobiles, 76; land subsidence, 152–153
Cambridge, Mass., 115
Canada, 66, 151, 224
Carbon monoxide, 66, 88
Central Park, 70–71, 232
Champaign-Urbana, Ill., precipitation, *65*
Charles River, 115
Chestnut blight, 244
Chicago, *137*, 145–146, 201, 204, 214–215, 221; influence of topography, 32–34; frost-free period, 62; visibility in, 62; plume of heat and dust, 64–66
Children, 274–275
Cincinnati, 66, 116; highways, *72*; solar radiation, 75; park influence on climate, 79–81; air pollution, 85–87; sultriness, 89; land use, 90–91
Cities: growth of, 3–6; definition, 5–6. *See also* Ecosystem, urban
Climate: urban, 51–96; difference between city and countryside, 52–58; planning measures, 90–95
Climatic dome, 59–62, 76–81
Climatic hazards, 174, 177–187
Cloudiness, *52*
Cockeysville, Md., 107
Columbia, Md., 51, 79, 115
Columbia River, 104
Concord, Mass., 130
Connecticut, 182
Construction: sedimentation and, 104–108, *142*; erosion and, 139, *141–142*
Coral Gables, Fla., 221
Crescent City, Calif., 189–190
Crippen, J. R., 109
Crookston, Minn., flood in, *175*
Cultural requirements of urban man, 15–19
Culture: definition, 15; influence on urbanization, 17–18
Cutting and filling, 41–43, 140, 143–145

Darlington, Wis., 175–176
Dasmann, Raymond, 261
DDT, 266
Decibels (dB), 196–198
Denver, 45–46, *137*, 236, 265
Desert Hot Springs, Calif., 175–176
Detergents, 109

91517

DATE DUE
